A Concise Nuxalk –
English Dictionary

H. F. Nater

Canadian Ethnology Service
Mercury Series Paper 115

Canadian Museum of Civilization

Canadian Cataloguing in Publication Data

Nater, H. F.

A concise Nuxalk-English dictionary
(Mercury series, ISSN 0316-1854)
(Paper / Canadian Ethnology Service,
ISSN 0316-1862 ; no. 115)
Includes an abstract in French.
Includes bibliographical references.
ISBN 0-660-10798-8

1. Bella Coola language – Dictionaries. 2. Indians
of North America – British Columbia – Languages.
I. Canadian Museum of Civilization. II. Canadian
Ethnology Service. III. Title. IV. Series: Paper
(Canadian Ethnology Service); no. 115.

PM675.N37 1990   497'.9   C90-098565-8

Printed and bound in Canada

Published by the
Canadian Museum of Civilization
100 Laurier Street
P.O. Box 3100, Station B
Hull, Quebec
J8X 4H2

Canadian Ethnology Service
Papers Coordinator:
Pamela Coulas

Canada🍁

OBJECT OF THE MERCURY SERIES

The Mercury Series is designed to permit the rapid dissemination of information pertaining to the disciplines in which the Canadian Museum of Civilization is active. Considered an important reference by the scientific community, the Mercury Series comprises over three hundred specialized publications on Canada's history and prehistory.

Because of its specialized audience, the series consists largely of monographs published in the language of the author.

In the interest of making information available quickly, normal production procedures have been abbreviated. As a result, grammatical and typographical errors may occur. Your indulgence is requested

Titles in the Mercury Series can be obtained by writing to:

Mail Order Services
Publishing Division
Canadian Museum of Civilization
100 Laurier Street
P.O. Box 3100, Station B
Hull, Quebec
J8X 4H2

BUT DE LA COLLECTION MERCURE

La collection Mercure vise à diffuser rapidement le résultat de travaux dans les disciplines qui relèvent des sphères d'activités du Musée canadien des civilisations. Considérée comme un apport important dans la communauté scientifique, la collection Mercure présente plus de trois cents publications spécialisées portant sur l'héritage canadien préhistorique et historique.

Comme la collection s'adresse à un public spécialisé celle-ci est constituée essentiellement de monographies publiées dans la langue des auteurs.

Pour assurer la prompte distribution des exemplaires imprimés, les étapes de l'édition ont été abrégées. En conséquence, certaines coquilles ou fautes de grammaire peuvent subsister : c'est pourquoi nous réclamons votre indulgence.

Vous pouvez vous procurer la liste des titres parus dans la collection Mercure en écrivant au :

Service des commandes postales
Division de l'édition
Musée canadien des civilisations
100, rue Laurier
C.P. 3100, succursale B
Hull (Québec)
J8X 4H2

Abstract

This dictionary lists in alphabetical order over 2000 Nuxalk morphemes, as well as sample words and sentences, gathered by the author at Bella Coola, British Columbia, between 1972 and 1983. The morphemes are numbered, and reference is frequently made to the author's Nuxalk grammar which appeared earlier in this Series (Paper No. 92).

Résumé

Dans ce dictionnaire, l'auteur énumère dans l'ordre alphabétique plus de 2000 morphèmes du Nuxalk, ainsi que des mots et phrases exemplaires, amassés par lui-même à Bella Coola (Colombie Britannique) entre 1972 et 1983. Les morphèmes ont été numérotés, et l'auteur fait allusion fréquemment à sa grammaire de la langue nuxalk, publiée plus tôt dans cette collection (Dossier n° 92).

CONTENTS

INTRODUCTION

This dictionary was written as a sequel to my "Stem list of the Bella Coola language" (1977) and "The Bella Coola language" (1984), and serves a dual purpose. Firstly, it has been my intention to update and expand the material contained in the stem list, which does not list the numerous Nuxalk bound morphemes (affixes and clitics), and is defective in other respects as well (consider e.g. the lack of information on transitivity or intransitivity of verb stems). (On the other hand, etymological data are not included in the present volume, but a separate volume dealing with such historical aspects of the Nuxalk language is in preparation.) Secondly, this dictionary meets the practical demands expressed by linguists and Nuxalk language students and instructors alike. For the linguists' convenience, I have inserted references to my Nuxalk grammar. An example: entry 826, the pronoun **nts** I, me, is followed by the parenthesized number code 25.2, which corresponds to section 25.2 of "The Bella Coola language," where several properties of the pronouns are discussed. Those Nuxalk language students and instructors who have an imperfect command of the language, or are lacking in vocabulary, should benefit from this dictionary as well. It is hoped that, eventually, an English-Nuxalk dictionary will also see the light.

A note on the use of **7** is in order. In "The Bella Coola language," the reader will observe this symbol rather more frequently than in this volume, more specifically so in word-initial position. In the dictionary, the occurrence of morpheme-initial **7** preceding **a** or a vocalic sonorant is limited: it is spelled only (1) after prefixes and proclitics, (2) in a few enclitics, (3) in some deictic roots, (4) in the root ***7m**. Examples are: (1) **alhpsts** I eat vs. **ka+7alhpsts+ma** maybe I will eat, **mt** to sit vs. **s7mtsta** seat, chair; (2) **qaaxla+7isu!** drink some more!, **alhpstumulhaw+7ilhu!** feed us first! (vs. e.g. **lhtnmts+alu** I tried to go up);

(3) ***7aw** proximity, ***7atu** use, contact, ***7alhay** slight distance (vs. **aw** yes, **atsi** boat, etc.); (4) derivations of ***7m** erect all contain **7** (e.g. **kus7m** having an erection, **as7mllxs** pugnosed vs. e.g. **musm** to spy, **asmús** three). Furthermore, **7** plays no role in the alphabetical order: entries such as **7lats** sea cucumber, **7na** determinative, and **7yanahu** turnip are listed under resp. **L, N,** and **Y.**

ALPHABETICAL ORDER, SPELLING CONVENTIONS, SYMBOLS, ABBREVIATIONS

The alphabetical order in which the Nuxalk morphemes are arranged in the
dictionary is the same as for English, but Nuxalk ' is treated as the
last letter in the alphabet (while 7 is ignored). Thus, the full alphabet (including di- and trigraphs) is: **a, c, cw, h, i, k, kw, kw', k', 1
and 1, 1h, m** and **m, n** and **n, p, p', q, qw, qw', q', s, t, t1', ts, ts',
t', u, w, x, xw, y, 7/'.**
Entries are numbered, sub-entries are listed alphabetically, but sample
words and sentences appear in random order; **nu-** in combination with suf-
fixes requiring this prefix is disregarded for alphabetical purposes.

The orthography of the Nuxalk phonemes, with the exception of 1, **m, n,**
is identical to the one employed in "The Bella Coola language." They
are tabulated as follows:

	I	II	III	IV	V	VI
A	p	p'		m	m	
B	t	t'				
C	ts	ts'	s	n	n	
D		t1'	1h	1	1	
E	k	k'	c	y	i	
F	q	q'	x			
G	kw	kw'	cw			
H	qw	qw'	xw	w	u	
I		7	h			a

(I = plain plosive, II = glottalized plosive, III = fricative, IV = consonantal sonorant, V = vocalic sonorant, VI = vowel; A = labial, B = dental, C = alveolar, D = lateral, E = palatovelar, F = postvelar, G = rounded velar, H = rounded postvelar, I = laryngal)

Doubling of **a**, vocalic sonorants, and the fricatives **s** and **lh** is a frequent phenomenon (see sections 5.2, 5.2.2, 5.3, 5.3.1 and 5.3.4 of "The Bella Coola language"); **mm, nn, ll, ii, uu, aa, ss;** doubled **lh**, however, is more economically rendered as **lhh**.
Syllabicity of **m̲**, **n̲**, **l̲** is indicated only where unpredictable (cf. section 4.5 of "The Bella Coola language"). Reduced vocalic sonorants are printed with a virgule superimposed: **nm̸nmk'** animal, **tɫtlkw** slippery, **mɫmnta** path, road, etc. (cf. sections 4.2.1.1 and 4.2.5).
Dragged vowels (see "The Bella Coola language," sections 1.8, 12.4.1, 16.4.2, 28.3.9 and 28.3.20.3) are spelled with an acute: **úlh+** (going) towards, **ts'ícw** five, **ts'klákt** ten, etc.
A rule of phonotactics ("The Bella Coola language," section 10.1) states that **u** cannot by preceded by **w**. Consequently, rounded velars and postvelars (and clusters thereof), too, are spelled without **w** before **u**: **xuta** dipnet, **squlh** bee, wasp, **k'utsci** maggots, **k'cusis** he looked at his face, **q'xuusnm** to be carving a face, etc. (cf. sections 3.2 and 9.4.2).

Other spelling conventions are:

(1) Enclitic strings are written together (i.e. without + intervening) when "immediate constituent" analysis separates the entire string from the preceding unit ("The Bella Coola language," 28.3.4): e.g. **alh7ay+matu** it may (**+ma**) be the case (**alh7ay**) indeed (**+tu**) vs. **ta+ mants+tski+tx** my father (**ta+mants+tx**), I presume (**+tski**).

(2) Parenthesized units are optional: e.g. **a(7)nayk** to want, desire =

anayk or a7nayk, alhaaq'likw(lhp) creeping juniper = alhaaq'likw or alhaaq'likwlhp, (nu-...)-aax behind, under = -aax or nu-...-aax, (+7)ats pl. demonstrative = ats (free form) or +7ats (enclitic), *clhh(+) away from = *clhh (verbal root) or *clhh+ (proclitical root), etc.

(3) In names of dances, persons, and geographical locations, the first letter is capitalized: e.g. **Milha** a type of dance, **Hamsa** a man's name, **Sk'yaax** a geographical name.

(4) Verbs belonging to the causative paradigm are marked as ending in ...tu- (examples: **alhpstu-** to feed somebody, **scuukstu-** to defeat a team). Here, the hyphen placed after the causative suffix -tu(-) serves to indicate that this suffix as such requires the addition of a causative pronominal suffix (for which see "The Bella Coola language," sections 14.4.1-3).

Symbols and abbreviations encountered frequently in the dictionary are enumerated below.

SYMBOLS

*   Bound form (root or stem not recorded in isolation). Examples: ***7m** erect, ***alh7alhcw** (tr.) to hurry somebody, ***(+)7atu** verbal deictic root conveying use or contact.

+   Boundary sign separating clitics from other units. Examples: **ka+** hypothetical, irrealis, future (proclitic), **alh+** at, relative to (proclitic), **+tuu** exactly, just, even, too (enclitic), **+lú** still, yet (enclitic).

- Boundary sign separating affixes from other units (incl. affixes). Examples: **alh-** stative-progressive (prefix), **tam-** iterative (prefix), **-ak** hand (suffix), **-ulh-ik-alh** top of foot (suffix string), **-al-** connective (infix), **-anlh-** side or corner (infix), **kanus-...-m** having a ... odor or flavor (circumfix), **unus(i)-...-m** to go somewhere with a purpose (circumfix).

^ Placed over **i, m, n, s, u, w**, or **-**, this symbol signifies telescoping. Examples: **yacyaakî** small mountain goat = /yac.yaaki⁀i/, **wa+7alqw'alm̂tsts** all my younger brothers and sisters = /wa+7al.qw'alm⁀mts-ts/, **q'am̂ut** to attend a funeral = /q'aw⁀mut/, **alhkan̂macw** to resemble each other = /alh-kan⁀nmacw/, **wa+st'lŝ** his cranberries = /wa+st'ls⁀s/, **snûats'ams** canine = /s-nu⁀wats'-ams/, **kasmiŵlh** golden eagle's egg = /kasmiw^ulh/. See also "The Bella Coola language," section 6.1.1.

1 First person.

2 Second person.

3 Third person.

ABBREVIATIONS

caus. = causativizing suffix or suffix belonging to the causative paradigm; dim. = diminutive derivation (e.g. **kɪklaacwi(i)** dim. (of **klacw** muskrat) = little muskrat); fem. = female; imp. = imperative; itr. = intransitive verb or suffix combining with intransitive stems; obj. = grammatical object (patient); pass. = passive paradigm; pl. = plural; sg. = singular; subj. = grammatical subject (agent); tr. = transitive verb, suffix combining with transitive stems, or transitivizing suffix.

REFERENCES

Nater, H.F. (1977). Stem list of the Bella Coola language. PdR Press Publications on Salish Languages 4. The Peter de Ridder Press. Lisse, Netherlands.

---- (1984). The Bella Coola language. National Museum of Man Mercury Series No. 92. Ottawa.

---- (1988). Nuxalk lexicon. Unpublished Ms.

DICTIONARY

A

1   ***a** remote (23.6.1)

2   **a+** = **wa+** (15.1, 16.3)

3   **a–** allomorph of **alh–** before **nu–**, **s**... (23.5)

4   **a–** locative prefix (23.6.1)

5   **+a** question marker (28.3.17, 28.3.24)

6   **+a**... syllable inserted between **–x** and enclitic (28.3.22.1)

7   **–a** intransitivizer (19.6)

8   **–aak** = **–ak**

9   **–aakas** formative suffix (22.2): **Tmcwaakas** a personal name, **Tsakwaakas** a personal name, **Alhkw'ntamaakas** the supreme deity

10   ***aalats'** = ***alats'**

11   **–aalh** = **–alh**

12   **–aalhh** = **–alhh**

13   **–aaq** = **–aax**

14   **–aaqws** = **–aqw's** (7.2, 20.2.2)

15   ***aax** to crawl: **icaaxlc, alhaaxlc** to crawl, **icaaxulmcayc** to be crawling on the ground

16   **–aax, –aaq** leg, step (20.2.1, 20.5.1); bush, tree, stick, wood (log, boat) (20.3.1); food, dish (20.3.1); name (20.3.1): **tipyaaq** to stand on one leg, be one-legged, **tsyaaxm** to take a step, **astistnmaaq** to have a stiff leg, **nmnmaax** both legs, **stiktl'aatl'qi** to have one leg shorter than the other, **paaxlhaax** to stand at the stern, **smawaax ti+ stn** one tree or stick, **p'uyaax** tree falls down, is felled, **taq'aax** dense bush, **t'xúlhaax** six trees, **nuts'lhaax** shade in the bush, **stnaax** timber, **tyaax ti+lhalas** boat is steady, **nuscwaax** pot or canoe is leaking, **st'saax** (tr.) to put salt in food, **xsaax** sweet drink, **wlaax** (tr.) to pour a drink, **nutsiqw'aaq** (tr.) to break a dish or pot, **asmúsaax+ts' wa+skwatstats+ts** I have three names now

(nu-...)-aax behind, under: (lower) end, rear, back, bottom, seat; sun, day, lightning; people, population (20.3.1): **kulhaax** back door, **asaaq** bottom of container, **assaax** mouth of river, **nup'iixmaax** exhaust fumes, **nust'cwmaaxta** bark on top of which **kalhst'cwmta** is placed, **anust'cwmaaxm** (tr.) to have something for a cushion, **anulhk'aaq** bottom has come off a bottle, **tcatl'saax** back of the house (outside), **ustqnkaaq** petticoat, **amataax** seat, chair, **nukwlaax** the sun is hot, it is a hot day, **nutayaaxm** lightning strikes, **alhɬtiɬkaɬ smawaax tiɬkaɬsuncw** some day (in the future), one of these days, **nuplcaax** village has been abandoned, population has disappeared, **nuyulaaxit tiɬ7apsulhɬt'ayc** they have massacred this entire population

nu-...-aax hole, rectum (20.2.1): **nup'atsaax** deep hole, **nutsqaaq** sewing needle, **nut'kwaax** to bleed from the rectum, **snuts'imnaax** rectum, **nuscntsaax** to be cowardly, **nutsakwaax** wolf

nu-...-aaq-layc bottom projection: chin; heel (20.2.1): **asaaqlayc** chin or heel, **nustpaaqlayc** to have a freckle on one's chin, **nusp'aaqlayc** (tr.) to hit somebody on the chin or heel

-aaq-tn-aalh pair of shoes (20.3.1): **músaaqtnaalh waɬqinxtsɬts** I have four pairs of shoes

-aax-ak wrist (20.2.1): **mucwmukwaaxakta** bracelet, **tuk'maaxak** to have a sprained wrist, **cmaaxak** (tr.) to break somebody's wrist, **skulhaaxak** wrist, **sp'aaxakayc** to have been hit on the wrist

-aax-alh ankle (20.2.1); step (20.5.1); day's/days' travel (20.5.1, 20.6.1); shoes; **skulhaaxalh** ankle, **sp'aaxalhayc** to have been hit on the ankle, **tuk'maaxalh** to have a sprained ankle, **matl'apaaxalh** to take a step, **nuksaaxalhm** to step backwards, **nuq'ayaaxalh** (tr.) to block somebody's way, **mntskaaqalhits waɬqinxɬts** I count the shoes, **smawaaxalh** one day's travel, **lhnúsaaxalh** two days' travel

(nu-...)-aax-alits tooth (20.2.1): **smawaaqalits** one tooth, **alhtmpaaxalitsm** (tr.) to have something between one's teeth, **tayaaqalitsayc** to have been hit on the teeth, **tskw'maaqalits** (tr.) to pull out somebody's tooth, **tsik'aaxalitsm** to use a toothpick, **nusp'aaqalits-ayc** to have been hit on the teeth

-aax-ams jaw, mandible (20.2.1): **asaaxams = skulhaaxams** jaw, **tqnk-aaxams** lower jaw

(nu-...)-aax-apsm back of neck (20.2.1): **asaaxapsm** back of neck, **sp'aaxapsmayc** to have been hit in the neck, **nutuk'maaxapsm** to have a sprained neck

-aax-ik roof (20.3.1): **tyaaxik** flat roof

-aax-ik-an behind the ear (20.2.1): **asaaxikan** behind the ear

-aax-ik-t strip (20.3.1): **tcaaxiktits ti+st'winlh+t'ayc** I cut this hide into strips, **qpaapqikti** narrow strip

-aax-ilh pubic hair (20.2.1): **tsatskwaaxilh** to have long pubic hair, **sxaaxilhm** to shave one's pubic hair

nu-...-aax-ulh-ank (= **nu-...-ulh-aax-ank**) button: **nutslhaaxulhank-aycts** a button has come off my shirt

-aax-us mouth of river (20.3.1): **assaaxus** mouth of river

-aax-uts beard, whiskers (20.2.1); edge, (other) side, across (river or road), at riverbank, sandbar; near or around fire; to shoot, shot; drink, smoke (cigaret) (20.3.1): **sxaaxutsm** to shave one's beard, **cwlaaxuts** (tr.) to pull somebody's beard, **xsaaxutsm** to apply vaseline to one's whiskers, **ts'waaxuts** to have a grey beard, **kulh-aaxuts** roadside, **mtaaxuts** to sit at the riverbank or around a fire, **kwnaaxutsayc** to walk on a sandbar, **nuklhmaaxuts** to cross a road, **tpyaaxuts** other side of river or channel, **Nunusqw'aaxuts** Jump Across (a geographical name), **tayamkis txwnayaaxutsam** I threw it across the river, **kulhaaxuts** to be near a fire, **alhkwlhaaxuts** pitchwood torch, **smawaaxuts** single-barrelled gun, **lhɲlhnúsaaxuts** double-barrelled gun, **sk'laaxutsm** to add cold water to one's tea or coffee, **xsaaxuts** drink is very sweet, **xitl'aaxuts** drink is lacking in sweetness, **wl-aaxuts** (tr.) to spill a drink, **nust'cwmaaqutsta** napkin, **nuksaaxutsm** to inhale smoke

17 **(nu-...)-aaxla** berries, juice, liquid (20.3.1): **lhlaaxla** (tr.) to clean berries, **nukw'pstaaxla** (tr.) to collect a liquid

18 **aaxlh** upstream area (23.6.1)

19 **aaxn** to have perceived an omen

20 **aaxqa**, *__aaxqn__ to urinate: **aaxqats c+a+sic** I am urinating blood, **aaxqayalus** to want to urinate, **s(7)aaxqalh** urine, **nu7aaxqnalsalayc** to accidentally wet oneself

21 **Aaxqlhmcani** a mythical name: daughter of Raven and Porcupine

22 *__aaxqn__ = **aaxqa**

23 **Acati** name of a location in the **Talyu** region

24 **acwlh** some (26.3.2): **alhk'yuktits wa+7acwlh+ts** I know some of them, **ka+putl'a+ma wa+7acwlh+ts** some of them may come

  *__acwlh__ vague, indeterminate, unidentified: **acwlhamcwtsinu** I cannot recognize you, you have become a stranger to me

25 **acws** to be audible, holler: **acwsm** (tr.) to holler at somebody, **acws-nic** (tr.) to hear something or somebody

  *__acws__ having perceived, learned: **acwsan** to be an expert, **acwsanta** expert, interpreter; a large type of seashell, conch, **acwsalc** to learn, **acwsalctimut** to study, be a student, **acwsalctu-** to teach somebody, **acwsalctnm** (to be a) teacher, **acwsalcta** school, college

26 **A7iis** a man's name

27 **-a7inixw** hunter, ... at hunting (21.2): **yaya7inixw** good hunter, **sc-a7inixw** unlucky hunter

28 **-ak**, **-aak** hand or paw (20.2.1); gloves (20.4.1.1, 20.5.1); work (20.5.1): **nanaak** grizzly bear's paw, **tspakm** (tr.) to wipe something with one's hand, **mntskaakits wa+ts'up'akt+ts** I count the gloves, **músaak wa+ts'up'akt** four pairs of gloves, **maslancwakts sksnmakts** I worked for one year, **numawaakmitsuti(i)** to be alone at work, **pipq'-aak** broad-leaved plantain

  nu-...-aak palm of hand (20.2.1): **assaak** palm of hand, **nusp'aap'kayc** to have been hit on the palm of one's hand

-ak-t tree branch (20.2.1): **slhip'nakt** tree branch, **suts'wakt** old man's beard lichen

29 ***akl** right: **alhakli** to be right, correct

30 **akwa, *akwn** (tr./itr.) to buy (something): **akwats c+ti+qw'xwmtimut** I am buying a car, **akwnuksaw** they are buying (things), **ic7akwkwa** to be shopping, **akwnutsm** to buy food for oneself, **nu7akwnalsim** general store

31 **akw'a** black diver (a bird): **aakw'kw'ayi** dim.

32 **akw'i** smoked salmon head skin

33 **akw'na** sea canoe: **as7akw'na** to travel by sea canoe

34 **-al-** connective (20.2, 20.2.1, 20.3, 20.3.1, 22.4)

-al-aalh line; base (20.3.1): **tslhalhlaalh** (tr.) to break a line, **kulhalaalh** foot of mountain, **amatalaalh** base of totempole

-al-aax-alh-t behind the lower leg (20.2.1): **asalaaxalht** hollow of knee, **stl'imnalaaxalht** Achilles' tendon

-al-aax-t rope, anchor, boat; parents (20.3.1): **tcalaaqtn** (tr.) to cut a rope, **tiixwalaaxtn** (tr.) to fasten a rope to a stake, **tilcalaaxt** anchor is catching hold of something, **ksalaaqtntx kulhuutsam!** pull the boat ashore!, **amatalaaxt** parent, **plcalaaxt** both one's parents have died

-al-aax-t-layc (under the) tongue, speech (20.2.1): **assalaaxtlayc** under the tongue (= **tqnkalaaxtlayc**), **tmscalaaxtlayc** to speak with a weak voice

(nu-...)-al-ak-t underarm, armpit (20.2.1): **astipalaktm** (tr.) to hold something under one arm, **sxalaktm** to shave one's armpit, **squplhalakt** hair under arm, **skulhalakt = suqw'walakt** lymph nodes in armpit, **qwsmalakt** to have perspiring armpits

-al-ulh boat; rope (20.3.1): **p'iixlayalulhts** my boat is drifting away from me, **numawaluulhi** to be alone on a boat, **scanmalulhts** my boat is wearing out, deteriorating, **qpapluulhi** thin string, **kwmaluulh** thick rope

-al-us meat, flesh, body; chest (20.2.1); fire, firewood; engine; all, everything (20.3.1): **p'alcalus** to recover, get well, **mukwaluuslh** red springsalmon, **ts'aaqaluuslh** white springsalmon, **tcalustnm** to cut up fish or meat, **tpyalus** one side of the chest, **nukmayalusts** my chest hurts (inside), **puxalus** (tr.) to poke the fire, **lhnúsalus** two fires, **kwmlhalus** wood stove, **sp'alustnm** to split firewood, **skw'-alustu-** to take an engine apart, **tsiqw'alus** (tr.) to smash up everything

-al-us desiderative (19.17.3): **alh7alhtsimalusts** I want to speak, **anusuqw'ptamalusnu+a?** would you like to have a smoke?

nu-...-al-us-tcw-ilh inner thigh (near groin) (20.2.1): **nukmayalustcwilhts** my inner thigh hurts, **asalustcwilh** inner thigh

nu-...-al-uulh-aak line in palm of hand (20.2.1): **nusmawaluulhaak** life line

35 **ala+** = **alhɬwa+** (16.3)

36 **-alas** formative suffix (22.3): **Nuxalkalas** a beach across **Ista**

37 **alatk** to miss (a shot), make a mistake: **alh7alatk** to be wrong, mistaken, **alatkuuts** to mispronounce, **nu7alatklayc** to swallow the wrong way, choke

38 **alatsicw+7iks?** how or what is the situation?, what has happened?: how is it (that ...)?, why is it?, what kind (is it)? (25.5, 25.5.1, 25.5.1.1): **alatsicwlhts+7iks?** what have I done?, what has come over me?, **alatsicwnu+ks sikwanatnu?** why are you crying?, **alatsicwnu+ks s7axw tl'apnu?** why are you not going?, **alatsicw+7iks wa+syut wa+yanicicw?** what kind of music do you like?, **alh7alatsicwnu+ks?** how are you?, **alh7alatsicwliwanu+ks?** how are you feeling?, **alh7alatsicwaalh +7iks ti+lhalas+tc?** what type of boat is it?, **alh7alatsicwaqw's+7iks ti+lhalasnu?** what color is your boat?, **alh7alatsicwanlh+7iks ti+nupnu?** what kind of shirt do you have?, **alh7alatsicwtus+7iks?** how will he do it?, **alh7alatsicwakmtum+ks ska+7alhliclics ti+nalhm+tc?** in which way is the ling cod going to be cooked?

39 *alats', *aalats' to report, tell something: aalats'i(i)ts+suts' c+
ti+qw'las ti+s7aalats'i(i) now I will tell another story, alats'itu-
minu I will tell you something, alats'tnmc to squeal on somebody,
alats'amktsut to tell something about oneself

40 –alayc = –aylayc

41 alc to wander, roam around

42 –alc inchoative suffix (= –lc) (19.16.3): acwsalc to learn, t'qalc
to float towards the shore, t'qalc (tr.) to paste something, ksalc
to get married, sxalc (there is an) avalanche

43 –alcw formative suffix (22.3): muqw'alcw having no flavor, bland,
musalcw to feel around for fish with a long tapered stick, syup'alcw
point of land, yumalcw sour, lip'alcw (tr.) to turn around a point

44 alh+ at, relative to (16.1, 16.4.1, 23.6.1)

45 alh– stative-progressive (23.5)

46 –alh, –aalh foot, (lower) leg, walking, tracks, shoes (20.2.1,
20.5.1); vehicle; food implement (20.3.1, 20.4.1.1); coming from the
sky, precipitation (20.3.1): mamalhaalhi to be walking slowly,
pukw'saalh tracks of the pukw's, tsixaalh new shoes, matsalh (tr.)
to launch a canoe, smawalh one boat or car, tsixaalh new boat or
car, mntskalh (tr.) to count cans or spoons, smawalh one cup, tsakwaalh long knife, tsiqw'aalh (tr.) to break a dish or cup, stnaalh
wooden spoon, mukwaalh ti+nu7am7amataaq it is a red dish, xsalh it
is raining heavily, alhwlalh rain, stl'xusmalh hail, st'axwaalh sunlight is too bright, asts'alh waterfall
nu–...–a(a)lh footsole (20.2.1); floor, road (20.4.1.1, 20.5.1): nu-
myaalh (it is a) wide road, icnukcalhclhit wa+mⲙmnta+ts they are
painting lines on the road, nust'cwmaalhta floormat
–a(a)lh–uts door(way) (20.3.1); food implement, dish (20.4.1.1):
anutapalhuts the door is wide open, tsiqw'aalhutsm c+ti+nu7am7amat-
aaqs+tc he has broken his dish

47 alhaaq'likw(lhp) creeping juniper

48 **alh7alhcw** (tr.) to hurry somebody: **alh7alhcwtsut** to rush, be in a hurry, **alh7alhcuutsm** to eat in a hurry, **alh7alhcwakm** to hurry one's work

49 **alh7alhtsim** to talk, speak: **axw+ts' alh7alhtsimaylaycs** he cannot speak anymore, **alh7alhtsimutstimut** to pretend to be talking; to say too much, talk too loudly, **nu7alh7alhtsimikts** I want to speak, **alh-7alhtsimusmtmacwi** to chat, **alh7alhtsiṁ** (tr.) to tell somebody something

50 **alh7apq** brave: **alh7alh7aapqm** to be a brave

51 ***(+)7alhay** secondary nominal deictic root: slight or increased distance (15.4.1.2): **alhays+ts** now

52 **(nu-...)-a(a)lhh** back of mouth, throat, breath, voice (20.2.1): **snut'inalhh** uvula, **nulhpalhhm** to stuff one's mouth (with food), **nusqwlhalhh** to have a fishbone stuck in one's throat, **nutl'lhlcalhh** one's throat is getting dry, **nukmayalhh** to have a sore throat, **nuk'mnalhh** to choke, **nunuts'saalhh** to have a loud voice, **nulhkw'aalhh** to have a big voice, **cwpalhh** to expire, die, **xlhalhh** hungry

53 **alhi** to be located, stay somewhere: **alhinicits ala+7awcw+ts** I think it is right there, **alhitxw!** bring it here!

54 **alh7ikw** (tr./itr.) to barbecue (something): **alh7ikutsm** to barbecue one's food, **alh7ikuulh** to bake bread on hot rocks, **iŝ7alh7ikwlh** to eat barbecued food

55 **alh7ilhp'** (tr.) to hold back, restrain, prevent someone from ...ing: **alh7ilhp'its ska+7usqas** I prevent him from going out

56 **Alhiqwis** a geographical name: Port John

57 **Alhku** Elcho Harbor

58 **alhkwilm** wild, shy: **alhiikwlm** it (animal) is shy

59 **alhk'ilhtu-** to wait for somebody: **alhk'ilhtnm** to be waiting

60 **alhlxw** (tr./itr.) to look at something, read: **alh7alhlxwim** he is being looked at, studied, **nu7alhlxwikts** I want to read, **alhlxwtnm** to be showing pictures, **wa+7alhlxwim** a show, movie

61 **alhmulh** beads

62 ***alh(7)n** to (have) accept(ed): **alhnmtum c+ti+...** he was given a ...,
wa+s7alh7naaxmts the name I gave, **alh7nimuttum c+a+st'ls** he was giv-
en cranberries

63 **-alhp = -lhp**

64 **alhps** to eat: **nus7alhpsmc** given to eating, **alhpstu-** to feed, give
somebody something to eat

65 **alhqw'alayclc** mature, having status: **alhqw'alaycalc!** oh high one!,
your majesty!

66 **Alhq'iixa** a man's name

67 **alhtsxwm** (tr.) to reprimand somebody

68 **alhtsxwmalh** to walk in slush

69 **Alhts'yaax** a man's name

70 **+alhtu** approaching realization (28.3.14): **alhk'cicw+ayalhtu?** are you
beginning to see it now?, **q'lumaw+ayalhtu?** are they still trying to
climb?, **ka+tl'apnu+alhtukw'** if you will be going some time in the
near future

71 **+alhu = +alu**

72 **Alhu7ntstimut** name of a season (around February)

73 **alhyacwmaax** leaves are fluttering in the wind

74 **alhyannm** to tilt, slant, incline, overhang

75 **-ali** formative suffix (22.3): **scali** jealous

76 **-aliits, -aliicts** tongue (20.2.1): **tsk'maliits** having a sharp taste,
tangy, spicy, **niiqwaliits** to have burnt one's tongue, **tcaliictsim**
his tongue was cut out, **kmayaliits** one's tongue hurts, **kulhaliits**
side of tongue

77 **-alimtsk** formative suffix (22.3): **paaxalimtsk** (tr.) to give out
names, **us7usxlhalimtsk** braggart, **napalimtsk** (tr.) = **iinalimtsk** (tr.)
to distribute food, **its'kalimtsk** (tr.) to distribute presents,
lhuts'alimtsk (tr.) to undress, uncover somebody
-alimtsk-ak: slalimtskak cone of fir or pine tree

78 **(nu-...)-alits** tooth (20.2.1): **plalits** to be toothless, **nutl'xwy-alitsts** I have broken a tooth

79 **alkw** herald, messenger

80 **(nu-...)-almc** breast, teat (20.2.1): **nmnmalmc** both breasts, **slhx-almc** left breast, **nupusmalmc** one's breasts are swollen, **nutcalmcim** she had a mastectomy, **nukmayalmc** to have sore breasts

81 **almk** to pole a canoe up the river: **ka+nu7almkmmis+tuts' awcwa** he will go poling up the river again

82 **Almtsi** a man's name

83 **(nu-...)-alps** surrounded, enveloped; in one's mouth (20.2.1): **t'q-alps** (tr.) to put extra clothing on somebody, **t'qalpsta** extra cloth-ing, **nu7itl'yukalpsm** to mumble, mutter

84 **(nu-...)-alqi, (nu-...)-alx(i)** back of head, neck, hair at nape of neck (20.2.1): **nuqat'alxm** to put one's hand in one's neck, **nutuk'm-alxi** to have a sprained neck, **nusp'alxyayc** to have been hit in the neck, **kulhalxi** back of head, neck, **kulhalxyalh** to stand behind some-body, **alhtsmq'malqi** to have curly hair (in the neck), **tsakw'alxi** to have straight hair

-alxy-apsm back of neck (20.2.1): **asalxyapsm** back of neck

85 **-als** surface (20.2.1); liquid container; side of hill or mountain (20.3.1): **xawisals** can, **st'sals** bottle, **ts'ikwnals** drinking cup, **stapals** steep mountainside, **slawsals** grassy mountainside, **kulhalst** hill- or mountainside

nu-...-als inner surface, dome: sky, ceiling; room, wall; hide, clothing, pants (20.3.1): **nusxaxlsm** the sky is clear, **nutasals** (tr.) to poke the ceiling, **numyals** large room, **numnlhatals** (tr.) to meas-ure a room, **numukwals** red wall, **wa+nutctl'uk'als+ts** (the rooms) up-stairs, **nutscwalsilh** it is dark in our house, **nuts'sals** noise in the house, **nut'cwalsm** to sweep the house, **nunaaxwmalsim** dance hall, **nu-qaaqlamalsim** liquor store, **nu7akwnalsim** general store, **nutasals** (tr.) to poke, tan a hide, **nusxals** (tr.) to scrape a hide, **nutsik'-**

alsta bone implement used for fleshing hides, **nu7aaxqnalsalayc** to accidentally wet one's pants, **nu7apsalsalayc** to accidentally defecate in one's pants

nu-...-als-aaqws visible part of eyeball (20.2.1): **nustpalsaaqws** (to have a) cataract of the eye

(nu-...)-als-iixw roof of mouth, palatal-uvular area (20.2.1): **tc-tl'uk'alsiixw** palate (= **asalsiixw**), **nutictsnalsiixw** uvula, **anulhqm-alsiixw** to have phlegm in the uvular area, **nu7iixwalsiixw** to have burnt one's palate

(nu-...)-als-ik-an ear (20.2.1): **nuplhtatlsikan** "to be thick-eared" = to be slow of understanding, **numnlhkwlalsikan** (to have) hair in one's ears, **nutakanalsikan** to have an earache, **nutayalsikanayc** to have been hit on the ear, **nut'kwalsikan** to bleed from the ear, **nu-tsqalsikan** to have a pierced ear, **nutsatskwalsikan** "to have long ears" = to be curious, **nutsuptsalsikanayc** to have plugged ears, **kulhalsikan** back of ear, **asalsikan** inner ear

nu-...-als-ilh aperture in wall: **sinuxyalsilh** window

-als-t outward appearance, behavior: **qw'lasalst** to act funny

nu-...-als-uts inside the mouth, voice (20.2.1): **nusxwatmalsuts** (to have a) blister in the mouth, **nuqlalcalsuts** one's mouth starts watering, **snuqlayalsuts** saliva, **nu7astcwalsuts** inside of mouth, oral cavity, **nuts'salsuts** to talk loudly

86 **alsqa** west (cf. 23.6.1): **tcalsqalh** west wind

87 **-alst** deprivative (19.15): **atmnalstts c+ta+mnats+tx** my son died "on me", **ulxalstn** (tr.) to rob somebody of all his possessions, **knic-alstn** (tr.) to eat somebody else's food

88 **-altm** season: **tsqwaltm** autumn

89 **-altswa** formative suffix (22.3): **spuuxaltswa** grey blueberry, **Niixw-altswa** a personal name

90 **(nu-...)-altwa** sky, weather, season (20.3.1): **nutscwaltwa** it is dark outside, overcast, **sk'laltwa wa+suncw** the weather is cold, **scaltwa**

bad weather, **scwᶖcwmaltwa** lightning, **lhqaltwa** wet season, **tl'lhaltwa** dry season, **xawisaltwa** metal-colored, grey sky, **alhk'caltwam** weatherman, **skulhaltwas wa+suncw+7ats** outer space, cosmos, **ayaltwa** the weather is changing, **alhqwyaltwa** cloudless sky

91 **+alu, +alhu** unreal: supposed(ly), almost, trying to ... (28.3.13, 28.3.24): **wa+mᶖmntsts+alu+7ats** these "unreal" (unnatural, abnormal) children of mine (i.e. offspring of human female and male frog), **wic +kwalu awcwa** they say it is supposed to be in here, **akwalhits+alu** I almost bought it, **putl'aw+alhu** they tried to come

92 **aluux, *aluuq** to be last, go behind: **al7aluuX̂!** be the last one!, **aluuxts alh+7inu** I am going after you, **aluuxamts ska+7alhits alh+ lhup** I will be with you for the last time, **Aluuqanm** a man's name

93 **(nu-...)-alx(i) = (nu-...)-alqi**

94 **-am** to become (19.16.1); ... times (26.2.6); ordinal (26.2.8): **tqnk-am** to go under something, **asmúsamtu-** to divide something into three pieces, **tpyaaxam** to cross a road or river, **kulhutsam** to reach the shore, **ixwam** to go on a journey, **ts'ícwlancwam+ts'** it has been five years, **maaskamnu+ks stl'apnu ulh+ts?** how often do you go to them?

95 **-ama, -amn-** tool, implement (21.2): **tiixwama** sledgehammer, **tl'alhama** clothesline, **its'amni** blanket

96 **ama7itsk** maybe: **ama7itsk alh7atmas+ts'** maybe he is dead already, **ama7itsk ka+putl's** maybe he will come

97 **am7amitkalh** barefoot

98 **amat** where something is; functioning as (20.3.3, 23.6.1): **am7amataaq = nu7amataaq** saucer, **amatalus** fireplace, **amataqw's** lair, bed, **am-7amatuuts** dishpan, **am7amatuutsi** dish, plate, **amataax** seat, chair, **amatlikt** coffin, **amatalaaxt** parent

99 **-amcw** autonomously (19.9): **napamcwits snus7ulxs** I discovered that he steals routinely, **alhnapamcwits** I know it intuitively, **ulamcwits ulh+ts wa+7its'amni+ts** I give them the blankets (which I have made myself), **acwlhamcwtsinu** I cannot recognize you, you have become a

stranger to me

100 **-amk** adjunct-incorporative; eventually, additionally, casually
(19.7, 19.7.1-3): **xlhalhamk** (tr.) to crave (food), **lhulhamk** (tr.)
to hear news about somebody, **tl'yukamk** (tr.) to discuss somebody,
smsmayamk (tr.) to tell a story about somebody, **nuyamlhamk** (tr.) to
sing of somebody, **aalats'amk** (tr.) to report on somebody, **yayaatw-
amk** (tr.) to be happy about, enjoy something, **tulwamktsut** to finally succeed, **atsiwltamkim** somebody got her pregnant, **tcamk** (tr.) to
use something for cutting, **qtsamk** (tr.) to cast out a net, **xapnamktsut** to mount a horse, **ulxamk** (tr.) to casually steal something,
tayamk (tr.) to casually cast something aside, **upkamk** (tr.) to mail
something out, take it to the post office (e.g. while shopping),
mntcwamk (tr.) to incidentally dip something up, **Alhmutsamk** Mystery
Dancer, **tl'apamk** (tr.) to get, catch something

101 **amlh** summer; springsalmon: **amlham** summertime, **a7mlhanmi** spring,
a7amlhi small springsalmon, **amlhtam** springsalmon season, **samlh**
sockeye salmon, **samlhtam** sockeye season

102 **a7mma = a7nna**

103 **-amn- = -ama**

104 **-ams** trap, wedge (20.3.1): **kawams** (tr.) to wedge something
(nu-...)-ams jaw, mandible (20.2.1): **tctl'uk'ams** upper jaw, **tqnkams**
lower jaw, **snûats'ams** canine, eyetooth, **tpyams** side of jaw

105 **amulh** to get one's share of food, serve oneself: **amulhtutits** I will
serve them their food, **amulhutsm = amulh**

106 **(nu-...)-an** temple; collarbone (20.2.1); corner (20.5.1): **nusp'an-
ayc** to have been hit on the temple, **asan** temple, **icniq'xman** to have
lockjaw, **sqwlhan** collarbone, **nucman** (tr.) to break somebody's collarbone, **slhq'an** collar, **as(s)an** corner, **nuniixwanayc** to have a
fire in the corner, **Stsatsxwan** name of a creek: Tatsquan, **tslhanta**
tweezer, **nut'qanta** stamp, **acwsan** expert
-an-ak (lump of) wrist (20.2.1): **spulhanak** lump of wrist

-an-alh (lump of) ankle (20.2.1): uslikw'analhts something rolled
on top of my ankle, spulhanalh lump of ankle

-an-ilh groin (20.2.1): st'lsanilh lymph nodes in groin, tuk'anilhm
to stretch one's hip joints

-an-uts sound coming from corner (20.5.1): asanuts a sound is coming from the corner

nu-...-an-aax-apsm side of neck (20.2.1): nusp'anaaxapsmayc to have
been hit on the side of the neck

us-...-an-ulh-iixw top of head (20.2.1): usklhanulhiixwts something
fell on my head

us-...-an-ulh-ik upper back (20.2.1): usklhanulhikts something fell
on my back

107 -ana formative suffix (22.2): snxana cricket, Snxana a personal
name, tl'upana cormorant, Tl'itsaplilhana the name of one of nine
supernatural siblings, xwiitsana restless, fidgeting

108 -anaats really, very (18.6): scanaats very bad, yayanaats very
good, lhkw'anaats very big, xitl'anaats very skinny, st'axwanaats
very difficult

109 analas funnel

110 analha (tr./itr.) to answer (somebody)

111 anana! ouch!, oh my!: ananay! = anana! + -i, ananaatsanay! exclamation expressing extreme pain, shock, or surprise

112 An7atsqwtulh a dance the performers of which occupy positions ac-
cording to rank or descent

113 -anaw allomorph of -aw after wic, lhup, lhmilh (25.2, 25.3)

114 a(7)nayk to want, desire: a(7)naykm (tr.) to want something

115 -ancw = -ncw

116 -ani formative suffix (22.2): tsimani horseclam, plxani inner surface of abalone shell, k'ucani butter clam, lhmk'mani weasel,
tl'akwani elbow, Pakwani a mountain at Kwatna, Nutscwani little bay
in the Talyu region, Nutciictskwani Necleetsconnay River, Uqw'wani

a mountain, **Nu7ip'utsani** a little bay west of **Nusilawat**, **Ts'sani** a man's name, **Yuyupaaxani** a location south of **Sit'xt**, **Quqani** a mythical bird

117 **anis** to deny: **axwtxw anisnu!** don't deny it!

118 **(nu-...)-ank** front of body, chest; side (of body or boat) (20.2.1): **asank** front of body, **tcalhyank = skulhank** side, **nusp'ankayc** to have been hit in the chest or side, **miank** wide canoe

-ank-aax-alh edge of roof (20.3.1): **kulhankaaxalh** edge of roof

-ank-alh standing in front: **assankalh** to stand in front of somebody

nu-...-ank-al-us side of chest (20.2.1): **nukmayankalusts** one side of my chest hurts

-ank-iixw side of head or face, cheek (20.2.1): **stsapankiixw** bone on side of head, **sp'ankiixw** (tr.) to hit somebody on the side of his face, **yulankiixw** (tr.) to stroke somebody's cheek

-ank-us side of face or hillside (20.2.1, 20.5.1, 20.5.2): **lhq'ank-us** (tr.) to slap somebody in the side of his face, **skulhankus** side of face, **kulhankus** hillside, **tpyankus** other side of hill, **tcitskw-ankuŝ ti+syup'alcw** other side of a point of land, **Ts'wankus** name of a location in the Bella Coola village

-ank-uts(-liits)-alh side of lower leg (20.2.1): **skulhankutsalh = skulhankutsliitsalh** side of lower leg, **tcastcwankutsliitsalh** inner side of lower leg

119 **ank'pts** mouse

120 **-anlh(-)** side or corner (20.2.1); cloth, sheet (20.3.1, 20.4.1.1): **pik'anlh** oil pants, **maaxtsanlh** grey clothes, **mukwanlh** red clothes, **alhtpanlh** spotted shirt, **tiq'anlhm** to sew one's clothes, **t'cwanlhta** clothes-brush, **tsqwanlh** wet clothes, **spikw'anlh** groundhog blanket, **yakyanlh** mountain goat blanket, **nulhxanlh** selfish, **nuyayanlh** generous

(nu-...)-anlh-aax-uts corner of mouth; lip (20.2.1): **nukmayanlhaax-uts** corner of one's mouth hurts, **nutcacnlhaaxuts** (tr.) to cut somebody's mouth in the corners, **tctl'uk'anlhaaxuts** upper lip, **tqnk-anlhaaxuts** lower lip

-anlh-ank side of body (20.2.1): **skw'panlhank** right side, **slhxanlh-ank** left side

-anlh-ank-us side of face: **skw'panlhankus** right side of face, **slhx-anlhankus** left side of face

(nu-...)-anlh-iixw side of head (20.2.1): **nukwlhanlhiixw** one side of one's skull is cracked, **axtsanlhiiqw** to lie facing sideways

-anlh-layc rib(s) (20.2.1): **smawanlhlayc** one rib, **lhnúsanlhlayc** two ribs, **cmanlhlaycayc** to have one or more broken ribs, **sp'anlhlaycayc** to have been hit in the ribs

-anlh-ulh-aqw's corner of eye (20.2.1): **sik'amanlhulhaqw's** the corner of one's eye is injured

121 **-anm** to become gradually or increasingly ...(er); (it is) the time (season) of ...; the time has arrived for one to ..., one must ... now (19.16.2, 19.16.2.1-3): **scanm** to wear out, **qxyuanm** to (seem to) become increasingly more useless, **staltmcanm** to work hard at becoming a chief, **t'lianm** dog salmon season, **sutkanmi** early winter, **ilhtsayanmts** it is time for me to start picking berries, **alhpsanmts** I must eat now, **Spuxanm** a personal name

-anm-aak hour, ... o'clock (19.16.2.4, 20.6.1): **smawanmaak** one hour, (it is) one o'clock, **maaskanmaak+7iks?** what time is it?

122 **a7nna, a7mma** hooded merganser

123 **antsns** orange(s)

124 **anu-** through, throughout, around, spread, across, (coming) out of (23.6.2): **anutiixw** tanning frame, **anusts'mlcaax** river delta, **anu-st'cwmaaxm** (tr.) to use something for a cushion, **anuputl'uts** water issues from one's mouth, **ti+kwl ti+7anuputl'** a hot spring, **anulixw-aax** (tr.) to chase somebody out of the house

125 **anu-** = **a-nu-** contraction of **alh-** and **nu-** (23.5): **anutplq'** (turned) inside out, **anutapalhuts** door is wide open, **anutsiixlh** (hole) dug

in the ground, **anukw'na** to be aiming, **anukits'm** whirlpool, **anup'lht** lukewarm, **anukalalhayc usqa** he has walked straight out

126 **Anulhcum** a geographical name

127 **anumaaxm** to groan under a heavy load

128 ***anuqum** (tr.) to limit, restrain, moderate: **anuqumakmx!** don't take too much!

129 **anuq'm** (tr.) to dare or threaten somebody

130 **anus-** to have lost, lack, be deprived of (23.2): **anuskwtmts** widow, **anuscnas** widower, **anusman** having lost one's father, **anuŝtan** having lost one's mother

131 **anusq'x** (tr.) to copy somebody: **an7anusq'x** (tr.) to continually copy people, **an7anusq'xmc** to be given to copying, be an imitator, **an7anusq'xuuts** (tr.) to copy somebody's voice

132 **Anuxawaqs** a woman's name

133 **-ap** 2 pl. subj. itr./tr./caus. (14.2, 14.3.1, 14.4.1), 2 pl. obj. tr./caus. (14.3.2, 14.4.2)

134 **apcw** (tr.), **apcwa** (itr.) to lift something: **apcwaynic** to manage to lift something, **apcwlxs** (tr.) to lift one end of, tilt something, **apcwaakm** to raise one's arm

135 **apls** apple(s)

136 **aps** to defecate: **nus7apsta** toilet, **nu7apsalsalayc** to accidentally defecate in one's pants

137 **Apsiis** a man's name

138 **-apsm** (side of) neck (20.2.1): **tcapsm** (tr.) to decapitate somebody, **skulhapsm** neck, **stl'kwapsm** (to have a) wart on one's neck, **alht'um-apsm** to have a "hickey" on one's neck

139 **apsu** (tr.), **apswa** (itr.) to blow on something: **nu7apswaakm** to blow on one's hands, **apswatuminu** I will blow it off (away) from you

140 **apsulh** to inhabit, populate, population, village: **axw ti+ka+7apsulh ala+7ats** there are no people living here, **apsulhilh alh+Nuxalk** we live in Bella Coola, **apsulham** to settle, establish oneself

141 ***ap'lu** eroded, hollow(ed out): **ap'lunk**, **ap'lunk** bare, exposed tree roots, **nu7ap'luiik** hollow tree

142 **aqs** halibut hook: **aaqsi** dim., **aqsm** to fish with an **aqs**

143 **-aqs**, **-qs**, **-ayqs** formative suffix (22.2): **T'uqwtaqs** a geographical name, **Anuxawaqs** a woman's name, **Qamaatslaqs** a man's name, **Lhalyaqs** a woman's name, **Ts'umqlaqs** a woman's name, **Ta7wisilaqs** a woman's name, **Tl'aqwmayqs** the name of a (mythical) supernatural child, **kwa7yalaqs** bluejay, **q'awlhtaqs** helldiver

144 ***aqw'** (tr.) to snarl, tangle something: **aqw'qw'alxyayc** one's hair gets entangled (in something), **icaqw'iixwalhaycts** I tripped over something

145 **aqw'an** steep riverbank or cliff wall

146 ***aqw'lh** downstream: **taqw'lh** downstream area, **Txaqw'lh** (people from) the north, Port Simpson, **ti+txaqw'lhankiixws ti+smt** lower side of a mountain

147 **aqw'm** herring are spawning: **si7aqw'm** time of the year when herring are spawning

148 **-aqw's** ground, soil, sand; berries (20.3.1); paint, color (20.5.1): **maaxtsaqw's** soil containing clay, **sts'ixaqw's** sandy soil, **sk'caqw's** black soil, **ip'aqw's** (tr.) = **mnts'aqw's** (tr.) to crush berries, **maliixwaqw's** (tr.) to mix paint, **pcaqw's** having a pretty color, **mukwaqw's** having a brown color; dancer's headband
(nu-...)-aqw's branches, wood; fire, ashes, stove; water (20.3.1); eye(s), sight (20.2.1): **tyaqw's** = **tl'axwaqw's** wood that is hard to split, **astuq'aqw's** knot in wood, **tiixwaqw'sta** nail, spike, **taq'-aqw's** clustered branches, **asaqw's** hearth, fireplace, **nutasaqw's** (tr.) to poke a fire, **nulhlaqw's** (tr.) to clean out a stove, remove the ashes, **miltmaqw's** water spills over, **nutsik'maqw's** dirty water, **nustqwaqw's** muddy water, **tyaqw's** = **nuq'saqw's** to stare, **tipmaqw'sm** (tr.) to catch sight of something, **squpaqw's** eyebrows
nu-...-aqw's knot; bed; bottom (20.3.1); eyeglasses, spectacles

(20.5.1): **nulicmaqw's** knot is slipping, **nuq'saqw's** knot is tight,
nulhnúsaqw's two are in bed, **asaqw's** bottom of water, **nut'xtaqw's**
bottom of cave, **nutsiqw'aqw's** (tr.) to break somebody's spectacles
nu-...-aqw's-an-ilh upper thigh (near groin) (20.2.1): **asaqw'sanilh**
lower aspect of groin (near genitals), **nuskw'maqw'sanilhayc** one's
hip is dislocated, **nukwﬁkwmaqw'sanilh** (to have) fat thighs

149 **aq'a(a)tcyu** swing: **aq'atcyum** to (play on a) swing

150 **aq'miixalhp** cottonwood

151 **aq'sn** (tr.) to hang, strangle somebody: **aq'sntsuut** to hang oneself

152 **aq'u** (tr.) to emprison: **alhaq'u** to be in jail, **aqw'witim+ma** he has
probably been committed to prison for a short time, **an7aq'uli(i)kw**
policeman, **nus7aq'ulikwsta** prison

153 ***as, *ass** base combined with lexical suffix: being (at) ... (20.2,
20.3): **asnalusaax = asalustcwilh** between the legs, crotch, **asnalus-
aqw's** bridge of nose, **aslxsnk** tail, **aslits'** side, **asan** corner; temple, **Asanani** Canoe Crossing, **asank** front of body; to be in front of
somebody, **assankalh** to stand in front of somebody, **asals** inner bark
of cedar; ceiling, **as(als)anuts** a sound is coming from the corner,
asalsiixw palate, **asalsuts** inner aspect of mouth, oral cavity, **asalsikan** inner ear, **asalxi** back of head, neck, **asalxyapsm** back of
neck, nape, **asalaaxtlayc** under the tongue, **asalaaxalht** hollow of
knee, **assaalh** footsole, **asalh** threshold, **assaak** palm of hand, **asaaq**
bottom of box, **asaaqlayc** chin; heel, **assaax** mouth of river, tidal
flats, **assaaxus** mouth of stream, **asaaxapsm** neck, **asaaxams** jawbone,
asaaxikan behind the ear, **asaqw's** bottom of water, riverbed; fireplace, **asaqw'sanilh** lower aspect of groin (near genitals), **asilh**
genitals, **assiilhuts** lips, **asik** middle finger, **assiik** spine, backbone, **asiknaluslxsak** between the fingers, **asiknaluslxsalh** between
the toes, **asiknalusaqw's** bridge of nose, **assiknalus** joints, **assik-
lqs** bow of boat, **asiklxs** nasal aperture, **asikalus** sternum, **asikalhh**
throat, **assikak** upper arm, **asikiixwalits** front teeth, **asikus** fore-

head, **asikulhaqw's** center of eye, pupil, **asiixw** smoke vent, **assiiqw** crown of head, top of tree, **asuts** front of house, **asutsaax** (to be) beneath the house, **asutsaaq** buttocks, posterior, **nu7asuusta** inner aspect of front door, **asulhaaxs ti+quna** base of thumb, **asuulhikalhh** front of neck, throat

154 **as-** to contain, have, use (23.2): **as7anulhts'aliitstut** they have the food prepared with Indian cheese, **asluta** to have brought, use a crowbar, **aŝulicts** to have brought food along, **aŝatl'a** to go by canoe, **asnuniixwik** to go by steamboat, **asmʎmntnalh** to use a ladder, **asxits'ak** to use an axe, **asnictnak** to use a saw, **as7asmnayak** to have a child

155 **ascw** seal: **aascwi** dim., **ascwaalh** seal's tracks, **nu7ascwlh** seal fat

156 **asi-** to consider the taste of something (23.2): **asisc** to dislike the taste of something, **asiya** to like the taste of something

157 **asikaax** small timber, underbrush

158 **asim** to pack a baby: **asimtnm** = **asimlt** to brood, hatch eggs

159 ***ask'** spread, divided: **ask'tmacwtum** he is torn between ... and ..., cannot decide where to settle

160 **asmús** three (26.2): **asmúsamtu-** to divide something in three, **asmús-anmutsts snuyamlhts** I sang three times, **asmúsamts stl'apts** I went three times, **asmúsaaxts s7alhaq'uts** I was in prison for three days, **asmúslancwts s7alhaq'uts** I was in prison for three years, **asmúsilh-ts s7alhaq'uts** I was in prison for three months, **asmúsaakts s7alh-aq'uts** I was in prison for three hours, **asmúslxs** sixty

161 **asqa** to be outside (23.6.1): **ala+7asqa+ts** outside, **asqaykus** front of house, **asqayaaxta** open shed where fish is dried, **asqayaaxnm** to take something outside to dry, **asqayalh** totempole, **asqayaalhi** small totempole

162 ***ass** = ***as**

163 **astam+ks?** where is it? (23.6.1, 25.5)

164 **Astas** a personal name

165   **astcw** to be inside (23.6.1): **ta+s7astcwlhts sxslcalhs wa+7alhwlalh +ts** once I was inside, the rain started to really pour, **wa+tsay alh+tu+7astcws tu+sulh+txw** everything that was in the house, **ta+ 7alhqulh ta+7astcw+tx** the book that was inside, **nu7astcwalsuts** inside of mouth, oral cavity

166   ***astip** to hold, clasp: **astipalaktm** (tr.) to hold something under one arm

167   **astsm** fresh fish

168   **asya** (tr./itr.) to butcher, cut up fish

169   **at** herring spawn: **atm** to collect herring spawn

170   **atl'a** to build a river canoe: **satl'a** river canoe, **aŝatl'a** to travel by river canoe, **satl'ayi** small river canoe, **nu7atl'ayk** (tr.) to hollow out a river canoe

171   **atl'anulh** gooseberry: **atl'tl'anulhp** gooseberry bush (/...ulh⁻lhp/)

172   ***atl's** behind, back, east, inland: **atl'salhiix!** step back!, **tc-atl'saax** back of house, **nu7atl'sasls** spacious cave, **nu7atl'siixw** head of river, **satl'suuts** tide coming in, **Atl'smc** Chilcotin native

173   **atma**, ***atmn** to die: **alh7atma** dead, **atmalikt** to be totally paralyzed, **atmnaak** to have a paralyzed hand, **sti7atmnus** to be paralyzed at one side, **sti7atmnusnimutts** my side seems to be paralyzed

174   **(+7)ats** demonstrative, pl. close (15.4.1.1): **ala+7ats** here

175   **atsaya** fox: **aatstsayi** dim.

176   **atsi** boat, canoe: **clh7atsinu+a?** have you got a boat?, **us7atsyam** to board a canoe

177   **(+7)atsi** interrogative form of **(+7)ats** (15.4.1.1)

178   **atsiwa**, ***atsiw(n)** belly, abdomen: **atsiwni** dim., **atsiwatinits** I have a bellyache, **atsiwlt** to be pregnant, **atsiwltlayc** she has become pregnant

179   ***ats'aaxlh** south: **tcats'aaxlh** south wind, **Ats'aaxlhmc** a tribal division in the **Talyu** region

180   **ats'i** to fish with a rod: **sats'ista** fishing rod, **iŝats'ista = ats'i**

181 **ats'ta** paddle: **ats'tni** dim., **ats'tnaluulh** paddle boat

182 ***(+)7atu** verbal deictic root conveying use or contact (15.4.1.3.2)

183 **-atwala** unique formative suffix (in **sts'its'xwatwalalhp**)

184 **at'** (tr.), **at'a** (itr.) to smear on, paint something: **at'ta** paint, **at'aaksta** paint brush, **an7aat'a** painter, **at'usm** to paint one's face, **at'liitsm** to paint one's body, **at'uulh** (tr.) to paint a house (exterior), **nu7at'als** (tr.) to paint a house (interior)
*at' (tr.) to cut up, smash something: **at'ulh** (tr.) to cut up, mash potatoes, **alhat'ulh** potato stew

185 **at'maakw** kingfisher

186 **aw** yes (29.4)

187 **-aw, -naw** 3 pl. subj. itr. (14.2)
-(n)aw+... 3 pl. subj. tr./itr. (28.3.20.1-6)

188 **-aw** emphatic imperative suffix (29.4.1)

189 ***(+)7aw, (+7)awa** verbal/spatial deictic root conveying proximity (15.4.1.3.1, 15.4.1.4): **ala+7awa** around here

190 **awanaaxkw** raft: **as7awanaaxkw** to travel by raft, **awanaaxkwit wa+ sts'laaxlh** they are going to transport the lumber by raft

191 ***(+)7awcw, (+7)awcwa** spatial deictic root (15.4.1.4): **ala+7awcwa** in here

192 **awk'awalh** blind

193 **awlh** (tr.) to follow somebody

194 **Awsti** a man's name

195 **ax+...** = **axw** (28.3.23)

196 **Axlxm** a personal name

197 ***axts** to lie down: **axtsm** to be lying down, **axtstmacw** to lie together, **nu7axtsaax** to lie on one's back, **axtsanlhiiqw** to lie facing sideways, **si7axtsuliits** nightgown, **Axtsikayc** a woman's name

198 **axxa!** exclamation of disgust: yuck!

199 **axxut** to cough

200 **axw** no(t) (27.1-7, 29.4): **axwtxw!** don't!, **axwlit** to deny or refuse,

axw ti+ka+... there is no ...

201 -axw, -naxw pl. imperative (14.2.4, 14.3.1.1, 14.4.1.1)

202 axwni, ic7axwni a small bird (thrush?)

203 ay, *a7i to manifest oneself, to be or act thus: alh7ay+atu? is it
really so?, alh7ay+matu it must be so, alh7aynaw+tuu c+lhmilh they
are exactly like us, alh7ay+tuu c+7nts s7alhpss "he is just like me
as he eats" = I am eating and so is he, axwtxw alh7aynu! don't do
it!, alh7ayliwa c+ti+squlh it looks like a bee, tlh/lhliwa alh+ti+
s7alh7alclikts+ts'n+tc (/...7ay⁻lc.../) he is quite strong for a
man of his age, alhnapits ti+7aytcw I know who did it, aytutim (it)
happened to them, axwtxw+ats' aytucw! don't do it again!, ayuts to
say, tell, ayu(u)tstimutx ska+nuyamlhnu! try to sing!, ti+7ayutsmim
+t'ayc ŝisyulhs this one which is said to be a sisyulh, ayalhtcutsm
to say over, repeat, ayalh to go, aytimutts+ma ska+tl'apts maybe I
will try to go, aynictinits people think I am that way, ayanmuutsts
ulh+... I went as far as ..., nu7ayanlhmik (tr.) to hate somebody,
ic7ayak to give away, ic7ayaklcts c+ti+7akw'nats+tc I have to give
my canoe away, alha7itimutis c+a+stl'yuks he did what he said he
would do, alha7yaalh to die, pass away, Alha7yu(u)ts Norwegian,
it7Alha7yuuts to speak Norwegian
ay s7ay (to be) any (25.9): ay s7ays wa+yanicits I like anything,
ay s7aynaw ala+smlhk+ts wa+yanictits I like any kind of fish, ay+ma
s7ays+tsk wa+7amats+tsk I figure he may be anywhere, ay txw s7aynaw
they were of many kinds, diverse

204 *ay, *ayaw, *ayu (tr.) to change, exchange, trade: ayawtsut to (become) change(d), ayaŵlhits ti+lhalas+tc I will alter the canoe,
ayaŵlhmts c+a+sq'lhkw+7ats I exchange my clothes, ayaŵlhiiqwmts I
exchange my hat, ayaŵlhiixwtmacwilh c+a+qaytilh+ts! = ayam̂tmacwilh
c+a+qaytilh+ts! let's trade hats!, ayaŵtsm to trade food, ayawanlh
(tr.) to alter clothes, ayawanlhm to trade clothes, it7ayawanlh-
tmacwilh! let's trade clothes!, nu7ayawalsm to change the sand on

the floor, **ayawsmtim wa+suncw+7ats** the world is changing, **ayawaakm-ts c+a+ts'up'akt** I change gloves, **ayam** to trade, **(ic7)ayamtmacw** to trade things with somebody, **nu7ayuik** (tr.) to change the contents of a receptacle, **nu7ayuaaxalusm** to give something in exchange, **ay-altwa** the weather is changing

205   **ayalhilaaxa** a small type of whistle: **Ayalhilaaxa** a woman's name

206   ***ayaw = *ay**

207   **-ayc** to have been ...ed (19.14.1); to (happen to) have completed one's ...ing (19.14.1.1, 19.14.1.2); to be in a ...ing state or position; to be able, manage (19.14.1.2); to have (19.14.1.2): **tcayc** to have been cut, **qwlxwayc** to have been hired, contracted, **walayc** to have been left, **skw'ayc** to be undone, **tmpaaxalitsayc** there is something (stuck) between one's teeth, **numnlhatayc** to have fathomed the water, **xwlhaycaw** they have brushed past, **tl'apayc** to have gone, **alhq'lumayc** to have climbed, **alhq'pstayc** to be tasty, **mtaaxutsaycaw** they are sitting around the fire, **iixwayc** to be burning, **ustcwayc** to manage to come in, to get in, **lhxwtayc** to be able to go through, **sqw'ikayc** to manage to jump over something, **axw tsikwaycts** I cannot move, **sucnayc** to have hands, **icnayc** to have feet, **itsnayc** to have teeth

  -ayc-tsut: maliixwayctsut to be mixed up, confused

  -ayc-nimut: tcaakaycnimutts I got my hand cut, **tculhankaycnimutts** I got myself cut in the belly, **tsik'aycnimut** to get oneself stabbed

208   **Aycts'mqa** a mythical woman's name

209   **ayk'** ancient, to be or take a long time: **alh+tu+7ayk'+txw** a long time ago, **ayk'ts alh+txw** I was there for a long time, **ayk'liwa** to be slow, late, **ayk'alh** to be slow in arriving, **ay7ayk'uutsts ti+ s7alhpsts** I am a slow eater, **ayk'malhh** not having eaten for a long time, to be very hungry, **ayk'mlh** old object, **ayk'mlhaalh wa+qinx** old shoes, **ayk'miis s7alhis** he stayed for a while

210   **-a(y)layc** to accidentally ...; to manage; to complete (19.14.3):

nupq'talayc to fart accidentally, **lq'aylayc** to conceive an idea, **lhut'aylayc** to catch a whiff, **q'pstalayc** to happen to have a taste, **alh7alhtsimalayc** to manage to speak, **ksnmakaylayc** to be able to work, **alhpsaylayclh** he has finished eating

211 **-aynic** (tr.) to happen or manage to ... something (19.14.4): **mus-aynic** to happen to feel something, **lq'aynic** to happen to think of, guess something, **q'pstaynic** to accidentally taste something, **apcw-aynic** to manage to lift something, **tsaaxnaynic** to manage to get rid of somebody, **q'lhkwaynic** to manage to repair something, **sts'apaynic** to manage to subdue somebody

212 **-ayqs = -aqs**

213 **ayts'aym** boa kelp: **snu7ayts'aymaqw's** boa kelp (in the water)

214 ***ayu = *ay**

C

215 **c+** by (means of), via, through (16.4.3)

216 **Calhasu** a woman's name

217 **ca7m** to gather gooseberries (by stripping the branches)

218 **cap'** to evacuate, escape: **cap'nicits** I let him escape, **cap'timut = cap'**, **nucap'ik** (tr.) to clean out a container

219 **cil** (tr.), **cila** (itr.) to nibble, gnaw at something: **ciluulhis ti+ 7apls** he is nibbling an apple

220 ***cip** (tr.) to lessen, diminish something: **cipayc wa+knicilh+ts** our food stuff is diminishing

221 **clh-** to have, possess (23.2): **clhmnalc** to have a child, **clh7atsi** to have a boat

222 ***clhh(+)** away from (16.4.4): **akwalhits t'ayc ticlhh+ta+Xala** I have

bought this from **Xala**, **ulxlhis t'ayc tsiclhh+7ilha7ilh** he has stolen this from her, **alhk'ctx wiclhh+t'axw!** look at it from over there!, **wiclhhts Holland** I am from Holland, **tsiclhhalhilh ts'ayc s7ixq'mlh** we are walking away from her, **ta+7imlk ta+ticlhhalhs ta+ mans+tx** the man who moved away from his father

223 **cli** penis: **ascli** to have a penis, **k'ilhcli** to have no penis

224 **cm** (tr.), **cma** (itr.) to snap, break something: **cmnalus** (tr.) to break something into pieces, **nucmik** (tr.) to break something in half, **nucmikta** deadfall for bear

*cm to be broken (cf. 17.3.1): **nucmcmiik** to have a broken spine, **cmak** to have a broken arm, **cmaaxak** to have a broken wrist, **cmlxsak** to have a broken finger, **cmiixwalst** to have a broken scapula, **nucmanlhlayc** to have a broken rib, **nucman** to have a broken clavicle, **cmaaxapsm** to have a broken neck, **cmcmi** pocket knife

225 **cmanwas** guardian spirit, spiritual guidance: **cmanwastimut** to follow one's intuition, be one's own counselor, **kalhcmanwastsut** to seek guidance, **ascmanwastumx, Mnaakays!** guide me, oh Lord!

226 **cnas** woman, wife: **anuscnas** widower, **cnasam+ts'** she is a woman now, **cncnaasi** girl, **cnaaslh** female animal, **cnasaaxta** female cousins; only female sibling in family, **skulhcnas** female cousins, **cnasuliits** woman's clothing, **cnasuliitsta ti+nup** it is a lady's shirt, **ascnastamim lha+7na c+ta+7na** she had a tryst with him, **cncnas** the name of a constellation

227 **cp** (?tr.) to dry a string by running it between the thumb and forefinger

228 ***cs** all, whole, entire (26.3.6): **csaalhaw stl'apaw** they are all going, **iscsiilh** to do something for an entire month
cs-uuts all: **csuuts wa+qwanilh** all the spoons, **csuutsilh s7alhilh ala+7ats** we are all here, **csuutsaw syanictits** I like all of them

229 **cuk', *cuuk** (tr.) to bathe somebody: **cuk'm** to take a bath, **nuscuuksta** bathtub, **nuscuk'msta** bathroom

230 ***cul** (tr.) to drill: **culta** drill, **culculm** to apply the firedrill, **alhculculuulh** biscuit, pilot bread

231 **cum** ice: **(s)nucumiixw** glacier

232 ***cuuk** = **cuk'**

233 **-cw** 2 sg. subj. tr./caus. (14.3.1, 14.4.1)

234 **cwaacwi, cwaacwcwi** light of weight: **cwaacwaalhi** to tread lightly

235 **cwilm** to itch: **nucwilmalsikan** to have an itchy ear, **nucwilmulhaqw's** to have an itchy eye

236 ***cwin** to have seen, be aware: **cwin(n)imut** to know that something is around or happening, **axw cwinimutts** I do not know what is going on, **nucwinnimutikts** I have a feeling that something is going on, **cwin-nmacwaw** they both heard something (simultaneously), **scwincw** omen

237 **cwiq'** cow parsnip, Indian rhubarb

238 **cwl** (tr.) to pull, grab: **cwliixw** (tr.) to pull somebody's hair, **cwlaaxuts** (tr.) to pull someone's whiskers, **cwla** to fight, wrestle, **cwlamtsinu** I will fight you, **unusicwlamaw ulh+lhmilh** they came to us with the intention to fight, **cwlcwla** to be wrestling

239 **cwm** warm: **cwmtsut** to warm oneself

240 **cwnalh** well, spring: **Nucwnalhayc** a geographical name

241 **cwp** (tr.), **cwpa** (itr.) to try to free or untangle something: **cwḿ-cwmptx!** keep untangling it!, **cwptsut** to try to free oneself, **cwḿ-cwmptsut** to struggle, press on (e.g. when climbing a mountain or going through thick brush), **alhcwpaycts+ts'** I am through with my work now, I am free, available

*cwp to come to an end, be released, come loose, relax, drop, lean: **cwplxs** end (e.g. of a story), **cwplxsnicits ta+7alhqulh+tx** I have finished reading the book, **cwplxslayc** to be at the end (of one's life), **nucwpaaxmtu-** to reach the end of the river, **nucwpiixwmtu-** to reach the end of the valley, **cwpakm** (tr.) to let go of, put down something, **cwpalhh** to die, pass away, **cwpaalh** one's foot slips, **uncwpts** my pants are coming down, **nucwpulhaaq** baby's diaper is coming off, **scwputs** drop-off in sea, **cwpank** (tr.) to lean something against something, **alhcwpanktsut** to lean on something, **alhcwpank-iiqw** deadfall for small game

242 **cwp'** (tr.), **cwp'a** (itr.) to unhook, untangle something: **cwp'uutsits ti+smlhk+tc** I take the fish off the hook, **cwp'uuts ti+tutup+tc** the trout is taken off the hook, **cwp'uuts(m̱)laycts** (the fish) freed itself from my hook

243 **cwts** (tr.), **cwtsa** (itr.) to discharge, remove, undo, unpart: to spill, pour out; to take apart, tear down, wreck: **cwtsm** to pour berries into a box, **nucwtsik** (tr.) to spill a granular substance (e.g. sugar) from a container, **nucwtsiklayc** to have spilled a granular substance, **cwtsalusm** to fall apart, **cwtsalustu-** to take something apart, **cwtslcakm** to wreck one's product, **Cwtsani** a man's name

244 **cwt'** to fall in, collapse: **cwt'uus** house collapses, **scwt'unt'uus** deadfall, **anucwt'uulh** there is a hole in the side of a bottle, **anu-cwt'aaq** there is a hole in the bottom of a bottle, **anucwt'ikiixw** there is a hole in the neck of a bottle, **cwt'nicits** I caught it (animal) in a trap

H

245 **ha7m** pigeon
246 **Hamats'a** Heiltsuk term for **Lxulhla**
247 **Hamsa** a man's name
248 **Hanu** a woman's name
249 **hatst!** = **hatsst!** = **tst!** = **tsst!**
250 **ha7u** tent caterpillar: **ha7ui** dim.
251 **Hawhaw** a mythical bird with a long beak

252 **Ḣaw(7)yat** name of a river

253 **huuqwat, uuqwat** term used to pacify a baby

254 **huyp!** a dance-cry

I

255 ***i** close (23.6.1)

256 **+7i...** interrogative marker (28.3.18.5.1, 28.3.24)

257 **+7i...k(a), +7it...k(a)** coercive-contrastive (28.3.19.1, 28.3.22.2, 28.3.24)

258 **-i(i), -y(i)** diminutive suffix (18.3, 18.3.1-3)

259 **-i-** euphonic vowel (19.3.1)

260 **-i-** 3 sg. obj. tr. (14.3.1)

261 **ic-** intensive-distributive (23.5): **ic7akwkwa** to be shopping, **ic-liikw'iitis** he is rolling it back and forth, **icp'iixlanaw** they are floating around, **icpqw'm** blizzard is blowing, **icmusa** to be feeling around (in the dark), **icnulhxlxsanmlayc** to wander around, **ic7ayak** to distribute presents, give item(s) away, **icntl'** it is very dark, **iclq'm** to be thinking, **ickaku** (tr.) to support a table leg that is too short (e.g. by putting a book under it)

262 **ica, *icn** lower leg, foot: **wa+7ic7icats+ts** both my feet, **icnayc** to have feet

263 **icaasnic** (**icaalasnic** in one song) (tr.) to search, look for something: **icaasnm** to be searching

264 **ica7i(i), in(7)ica7i(i)** to be incomplete, defective; to almost or soon ...: **alh7ica7i** baby with a physical defect, malformed, **ica7i-timut** to be lost, wandering around, **in7ica7i(i)naw ska+tl'apaw** they will go soon

265 **iclh** to have arranged a date with a woman: **iclhts ulh+7ilh** I have dated her

266 **Iclhacwani** a man's name

267 ***icn = ica**

268 **iculh** mother of illegitimate child: **s7icu(u)lhh** illegitimate child, **alh7icu(u)lh** wild, shy

269 **-ii = -i**

270 **-iik = -ik**

271 **iiklhii, *iklh** near, close: **iklhlci** to come closer, **alhtam7iklhlc-aalhi** to make a gradual approach

272 **-iilh = -ilh**

273 ***iin = *in(a)**

274 **i7ipts, iipts** to dream: **i7iptsnictsinu** I dreamt of you, **i7iptsilh** to have a wet dream, wet the bed

275 ***iiqm = iixm**

276 ***iiqw = iixw**

277 **-iiqw = -iixw**

278 **iixlhp** yellow cedar: **ic7iixlhp** several yellow cedars, **Nu7iixlhp** Nelson Creek

279 **iixm, *iiqm** to stink: **iixmaalh, iiqmaalh** to have stinking feet, **nu-7iixmik** vessel stinks, **iixmlc** to begin to stink

280 **iixsa, *iixsn** medicine: **nu7iixsnutsta** poison, **nu7iixsnutsayc** to have been poisoned

281 **iixw, *iiqw** to burn: **nu7iixw** to burn one's throat, **iixwlaycts** I burnt my pot, **iixwtu-** to burn something, **iixwlits'** to burn one's skin, **iixwak** to burn one's hand, **iiqwaliits** to burn one's tongue, **iixwayc** it is burnt, **nus7iixwtsta** oven, stove, **iixwsulh** to build a fire, **Ic7iixwtimut** a woman's name, **ic7iixw** red cod, **ic7iixwtalhp** red alder

282 **-iixw, -iiqw** top, head, hair; sprout (20.2.1); hat, lid, lock, door (20.5.1): **tctl'uk'iixw** the top of something, **nu7mtiixwayc** to sit on

top of something, **tqwmiixwayc** to be hanging over a rail or line,
assiiqw crown of head; plant top, sprout, **pliixw** headless, **piq'iixw**
having a broad head, **nuk'tsiitsqw** to bump one's head, **p'wîixw** halibut head, **mnts'iixw** having blond hair, **mukwiixw** having red or brown
hair; red lid, **pusiixw** = **putl'iixw** to bud, sprout, **tslhiixw** (tr.),
tslhiixwa (itr.) to weed plants, **tayamkiixwm** to throw away one's
hat, **tpiixw** lid, cover, **tpiixw** (tr.) to close something, **skw'iixw**
(tr.) to unlock something, **nutpiixw** next door

-iixw-aax-ilh pubic hair: **lhliixwaaxilhnm** to pull out somebody's
pubic hair

-iixw-ak tip of finger, fingernail (20.2.1): **cmiixwak** to have a
broken fingernail, **tl'piipqwakm** to cut one's fingernails

-iixw-alh tip of toe, toenail (20.2.1): **scwtl'iiqwalhmtsinu** "I
missed you by a toe" = I could not jump as far as you, **tl'piipqwalhm** to cut one's toenails, **k'tsiixwalh** to bump one's toe, to trip,
q'awiixwalhayc one's toes have gotten hooked on something

-iixw-als-t shoulder (20.2.1): **alhpuspusmiixwalst** to have a swollen
shoulder, **tuk'miixwalst** to have a sprained shoulder, **sp'iixwalstayc**
to have been hit on the shoulder, **tsik'iixwalst(n)** (tr.) to stab
somebody in the shoulder, **sak'amiixwalst** to have an injured shoulder, **skulhiixwalst** shoulder

-iixw-als-t-uts-ak elbow (20.2.1): **sts'iixwalstutsakts** (I fell into
a puddle and) water splashed up from my elbows, **anulhkwmiixwalstutsakmlhits** I have carried it by (hanging it over) the elbow, **k'ts-
iixwalstutsak** to have an injured elbow, **sp'iixwalstutsakayc** to have
been hit on the elbow, **skulhiixwalstutsak** elbow, upper arm

-iixw-an head of penis (20.2.1): **skulhiixwan** head of penis

-iixw-layc knee (20.2.1): **tuk'miixwlayc** to have a sprained knee,
t'tsiixwlayc (tr.) to tap somebody on the knee, **sp'iixwlaycayc** to
have been hit on the knee, **nmnmiixwlayc** both knees, **kmayxwlayc**
one's knee hurts

-iixw-nk hip(bone) (20.2.1): **sp'iixwnkayc** to have been hit on the hip, **cmiixwnk** (tr.) to break somebody's hip

283 **iixwsila** to miss a meal: **iixwsilanictscw** it is your fault that I missed the meal

284 **-ik, -iik** top surface: roof, table top (20.3.1): **nust'cwmikta** table cloth, **tspiikta** cloth used to wipe the table, **sxik** (tr.) to scrape a surface, **anupipk'miik** sparks are coming from the chimney, **tpik** (tr.) to stretch a hide on a frame, **tkwik ti+kulhik+tc** the roof is dirty, **stapik** steep roof, **plikm** to capsize

(nu-...)-i(i)k back (20.2.1); desiderative (19.17.3): **sxp'ik, sxp'-iip'k** spine, **sqwlhik** dorsal fin, **nututkw'mik** to sprain one's back, **nucmcmiik** to have a broken spine, **alh7alhtsimikts** I want to speak, **anusuqw'ptamiknu+a?** do you want to smoke?, **nutl'apikts** I want to go, **nûn̲ts'ikm** (tr.) to want to kill somebody

nu-...-i(i)k mind (20.2.1); hollow, contained inside; middle, half, in two (20.3.1): **nutsutik** to think, **numaliixwikayc** to be mentally confused, **nuniixwik** "(having) fire inside" = steamboat, **numatsikta** boards on bottom of canoe, **nutkwik ti+satl'a+tc** the canoe is dirty inside, **nutupmik** something is frothing in a vessel, **nutspik** (tr.) to wipe a pot clean, **nusxik** (tr.) to scrape a pot clean, **nuscwmik-laycts** I burnt my pot, **nut'tsik** (tr.) to break an egg, **nutcikim ti+kw'las+tc** his belly was cut open, **nutpîik** next room, **nu7ap'luiik** hollow tree, **snut'xtiitk** seed, stone in fruit, **inulh ti+nutpîk** the other half is yours, **nutcik** (tr.) to cut something in two, **nustq'-iktmacw** to be joined together, **anutqwmik** to hang draped over something, **nutiq'ik** (tr.) to sew together, **nut'upik** (tr.) to split a rock in half, **nutslhik** (tr.) to break something in half, **nukalik** center, middle, half

-ik-ak upper surface of hand (20.2.1): **skulhikak** upper surface of hand

nu-...-ik-ak upper arm (20.2.1): **nutlhilhkak** biceps, **nusp'ikakayc**

to have been hit on the upper arm, **nusquplhikaak** hair under arm,
anustnmikak to have a stiff elbow, **asikaktu-** to carry something on
the elbow

-ik-alh ground surface (20.3.1): **sts'ixikalh** sandbar, **slawsikalh**
grassy plain, meadow

(nu-...)-ik-alh shin (20.2.1): **squplhikalh** hair on shin, **ts'xlhnik-
alh** (tr.) to kick somebody in the shin, **sp'ikalhayc** to have been
hit on the shin, **skulhikalh = uts'ikalh** shin, **nukmkmaykalh** to have
a pain in the shin, **sts'qiiqkalh** marrow

nu-...-ik-alhh throat (20.2.1); what one eats, food: **asikalhh =
snukalikalhh** throat, **anumnlhatikalhhm** to eat with moderation

nu-...-ik-als inner ear (20.2.1): **nusquplhikals** hairs in ear

nu-...-ik-al-us chest (20.2.1): **nusp'ikalusayc** to have been hit in
the chest, **nusxikalus** (tr.) to shave somebody's chest hair off, **nu-
kmaykalus** to have a sore chest, **nuqat'ikalusm** to fold one's arms

-ik-an ear (20.2.1): **tcikanim** his ear was cut off, **taykanayc** to
have been hit on the ear, **tsqikan** (tr.) to pierce somebody's ear,
tsatskwikan to have long ears, **iixwikan** to have frostbitten ears

(nu-...)-ik-aqw's center of eye, pupil (20.2.1): **mAmnts'ikaqw's** to
have hazel eyes, **numukwikaqw's** to have brown eyes

nu-...-ik-aqw's bed (20.3.1): **nuspuxikaqw's** feather bed

nu-...-ik-iixw in the head; crown of head (20.2.1): **nukmaykiixw** to
have a headache, **nukwlhikiixw** the crown of one's head is cracked

nu-...-ik-iixw-alits (front) teeth (20.2.1): **asikiixwalits** front
teeth, **anutl'xmikiiqwalitstimut** to crack something between one's
teeth, **anuxwixwqw'mikiiqwalits** to grind one's teeth

nu-...-ik-layc tube, tire (20.3.1); penis (20.2.1): **nup'siiklaycayc**
to have a flat tire, **nu7its'tiklayc** to ejaculate, **nu7ipiiklayci** to
have a thin penis, **anuxuxumiiklayc** to have gonorrhoea

nu-...-ik-lxs nose, nostrils (20.2.1): **nupiq'iklxs** to have a flat
nose, **nutsqiklxs** to have a pierced nasal septum, **anutsxmiklxs** one's

nose is dripping, **squplhiklxs** hairs in nose, **nmnmiklxs** both nostrils, **nusp'ikllxs** (tr.) to hit somebody on the nose, **nukmaykllxs** one's nose hurts

nu-...-ik-lxs-ak tip of finger (20.2.1): **nukmayklxsak** one's fingertip hurts, **nusp'ip'kllqsakayc** to have been hit on the fingernails

nu-...-ik-lxs-alh tip of toe (20.2.1): **nulhkw'miklxsalh** to bump one's toes, **nusp'ip'kllqsalhayc** to have been hit on the toenails

-ik-nalus joint; between two houses: **assiknalus** joints, **assiknalus** between two houses

nu-...-ik-t-ak middle of season: **nukaliktak ti+sutk** midwinter

nu-...-ik-ulh-aqw's center of eye, pupil (20.2.1): **numnts'ikulhaaqws** to have hazel eyes, **nuts'wikulhaqw's** to have grey eyes, **nutsimikulhaqw's** to bump, get hit in the eye

-ik-us part of house (20.3.1): **tcatl'sikus** back room, kitchen, **asqaykus** outside front of house

nu-...-ik-us forehead (20.2.1): **asikus = skulhikus** forehead, **snuqmqmikuus** soft spot on baby's head, fontanelle, **nusp'ikus** (tr.) to hit somebody on the forehead, **nuqat'ikusta** headband of packstrap

nu-...-ik-uulh body, flesh: **nutsakwikuulh** long-bodied, tall, **nuxupikuulh** (tr.) to insert something in a hole, **nutatkanikuulh** half--ripe fruit

-ik-uus blade (20.3.1): **tipîkuus** single-bladed axe, **nmnmikuus** double-bladed axe

-ik-uuts edge (20.3.1): **kulhikuuts** edge, **tqnkikuuts** lower edge

285 **ika+ = ka+** (28.2.1.2.2.2)

286 ***iks** (tr.) to drag something: **alh7iks** (tr.), **alh7iksa** (itr.) to drag something, **anu7iksaaq** (itr.) sleigh, (tr.) to pull something on a sleigh

287 **ikw** absorbent material made of cedar bark

288 **ikwlhamk** (tr.) to throw aside, discard something: **ikwlhamkayc** to fall full length

289 **ikw'lst** rockslide

290 **ik'ax = ik'axw** (28.3.23)

291 **ik'axw = k'axw** (27.6)

292 **ik'nuas** fog: **ik'nuasmtap+a?** did you have fog?

293 ***il** (tr.) to pass, go around something: **il<u>l</u>xs** (tr.) to go around a point, **ilus** (tr.) to go past somebody, **ilusayc** to ba able to pass, **ilusaynic** (tr.) to manage to pass somebody, **s7ilusaycsta** passage, **nu7iliilh** (tr.) to coil a rope, **ilayc** to go around, **s7il7ilayc** rainbow, **ilaaxayc** to visit, **nu7ilulhaaqta** diaper, **nu7ilals** (tr.) to line a wall, **Ilikusaycsta** a geographical name

294 **-ila** formative suffix (22.2): **mukwila** boy reaching puberty, **Tsuus-ila** name of a small bay, **mtl'msila** to somnambulate, **qw'aykila** small red cod, **iixwsila** to miss a meal

295 **ilh+** indefinite article, fem. remote sg. (15.1)

296 **(+7)ilh** definite (article), fem. remote sg. (15.4.1.1)

297 **-ilh** 1 pl. subj. itr. (14.2)

298 **-ilh, -iilh** ring-like (20.4.1.1); relation, relative (20.3.1); months (20.6.1); pertaining to genital area or sexual intercourse (20.2.1): **Sts'kiilh** name of a former village, **músilh wa+ym̷yucw** four bracelets, **alhts'ktiilhilh ulh+ts** we are closely related to them, **ixwilh alh+7nts** he is a distant relative of mine, **músilh** (to do something for) four months, **asilh** private parts, **sxwatilh** urine bladder, **tlhilh** to copulate in an aggressive manner, **tsixilh** to be newly wed

nu-...-i(i)lh circle, ring, hoop (20.3.1, 20.3.5); (female) private parts, vagina (20.2.1); backbone of salmon: **nu7iliilh** (tr.) to coil a rope, **nukaliilhtnm** to play at ring-throwing, **nuyalqiilh** hoop, **nusp'ilhayc** to have been hit in the genital area, **numîlh** to have a large vagina, **nut'kwilh** to bleed from the vagina, **splilh** vagina, **snumnts'lhtaylh** bloody part of salmon backbone, **nusxilh** (tr.) to scrape out the bloody part of salmon backbone

-ilh-alh month's travel (20.6.1): **ismawilhalh** one month's travel, **ilhnúsilhalh** two months' travel

(nu-...)-iilh-uts lips (20.2.1): **assiilhuts** both lips, **tqnkiilhuts** lower lip, **tctl'uk'iilhuts** upper lip, **nusp'iilhutsayc** to have been hit on the lip(s), **nupusmiilhuts** one's lips are swollen

299 **(+7)ilha7ilh** demonstrative, fem. remote sg. (15.4.1.1)

300 **ilhicw** shaded pool where fish congregate: **Ilhicwani** wife of North Wind

301 **ilhk'** (tr.), **ilhk'a** (itr.) to delouse somebody: **ilhk'iixwtsinu** I will delouse your head

302 **ilhm** standing up, erect, vertical, steep: **ilhmals** steep mountain side, **nu7ilhmalh** steep road, **ilhmik** steep roof, **ilhmuuts** steep shore, **alh7ilhm** standing up, erect, **alh7ilhmuutsaycts ala+tmcw+7ats** I am standing on the riverbank, **s7anu7ilhmik** mast

303 **ilhtsay** to pick berries: **q'slits'lhts s7ilhtsaylhts ka+sqaluts** I have been busy picking berries

304 **ilht'mlh** flea: **ilht'mlhim+ma ti+wats'+tc** the dog must have fleas

305 **+7ilhu, +7ilhú** imperative enclitic: ... first!, ... for a while! (28.3.20.3)

306 **ilhul** to be away for one day

307 **+7ilhuukax = +7ilhu** (28.3.20.4)

308 **Ilitmay** a woman's name

309 **ilk** mission bells (plant and edible bulbs)

310 ***ilt** (tr.) to put a cover over something: **kalh7iltta** bed sheets

311 **im** (tr.) to have sexual intercourse with somebody: **nus7iṁc** to be preoccupied with having sexual intercourse

312 ***im** (tr.) to connect, tie (up), wind string: **imnalusta** knuckle, **im-alht(n)** (tr.) to tie up a canoe, **imulh** (tr.), **imulha** (itr.) to roll up, wind a string, **s7anu7im** centipede

313 **-im** 3 sg. pass. tr. (14.3.3)

314 **imanta** bird's nest: **imantni** dim.

315 **imlk, *imlaakw** man, male: **im̲ml̲lki** boy, **imlkam+ts'** he is a man now,
imlkaaxta male cousins, **s7imlkuliitsta ti+nup** it is a man's shirt,
as7imlktamim ta+7na c+lha+7na he had a tryst with her, **imlaakwlh**
male animal

316 **imts** nephew, niece: **wa+7imtsmtsts** all my nephews and/or nieces

317 **-imut** reflexive suffix (19.10.4): **mnlhimut** to have a rest, **nmpimut**
to go aboard, **nukw'ptimut** to have one's fill of food, **iximut** fish
is spawning, **alh7nimuttum** he was given something

318 **in = n**

319 **ina, *in(a), *iin** (tr.) to bestow, present: **inatsx c+ti+smlhk+tc!**
give me the fish!, **inayclhilh c+7ats** these have been given to us,
iinalimtsk (tr.) to distribute food

320 **inacw** morning: **inacuts** to have breakfast

321 **inic-** more, in addition (23.6.2): **inic7ixw+alhu?** is it much further
yet?, **inicmawalhtxw!** let there be another bottle!, **wa+7inic7alhhi**
the remaining ones, **inictl'mstanaw+lhu ka+putl'** there will still be
more people coming, **inicknicim+malhu alhi** maybe there is still some
(more) food left

322 **in(7)iqw'i** a brave, hero: **in7iqw'im** to be brave

323 **inu** you (sg.) (25.2): **inu+aku?** is it you then?, **inulh t'ayc** this is
yours, **inutxw ti+ka+tl'ap!** may you be the one to go!, **inu ti+s-
tl'yukts** you are the one I am talking about

324 **inut+7iks?** what did he say? (25.5, 25.5.1.1, 25.5.5): **in7inutnic-
tscw+7iks?** what do you think I said?, **axw in7inuts** he did not say
anything

325 ***ip** narrow, thin: **nu7ipii** narrow, **nu7ipaalhi** narrow road, **ipliikti**
narrow space, **nu7ipiilhi** to have a small vagina, **nu7ipiiklayci** to
have a small penis, **S7iipnaluusi** a geographical name

326 **ipatsut** to store food: **nus7ipatsuutsta** larder, **nus7alh7ipatsuutsta**
refrigerator

327 **ipts** moss: **iptsliits** bark with moss on it, **iptslcik** moss starts to

grow on the roof, **iptsaak** lichen, limb moss, **iptsikit** they covered it with moss

328 **ipu** (tr.), **ipum** (itr.) to hide something: **iputsut** to hide oneself

329 **ip'** (tr.), **ip'a** (itr.) to catch, grab, hold, squeeze something: **ip'uulh** (tr.) to catch a ball, **alh7ip'ulhnm** to play lahal, **in7ip'-uulhla** catcher in baseball game, **in7ip'uutsta** fork, **alh7ip'utsm** to refrain from speaking, **s7ip'ama** handle, **anu7ip'iklxsm** to squeeze one's nose, **ip'aqw's** (tr.) to crush berries, **ip'aaxnm** to be extracting juice from berries, **Nu7ip'utsani** a bay west of **Nusilawat**

330 **Ip'ats'xti** a mythical name

331 **ip'tuus** to close one's eyes firmly

332 ***iq'** (tr.) to touch, disturb, move something: **axwtxw iq'aytucw!** do not disturb it!, **iq'usm** to move one's face around, **iq'alhm** to move, **iq'akm** (tr.) to touch, disturb something, **iq'tsut** to stir, move

333 **iq'im** (tr.) to braid somebody's hair: **iq'imtsinu** I will braid your hair, **iq'imtsut** to braid one's hair, **alh7iq'imaw** they have braids

334 **Iq'talikw** a personal name

335 **iq'uts** (tr.), **iq'utsa** (itr.) to rasp, file something: **iq'utsaktsx!** file my tool!, **iq'utsta** file, grindstone

336 **is-** to gather; to consume (23.2): **iskwmlh** to gather firewood, **is-7uk'uk'** to gather skunk cabbage leaves, **istii** to drink tea, **iŝlala-q'alh** to eat something fried, **iŝ7alh7ikwlh** to eat something barbecued, **is7iŝlaax** to always eat much, **istuc** (tr.) to butcher fish, **iŝmnts'aqw'stumulhx!** make us berry juice to drink!

337 **is-** intensive-prolonged (23.5): **ismúsilhalh** to travel for four months, **iscsiilh** to do something for an entire month, **istsk'nimut** to pine, be lonesome, homesick, **istscwimits sksnmakts** I worked enough, to my capacity, **istscwimit ti+7amlh** they are busy throughout the summer

338 **is7iisk(s)lhi** to whisper

339 **ismts'm** to dip one's food in eulachon grease

340 **isq's** (tr.) to singe the hairs off a pelt

341 ***issa** (tr.) to put earrings on somebody: **alh7issa** to be wearing earrings, **issa(a)ta** earring, **issaatatit** they made her wear earrings

342 **issut = isut**

343 **Ista** a geographical name: **Istamc** native of **Ista**

344 **ists'kw** (tr.), **ists'kwa** (itr.) to wet, splash water on something: **ists'kwiixw** (tr.) to water plants, **ists'kus** (tr.) to splash water on somebody's face, **ists'kwalus** (tr.) to sprinkle water on, extinguish a fire

345 **+7isu** imperative enclitic: ... again!, ... some more! (28.3.20.2)

346 **isut, issut** to paddle, travel by canoe: **isutus** to have a sunburnt face (having spent much time canoeing)

347 **it-** to speak (23.2): **itts'xlh** to speak English, **itNuxalkmc** to speak Nuxalk, **it7Atl'smc** to speak Chilcotin

348 **it-** to wear, clothing (23.2): **itkuut** to wear a coat, **itpik'uulh** to wear an oil coat, **ittsq'ts** I tore my clothes, **itkits'anlh** (tr.) to wash somebody's clothes, **itlhulhts'uulh** wearing no clothes, naked, **it7ayawanlhtmacw** to trade clothes

it-...-am to don, put on: **itnupam** to put on a shirt, **itsk'canlham** to dress in black

349 **+7it** imperative enclitic (28.3.20.1)

350 **+7it...k(a) = 7i...k(a)** coercive-contrastive (28.3.19.2, 28.3.22.2, 28.3.24)

351 **itl'** (tr.), **itl'a** (itr.) to shift, move something: **nu7itl'aaq** (tr.) to move a pan to another burner, **nu7itl'ik** (tr.) to transfer the contents of a pot, **itl'alh** (tr.) to make somebody walk, **itl'aalh** (tr.) to move somebody's foot, **itl'alhm** to move, walk, **itl'alhm** (tr.) to move off somebody's path, **itl'aalhm** (tr.) to move something with one's foot, **itl'tsut** to move over, step aside, **iciitl'a** to play checkers

352 **itqu** (tr.) to haul, tow something: **ka+7alh7itqwwaylayctumcw+a c+ti+**

qw'xwmtimutts+tc? will you be able to tow my car?

353 **its** (tr.) to rub, scrub something: **itsulmcta** brush used for scrubbing the floor, **alh7itsiik** washboard, **itsliikta** tool used during a massage

354 **itsa**, ***itsn** tooth: **iitstsni** dim., **itsaatimut** false teeth, **k'ilh-7itsa** to be toothless, **itsnayc** to have teeth

355 **itskw** to be remote, out of the way: **itskwix!** let me pass!, **itskw-alhix!** get out of my way!, **itskwnulitxw!** move it a little further!, **alh+ta+7itskwilh+txw** some months ago, **Nutciictskwani** Necleetsconnay River

356 ***itsn** = **itsa**

357 **Itsu** a woman's name

358 **its'ama**, **its'amni** blanket: **its'amayanm** to don a blanket

359 **its'kalimtsk** (tr.), **its'kalimtska** (itr.) to distribute presents

360 **its't** (tr./itr.) to squirt (on or into something): **nu7its'tiklayc** to ejaculate, **nu7its'talsikanaycts** somebody squirted water into my ear

361 **ituuxt** to go fishing for one day

362 **ix** (tr.), **ixa** (itr.) to grind, apply friction to something: **alh7ix-aalhm** to shuffle, drag one's feet, **iximut** "rubbing oneself" = fish is spawning

363 **ix-** = **ic-** (23.8)

364 **ixixi** snow goose

365 **ixqlm** to swim

366 **ixw** far, remote: **ixwam** to go on a long journey, **Ixwik** a geographical name

367 **i7yum** animal howls

K

368 **...k, ...ka** contrastive (28.3.19, 28.3.22.2, 28.3.24)

369 **-k** reduced allomorph of **-ik** found in e.g. **slaq'k, lhkw'mk, almk, k'matk**

370 **ka+ks?** which is it? (25.5, 25.5.2, 25.5.5)

371 **ka+** hypothetical, irrealis, future (28.2.1)

372 **ka-...-s** next, following (23.7): **kamalacws** next year, **kaynucs** to-morrow, **ka7a7amlhanmiis** next spring, **kanukaliks** at noon (said in the morning)

373 **...ka = ...k**

374 **kakaatsii** cute, charming

375 ***kal** right, straight, in the proper way or place: to go straight; to act suitably; to detect, find, meet: **nukalalhtxw wa+m∧mnta+ts!** follow a straight path!, **nukaluutsts** it went right into my mouth, **nukaliilhnm** to play at ring-throwing, **alhkalliwa** handy, adroit, **alhkaltcwm** (tr.) to guide, look after somebody, **alhkaltcwmitsut** to look after oneself, behave, be careful, **kaluuts** to use the right word, **kalxs** to arrive at the right time (/kal⌃lxs/), **nukalnicim c+ a+skwatstas+ts** he is given his rightful name, **nukaklstcutsm** to pre-pare one's food, **kalaalhm** (tr.) to find somebody, **kalaaqwsm** (tr.) to detect, descry something, **nukaltsinu** I will meet you, **kaltmacwm** (tr.) to meet somebody, **nukaltimut** "to be met by oneself" = to re-turn to where one comes from

nukalik center, middle, half: **nukalik ti+suncw** noon, midday, **nukal-ik ti+sntl'** midnight, **anukaliiklh** afternoon, **nukalikutstam** lunch-time, to have lunch, **snukaklikaycs wa+sulut+ts** the middle of the channel, **nukaliktak ti+sutk** midwinter, **anukalikayc** center beam, **anukalikuuts** half tide, **nukalikuulhla** half moon, **anukakliktmaculh = nukalikuulhla, nukakliktmacwtuts ulh+7inu** I will give half to you

376 **Kalastakw** a mythical woman's name

377 **kalh-, kas-** to gather, collect, pursue, hunt (23.2): **kalhnʉ́nmk'** to hunt animals, **kalhmaaxts** to collect clay, **kalhqax = kasqax** to hunt rabbit, **kaŝmlhk** to fish, **ikalhcʉ́cnastimut** to seek a wife

378 **kalh-** down, below, under (23.6.2): **alhkalhk'ctsut** to look down from a height, **kalhst'cwmta** cedarbark mattress

379 **Kalqm** a mythical woman's name

380 **Kalyaakas** a mythical man's name

381 **kamalh+** if (28.2.2)

382 ***kan** to be hit, bumped, hurt: **kannic** (tr.) to hurt somebody accidentally, **kannimut** to hurt oneself accidentally, **kannmacw** to bump into each other, **alhkañmacw** "to have collided together" = to resemble each other

383 ***kan** unspecified location: **kanmcnu+ks?** from which country are you?

384 **kanani** bracket fungus

385 **kanic, *kancw** (tr.) to wait for, worry about somebody: **kanicilh** we are waiting for him to come, **kancwlctits** I am beginning to worry about them (they should have been here by now)

386 **Kanilhkas** a woman's name

387 **Kanilhmay** a woman's name

388 **kanus-...-m, nus-...-m** having a ... odor or flavor (23.7): **kanuŝcm** having a bad odor/flavor, **kanusyam** having a good flavor, sweet, **kanuslhuk'm** having a horrible odor/flavor, **kanusxawism** having a metallic flavor, **kanuŝt'sm** having a salty flavor, **nusyamutsmits** I like its flavor

389 **kap'ay** humpback salmon: **kaakp'ayi** dim., **skakp'ayslh** small biting fly that abounds during the humpback salmon season, **kap'aytam** season of the humpback salmon

390 **kas- = kalh-** (377)

391 **kasmiw** golden eagle: **kasmiwi** dim., **kasmiŵlh** eggs of golden eagle

392 **kastsaw** to expect more: to bargain for more than the other party is

willing to give; shaman awaiting power

393 **kats'an** tail: **kaakts'ani** dim.

394 **Kats't** Brynildson Bay

395 **kaw** (tr.) to accomodate, support, prop, pile; to transport, carry, bring, deliver: **kawaalhta** footstool, **nukawalhm** to climb on a chair in order to reach something, **nukawaaxta** seat, chair, **kawams** (tr.) to wedge something, **kawlstaw+ts' c+a+t'xt+7ats** they pile these rocks on top, **kawnkta** fat around kidneys, **kawtim ulxlh** they were taken up the river, **ickaku** (tr.) to pack things around, **nukaŵts-tinilh** people bring us food, **kawalh** (tr.) to walk somebody home, **kawak** (tr.) to give somebody a job, **kulhkaṁut** to pay a prostitute

396 **kaycii** to be very or too ...: **kaycii st'ŝ** it is very salty, **kaycii-naw s7ixwaw** they are too far away

397 **kaynucs** tomorrow: **kaynucsakmits+ma** I may do it tomorrow

398 **kc** (tr.), **kca** (itr.) to draw a straight line on something: **icnukc-alhclhit wa+mʎmnta+ts** they are painting lines on the road, **kclqs** (tr.) to strike a match

399 **Kiicpiixwlayc** a man's name

400 **Kikiilha** a man's name

401 **kikya** grandmother: **kiikya** great-grandmother

402 **kikyu** (tr.), **kikyum** (itr.) to chew something: **nukikyûtstx!** chew the food for him!, **sisikyumaaxalits** molars

403 **Kilhaax** a woman's name

404 **kilm** to curl up, shrink: **nukilmanlhts** my dress has shrunk

405 **Kimilhqan** a mythical woman's name

406 **kinkin** water parsnip (root): **kinkinlhp** water parsnip (whole plant)

407 **kip'** (tr.), **kip'a** (itr.) to grasp, pinch: **kip'ta** clothespin, **kip'-aaksta** clamp, **kip'lxsalhm** (tr.) to grab something with one's toes

408 **kits'** (tr.), **kits'a** (itr.) to twist, wring something: **kits'm** to twist cedar bark, **alhkits'liktn** it is twisted, **kits'anlhm** to wash one's clothes by hand, **nuskiitsta** washtub, **kits'maaxalh** to twist

one's ankle, **kinkits'muutstimut** to contort one's mouth, grimace, **anukits'm** whirlpool, **anukits'miixw** back eddy

*kits' to be twisted (cf. 17.3.1): **kits'us** having a twisted face, **stikits'ank** lopsided, **Nukits'** "twisted water" = Hagensborg

409 **klacw** muskrat: **kɪklaacwi(i)** dim.

410 **klh** (tr./itr.), **klha** (itr.) to fall, drop something: **klhm** to take dried fish down (in smokehouse), **klh ti+snx+t'ayc** the sun is setting, **usklhanulhikts** something fell on my back, **usklhanulhiixwts** something fell on my head, **klhnimut** to slip and fall, **nuklhakts** it fell from my hand, **nuklhutsts** it fell out of my mouth

411 **klh7an** to menstruate: **sklh7anlhh** menstrual discharge, **sklh7ans tsi+ xwⁿxwnm** scarlet spots on maple leaves

412 **klhc** to be awake: **alhklhciktinits** somebody stayed up (waiting) for me, **alhklhciknm** to be a night-watchman

413 **klhm, nuklhm** to cross: **nuklhmts c+7ats ala+7anuxum+7ats** I am going to cross the river now, **nuklhmaaxuts** to cross the road, **nuklhmikts** I want to go across, **Sinuklhm** Canoe Crossing, **nus(7)alhklhm** seven

414 **kɪkl** herring: **kɪklta** herring seine

415 **klklii** to be slow, take one's time: **klkliliwa** to be sort of slow

416 **Kltiilh** Cascade Inlet

417 **kma** to be in pain: **kmalayc** to be ill, **nukma** to have a stomach ache, **kmayankts** my side hurts, **nukmaykalusts** my chest hurts, **kulhkmats** my penis hurts, **nukmayalmcts** my breasts hurt, **nukmayklxsakts** the tip of my finger hurts, **kmayulhikakts** the back of my hand hurts, **nukmayalhhts** my throat hurts, **nukmayaaxts** my rectum hurts, **nukmayaalhts** my footsole hurts, **nukmaykiixwts** I have a headache, **kmayaaqalitsts** I have a toothache, **nukmayalsikants** I have an earache, **kmayalusts** I have a cold, **kmayulhikts** my back hurts, **nukmayuulhnnakts** my testes hurt, **kmayulhaqw'sts** my eyes hurt, **kmalxsts** my nose hurts, **Nuskmata** a mythical woman's name

418 **kmap's** (tr.) to put heated rocks in water: **kmap'stx!** put the heated

rocks in the water!, **kmap'sta** pliers used for putting hot rocks in water

419 **knic** (tr.) to eat something: **snknic** food

420 **kntaw** dear (term of address)

421 **knum** smoked fish fillet: **nuknumta** box in which **knum** is stored, **us-knumayc** "to crave **knum**" = to be very hungry, starving

422 **kp** each, every, all (26.3.7): **kplhaw+atu sputl'lhaw?** have they all come?, **kpuslhaw+atu?** did each of them get his share?, **kputstutanx!** give each of them something to eat!, **kpustxw ska+nut'qanicw!** put a stamp on each!, **ala+7alhkp wa+tsay suncw** every day, **alhkpiixwaw skmalaycaw** they all are ill, **alhkputsmits wa+smayusta+ts** each story is mine, **anayks ska+kpalhmis wa+tsay alh+txw** then he wanted to go to all places, **kpakmit s7usmntacwit** they have finished skimming it, **Anukpalslay** a woman's name

423 **ks** rich, nutritious: **ks t'ayc ŝnknics** this is rich food

424 **ks** (tr.), **ksa** (itr.) to take off, pull (off) something: **kstx!** pull it off!, **ksm** to pull or reel in (net or fishing line), **ksiixwm** to take one's hat off, **ksaalhm** to take one's shoes off, **ksuulhm** to take one's pants off, **nunuksaaxutsm** to breathe deeply, **anuksutsm** to inhale, **nuksaasktmacw** to play at tug-of-war, **ksalaaqtntx kulhuuts-am!** pull the canoe ashore!, **axw ksalhaycts** I cannot get it off my feet, **nuksaaxalhm** to retreat, walk backwards, **ksunsulhayc** to have convulsions, **alhksulh** "money removed" = cheap, **ksalc** to get married *ksnm** to be domestically active: **sksnmsta** hunting area, **ksnmak** to work, **ksnmaktu-** to make somebody work, **axw ksnmakaylaycts** I cannot work

kstu-, **kstcwa** (itr.) to do, make, fix: **kstcwaynicits+ts'** I already did it, **kstcwatumulhx!** fix it for us!, **tu+kslhtcw+txw** the ones who have made it, **kstcutsm** to fix (prepare, store) one's food, **kstimut** to work, **kstimtimut** to be diligent

425 **+ks** interrogative marker (25.5, 28.3.18.5, 28.3.24)

426 **ktl'ii** short: **ktl'lci** to become shorter, **ktl'atl'aalhi** to be short-
-legged, **ktl'aatl'qi** short tree, **kuulhktl'i** to have a short penis

427 **+ku** attenuative: ..., sir/madam, ... then? (28.3.11, 28.3.24)

428 **+kuks** but, unexpectedly, on the contrary (28.3.18.1)

429 **kukwpi** grandfather: **kuukwpi** great-grandfather

430 ***kul** to (want to) borrow: **kulakts ulh+7inu** I want to borrow your
tool, **kululhiixwts ulh+7inu** I want to borrow your hat, **kululhs c+
ta+lhalas** he borrowed a boat, **kulits'ts c+ti+7its'amninu+tc** I want
to borrow your blanket (/kul⁼lits'-ts/), **kulaktumx c+ti+qulhquulh-
tanu+tc!** lend me your pencil!, **kululhiixwtumx!** lend me your hat!,
kululhtumx! lend me your vehicle!

kult to borrow: **kultts c+ti+nictanu+tc** I will borrow your saw, **kul-
tstumx c+ti+7ictaala!** lend me a dollar!, **kultiixwtumx!** lend me your
hat!

431 ***kulh** base combined with lexical suffix (20.2, 20.3): **kulhnk** base
of tree; foot of mountain, **kulhnkaaxalh** edge of roof, **kulhnalus**
channel, **kulhlxs** tip of pointed object, **kulhlxsanilh** hip, hipbone,
kulhank side, **kulhankus** hillside, **kulhals** wall, **kulhalsikan** back of
ear, **kulhalxi** back of head, neck, **kulhalaalh** base of mountain,
kulhaax back door, **kulhaaxuts** roadside; to be near a fire, **kulhaax-
utstxw!** put it near the fire!, **kulhik** roof, **kulhikuuts** edge, **kulh-
ikalh** to stand behind somebody, **kulhuts** edge, rim, **kulhuuts** shore,
beach, **kulhuutsalh** to be on the shore, **kulhutsam** (to go) towards
the shore, **kulhulmc** earth, land, ground, **kulhkwlhulmc** earthbound
spirit, ghost, **kulhulhuus** bow of boat, **kulhaliits** side of tongue
*skulh body part (20.2): **skulhnk** buttocks, **skulhnalus** joint, **skulhnalusaqw's** bridge of nose, **skulhnaluslxsak** web-like structure between the fingers, **skulhlxsalh** toe, **skulhlxsak** finger, **skulhapsm**
neck, **skulhank** side, **skulhankus** side of face, **skulhankutsalh** side
of lower leg, **skulhankutsliitsalh** = **skulhankutsalh**, **skulhalakt**
glands in armpit, **skulhaaxams** jaw, **skulhaaxalh** ankle, **skulhaaxak**

wrist, **skulhikalh** shin, **skulhikak** upper surface of hand, **skulhikus** forehead, **skulhiixwalst** shoulder, **skulhutsak** lower arm, **skulhuutslayc** nipple, **skulhuulhan** temple

432 **kulh-, kus-** (having) much/many, being very ... (23.2, 23.8): **kulhpapink** there are many snakes around, **kulhpats'alhta** "having many awls" = Scottish thistle, **kulhtaala** having much money, rich, **kulhk'ay** there is much snow, **kulhya** "very good" = clean, **kuŝtpuusps** having many freckles on the face, **kuŝtlh** very strong, **kuŝkw'alhla** very friendly

433 **kulh-, kus-** penis (23.3, 23.8): **kulhtsaakw** to have a long penis, **kulhtscwi** to have an average-sized penis, **kulhnaq'tm** to be sexually impotent, **alhkulhnmnmaaxim** he is unable to urinate, **kulhkaṁut** to pay a prostitute, **kus7m** to have an erection, **alhkuŝuq'** circumcised

434 **kupi** coffee: **nukupiita** coffeepot

435 **kup'** (tr.) to skewer, run a stick through something: **kup'm** to put fish on a barbecuing stick, **kup'sta** skewer, barbecuing stick

436 **kus-** = **kulh-**

437 **kusi** potatoes: **nukusyals** root cellar, **nukusita** potato bed

438 **kusu** pig

439 **kuut** coat: **itkuut** to wear a coat

440 **+kw** quotative: reportedly, it is said that ... (28.3.10, 28.3.24)

441 **-kw** formative suffix (22.3): **Statikw** a man's name, **Tswaakilakw** a man's name, **tsk'alhkw** devil's club, **ts'xlhmkw** drowned, **tsnkw** self

442 **Kwaasla** Smith Inlet

443 **Kwaaxila** a man's name

444 **kwakwas** small type of owl

445 **kwanat** to cry, weep: **skwanat** mourning song, **nuskwanatmc** given to weeping, **Kwanatulhayc** a geographical name: Crying Rock

446 **kwatasyan** Dolly Varden trout: **kwataasyani** dim.

447 **kwa7yalaqs** bluejay: **kwa7yalaaqsi** dim., **kwa7yalaqsaqw's** blue

448 **kwayx** powdery, dusty: **Kwayxus** a woman's name, **alhkwayxuulh** bannock

449 **kwcw** (tr.) to match, fit something: **axw alhkwcwts alh+tc** it (clothing) does not fit me, **kwcwaycts ulh+tc** it fits me, **kwcwaqw'stmacw-
ayc** the colors match

450 **kwcwm** (tr.) to place near a fire, to warm something: **kwcwmtsut** to
warm oneself, **kwcwmtu-** to warm something up

451 **kwikwtik** having a rough surface

452 **kwilh** (tr.), **kwilha** (itr.) to crush, crumble: **kwilhulh** (tr.) to
crush cooked food; to clear an area of rocks, **kwilhkwlha** to rummage

453 ***kwitl'** (tr.) to stir, disturb something: **alhkwitl'** (tr.), **alhkwitl'a** (itr.) to stir a liquid, **anukwitl'm** something is stirring
in the water, the water is rippling

454 **kwit'** (tr.), **kwit'a** (itr.) to crowd, squeeze in, wedge, separate:
kwit'alhnictscw = **kwit'liwanictscw** you are in my way, **kwit'aaxlayc**
to be stuck in a crowd, **csuuts s7alhkwit'iks** all doors are locked,
kwit'ulmc (tr.) to break up, loosen soil

455 **kwl** warm, hot: **nukwlaax** it is a hot day, **kwlaltwa** warm weather or
season, **nukwluts** the weather is hot, **alhkwltsut** to warm oneself,
nukwĭkwli lukewarm
***kwlc** to become warm (/*kwl⁻lc/): **kwlctu-** to warm something up, **nu-
kwlcuts** the weather is warming up

456 **kwlamk** (tr.), **kwlamka** (itr.) to distribute, hand out gifts: **kwlamk-
usnm** to be handing out food, **kwlamkusaycts** I received my share,
kwlamkuslhits c+lha+cnaslh I have given him a woman

457 **kwlh** (tr.) to crack, split something: **alhkwlh** cracked, **nukwlhiktx!**
split it!
***kwlh** to be cracked (cf. 17.3.1): **kwlhulhiixwlaycts** my kneecap is
cracked, **nukwlhik ti+satl'ats+tc** my canoe is cracked, **nukwlhikiixw**
jar has a crack near the lid, **anukwlhuulh** bottle is cracked on one
side, **anukwlhuuts** neck of bottle is cracked, **alhkwlhals** bottle has
a crack running from the neck to the bottom, **nukwlhaaq** bottom of
bottle is cracked, **alhkwlhalusm ta+7assaaq** bottom of bottle is all

cracked up, **alhkwlhaaxuts(ak)** pitchwood torch, **Kwlhani** a woman's
name

458 **kwm** thick, bulky: **kwmkwmalh** having thick legs, **kwmaluulh** rope is
thick, **kwmuulhla** fat person, **kwmuuts** big whistle used in **Sisawk**
dance

459 ***kwma** to wish the best, say farewell: **kwma+7it!** goodbye!, to your
health! (sg. addressee), **kwmanaw+it!** goodbye!, to your health! (pl.
addressee), **ax+ku kwmanu!** we will meet again!

460 **kwmay** worm: **kwmaytim ti+knum** the knum is infested with worms

461 **kwmlh** firewood: **kulhkwmlh** there is an abundance of firewood, **kwmlhalus** wood stove, **nukwmlhta** woodshed, **iskwmlh** to gather firewood

462 **kwn** (tr.) to get, take, bring something: **kwntsinu** I will take you
with me, **kwnm** to go and get something, **alhkwntx!** bring it!, **kwnutsm**
to get oneself something to eat, **kwnaaxsta** box used for storing
food, **alhkwntsis ta+mans+tx c+a+sluq'** he took eulachon grease to
bring to his father, **nukwnus** (tr.) to coil a rope, **nukwnalh** (tr.)
to follow somebody, **kwnikusayc** to walk on the riverbank, **kwnaaxutsayc** to walk on a sandbar

463 **Kwn7na** a man's name

464 **kwntsalha** a type of canoe

465 **kwpalh** liver: **kwpalhplhi** dim.

466 **kws** rough: **Kwsalh** a man's name

467 **kwsaslhm** to go somewhere in vain

468 **kwst** entire skin surface, exterior aspect of body

469 **kwtl'** (tr.), **kwtl'a** (itr.) to place on the ground, plant something,
put in place, arrange: **kwtl'us** (tr.) to pile things on the floor,
alhkwtl'ikayc alh+ti+7alhqulh+tc it is lying on the book, **kwtl'ik-
ayctu-** to put something on top of something, **alhkwtl'tmacwtu-** to
place objects side by side, **kwtl'tx wa+nusk'ctnulhaqw'stanu+ts!** put
your glasses on!, **skwtl'lhp** seed, **alhkwtl'** plant, **kwtl'aycs+kw ska+
kmalaycs** he was contaminated and fell ill, **kwtl'nalus** (tr.) to in-

sert something, **kwtl'aaqalitsm** to put one's false teeth in, **nu-kwtl'uts** "words planted in mouth" = (to be a) liar, **nunukwtl'uutsm** to tell lies, **nukwtl'aaq** (tr.) to boil something in a pot, **iŝnu-kwtl'aaqlh** to eat boiled food, **alhkwtl'tu-** "to cause to be deposited" = to give something as security, to pledge

470 **kwtmts** husband: **k'ilhkwtmts** = **anuskwtmts** widow

471 **Kwtsaax** a man's name

472 **kwtsus** young mountain goat

473 **kwtus** (tr.) to lower somebody's face to the water: **kwtusm** to lower one's face to the water (in order to drink from it)

474 **kwwaaxa** (tr.) to fool, mislead somebody

475 **+kw'**, **+k'u** frequently, repeatedly (28.3.12, 28.3.24)

476 **kw'alc** scorched: **kw'alcnicits** I scorched it, **kanuskw'alcm** it smells scorched

477 ***kw'alh** good, complete, grown: **kw'alhtu-** to raise a child, **kw'alh-tnmc** to be raising a child, **k'ilhkw'alhtcw** having no parents, waif, **kw'alhliwa** handy (object), **kw'alhla** friendly, amicable, **kuŝkw'alhla** very friendly, **k'iŝkw'alhla** unfriendly, hostile
kw'alhtn (tr.) to delineate, outline, shape, mark: **kamalh+kw'alhtn-im wa+suncw+7ats** when the universe was created, **tmkw'alhtnaalhayc** only his footprints remained, **kw'alhtnaynicits+ts'** now I see, understand (what somebody is talking about), **kw'alhtnakm** (tr.) to mark something, **alhkw'alhtnakm** marked, a sign, **kw'alhtnta** plan(s), intentions(s)

478 **Kw'alhna** Kwatna: **Kw'alhnamc** Kwatna native

479 **kw'atsa** (tr.) to shake something: **nukw'atsayktx!** shake the container!, **kw'atsayaakm** to wave one's hand, **kw'atsayusm** = **kw'atsayxwm** to nod affirmatively

480 ***kw'cw** to look out, be observant: **alhkw'cwmitsut** to be cautious, careful, **kw'cwmitsutstu-** to make aware of risk, caution somebody

481 **Kw'ixlakilakw** a man's name

482 **kw'la** belly, abdomen

483 **kw'lh** (tr.), **kw'lha** (itr.) to pour out, fill something with a liquid: **nukw'lhiik** (tr.), **nukw'lhiika** (itr.) to fill a container with liquid; to can fish, **nukw'lhta** stomach, **Nuskw'lh** Nasku Bay

484 **kw'liwas**, **kw'lwas** brother-in-law

485 **kw'lsi** gills of fish: **kw'lsyams** fish cheeks

486 **kw'lwas** = **kw'liwas**

487 **kw'n** (tr.), **kw'na** (itr.) to point at something: **nukw'n** (tr.), **nukw'na** (itr.) to aim at something, **kw'nustits** I'll show it to them, **kw'nusnm** to be showing things to people, **kw'nmiixw** to nod affirmatively

kw'nta plan, decision, resolution, instruction: **alhkw'ntnaaktinits** somebody showed me how to do it, **alhkw'ntaliwa** (tr.) to instruct, tell somebody what to do, **kw'ntatsutts ska+qw'xwmts** I decided to move, **Alhkw'ntam(aakas)** the supreme deity, **ickw'nta** (tr.) to marry off, give one's daughter away in marriage, **ickw'ntatss ta+mants+tx ulh+ti+kwtmtsts+t'ayc** my father gave me in marriage to this husband of mine, **alhkw'ntatnm** to have arranged a meeting, to be having a date

488 **kw'ni** fur seal: **nkw'nî** dim.

489 **kw'p** right, straight: **nukw'paalh** road is straight, **kw'piiqwamtuts** I straightened it, **kw'plctu-** to explain something, **nukw'plcutstnm** to analyze, interpret (a text), **kw'panlhutstimutx!** say it the right way!, **nukw'panlhik** to be helpful, **nukw'panlhaax** to go with the wind (in a boat), **nukw'palh** (tr.) to (go and) meet somebody, **kw'puts** fishing net, **kw'puuptsi** small fishing net, **nukw'putsals** net loft
***skw'p** (to the) right: **skw'paalh** right leg or foot, **skw'palmc** right breast, **skw'panlhaqw's** right eye, **skw'pankslh** right side, **skw'paakslh** right hand, **skw'paaqslh** right leg

490 **-kw'p** fathom (20.6.1): **makw'p** one fathom, **lhwaaskw'p** two fathoms

491 ***kw'pst** (tr.) to (re)arrange, restore: **kw'pstayc** to have recovered,

sober up, **kw'pstakm** (tr.) to repair something, **kw'pstalus** (tr.) to stoke a fire, **Kw'pstaltalusm** a woman's name, **nukw'pstaax** (tr.) to offer somebody a seat, **kw'pstutsm** (tr.) to repeat a word (and say it) properly, **nukw'pstaaxla** (tr.) to collect a liquid

492 **kw'pt** to become saturated (with water): **alhkw'pt** to be waterlogged, **kw'pttu-** to soak something in water, **nukw'pt** to be satiated, full from eating

493 **kw'pwalht** wing, flight-feather: **kw'pupwaalhti** dim., **askw'pwalhtulh-iiqw** to wear a feather bonnet, **tamkw'pwalhttu-** to make wings for somebody

494 **Kw'qwla** Clayton Falls

495 **kw's** to be somebody's steady date, fiancé: **kw'smtmacwaw** they are engaged, **iskw'ismtmacwaw** they (animals) are constantly mating

496 **kw'wa** (tr.) to bake food around a fire

497 **kw'wams, skw'wams** dimple in cheek

498 **Kw'yay** name of a Heiltsuk village west of **Na7mu**

499 **k'acw** to be empty, absent, nothing (26.3.8): **k'acwlhts** I have been away, **tick'acw** to catch nothing, **nuk'acwiik** container is empty, **nuk'aculhiik** house is empty, **k'acwlxslayc** the road ends

500 ***k'alh** (tr.) to whirl: **k'alhm** top (toy), **sk'alhk'alh** sling (weapon)

501 **k'am-** equal, same, coincidentally (23.5): **k'am7ayliwanaw stalawsaw alh+ta+smawilh+tx** they got married in the same month, **k'amtsaylh-tuts ta+tl'aplhtuts ulh+7inu in t'ayc** I have given you and him the same amount

502 **k'amk'** bull kelp: **k'amk'uk's** a mass of bull kelp

503 **k'amwas** young beaver (= **k'manwas**)

504 **k'anawilh** bow of boat: **k'anawilhts+7its'ik** and then I will be at the bow

505 **k'ankuus** deadfall: **k'ankuusm** to use a deadfall

506 ***k'apat** sharp: **k'apatuts** sharp blade, **nuk'apatlxs** sharp point,

k'apatutslctu- to sharpen a blade, **nuk'apatlxslctu-** to sharpen a point, **k'ak'patutslhp = ak'patutslhp** spruce needles

507 **k'aputs** sucker fish: **k'ak'puutsi** dim.

508 **k'aqas** crow: **k'aqaasi** dim.

509 **k'awn** blackmouth springsalmon

510 **k'ax+...** = **ax+...** (27.6, 28.3.23)

511 **k'axw = axw** (27.6)

512 **k'ay** snow: **k'aymtinilh** we are having snow, **kulhk'ay** there is much snow, **ayk'aym** it is snowing

513 **k'c** (tr./itr.) to see, look (at something): **k'ctx!** look at him!, **k'cx usqa!** look outside!, **ka+k'ctsinu+matuts'!** (I will) see you later!, **k'ctxw tqwntl'!** make him look this way!, **k'ctmacw** to see each other, **alhk'cits** I see it, **alhk'c tc usqa** he is looking outside, **nuk'calxim** to look back, **alhk'calhits** I saw where he went, **alhk'custss** he looked me in the face, **k'caktsinu** I look at your hand, **nuk'c** (tr.) to inspect a net for fish, **nuk'cik** (tr.) to look into a container, **alhk'cancankm** to keep looking around, **anuk'cikaktulht** they always look at everything we do, **k'cuusnm** to look at a newborn infant, **sk'cta** telescope, **nusk'ctnulhaqw'sta** (...aaqws...) glasses, spectacles, **nusk'cikulhaqw's** center of eye, pupil, **alhtamk'c** (tr./itr.) to wait for, expect somebody, **ick'icit** they keep checking it

514 **k'icw** (tr.), **k'icwm** (itr.) to gnaw at something: **alhk'icw** it has been gnawed at

515 **k'ilh-, k'is-** lacking, not having (23.2, 23.8): **k'ilhmnta** to have nowhere to go, wander around aimlessly, **k'ilhman** to be fatherless, **k'ilh7amatalaaxt** orphan, **k'ilhcnas** to have no wife, widower, bachelor, **k'ilhkwtmts** to have no husband, widow, single woman, **k'ilh-7itsa** toothless, **k'ilhnús** "(ten) minus two" = eight (/k'ilh⁻lhnús/) (26.2), **k'ilhtcumat** to have lost one's way, **k'iŝts'kaak** to be clumsy, **k'iŝts'kuuts** to mispronounce, **k'iŝlq'** mindless, stupid, **k'iŝmaw**

"(ten) minus one" = eight (26.2)

516 **k'im** (tr.) to look for a needed object (e.g. tool, part or material needed to complete one's work): **sk'im** needed object

517 **k'inacw** crab: **k'ik'naacwi** dim.

518 **k'ip** to erode: **k'ipuuts** riverbank is eroding, **k'ipllxs** point of land is eroding

519 **k'ipt** red elderberry: **ink'iptlhp** red elderberry plant, **k'iptulh** wine made of red elderberries

520 **k'is- = k'ilh-**

521 **k'ita** little finger: **sk'italxsalh** little toe

522 **k'ita** herring rake

523 ***k'l** coagulated, frozen, stuck: **k'lulmc** frozen ground, **nuk'laax** to be iced in
*k'lc (/***k'l⌐lc**/) to coagulate, solidify, freeze; to become stuck, be glued: **nuk'lc** water is freezing, **nuk'lcaaxilh** we are getting iced in, **k'lctu-** to freeze or glue something, **nuk'lculhaaxts** I am sticking to my seat, **lk'lcaakts** something is sticking to my hand, **k'lcta** glue

524 **k'lat** steelhead trout: **lk'laati** dim., **lk'laatlh** cutthroat trout, **Nuk'lat** name of a bay situated southwest of **Alhku**

525 **k'lay** bark of western birch: **lk'laylhp** western birch

526 **k'lht, k'lhtn** (tr.), **k'lhtna** (itr.) to brace, support something: **nuk'lhtnik** (tr.) to boil half-smoked fish in a container with little cedar sticks on the bottom, **nuk'lhtnaaq** (tr.) = **nuk'lhtnik**, **k'lhtnta** supporting pole

527 **k'm** (tr.), **k'ma** (itr.) to bite something: **k'mamsm** "to bite one's jaw" = to check oneself, not say anything, **k'mlhtinits** "I have been bitten" = I have hooked a fish, **alhk'ma** to be holding something in one's mouth
*k'm (tr.) to squeeze in, catch in trap: **k'ma**, ***k'mn-** to be stuck, trapped, **mk'mlqsakta** "finger-squeezer" = finger ring, **k'maalhta**

trap, **k'maalhayc** animal is trapped; one's feet are trapped, **k'maak-sta** clamp, vise, **alhk'mnaalhts** my shoes are too tight, **mk'mats ala+nupts** my shirts are too tight, **nuk'mnalhh** to choke, **kukulhk'ma** to have the hiccups

528 **k'mani** smelt (fish)

529 **k'manwas = k'amwas**

530 **k'matk** to stay overnight: **k'matkilh ala+7awcwa** we will spend the night here

531 **K'mckw'itxw** Kimsquit

532 **k'mlh** abdominal fin

533 **-k'mt** day(s) (20.6.1): **músk'mt** four days, **lhwaask'mtam** s...s he ...ed for two days

534 **k'musm** to do something for an entire year, complete an annual cycle, celebrate one's birthday: **k'musmakaw sksnmakaw** they worked for a year, **k'musmalh** to spend a year travelling, **yayaatwii ti+sk'musm-nu!** happy birthday!

535 **k'nm** to shake, tremble: **k'nmnicis** he shook it, **alhk'nmakts** my hands are trembling

536 **k'nts** sperm whale: **nk'ntsi** dim.

537 **k'ts** (tr.), **k'tsa** (itr.) to chop, cut with an axe: **k'tsaax** (tr.) to cut down a tree, **k'tsuulh** (tr.) to chop up a log, **nuk'tsiiqw** (tr.) to cut the top off a tree, **nuk'tsiktx!** cut it in half!, **k'tslqsak-ayc** his finger was chopped off, **sk'ts** "that which fells one" = disease, illness

538 **k'tsaatsay** licorice fern

539 **+k'u = +kw'**

540 **k'ucani** butter clam: **k'uuk'caní** dim., **k'ucanyalh** screw, **k'ucanita** screwdriver

541 **k'ult** porpoise: **k'uk'ulti** dim., **k'ultaalh** running shoes

542 **k'umts'** dried clams: **k'umts'm** to put clams on a stick and hang them in the smokehouse to dry

543 **k'up** to press (down), lower, crouch: **k'uplc** (tr.) to stalk, sneak up on somebody, **unk'upt** to press hard when defecating

544 **k'us** it is calm, there is no wind: **nuk'us** the water is calm, **k'usm-tinilh** we have no wind, we are becalmed

545 **k'utsci** maggots: **k'uukw'tscî** dim.

546 **k'yuk** (tr.) to identify, recognize, know somebody: **k'yuktx!** find out who he is!, **alhk'yukits** I know him

L

547 **+(7)l...** interrogative marker (28.3.24)

548 **-l-** connective (22.4)

549 **-la** formative suffix (22.2): **Piisla** name of a stream, **Kwaasla** Smith Inlet, **Q'umaanakwla** a chief's name

550 **laakts** squirrel: **laaktsi** dim.

551 **Laaqwamays** a mythical man's name

552 **-lacw, -lancw, -slancw** year (20.6.1): **malacw** year, **maslancwakts sksnmakts** I work for one year, **lhwaaslancw** two years, **asmúslancwts s7alh7aq'uts** I have been in prison for three years, **mawlxslancwamts +ts'** I am twenty years old now

553 **lahal** lahal (a game)

554 **lalam** to pole a canoe up the river: **Lalamani** a man's name

555 **lalaq'a** (tr./itr.), **lalaq'am** (itr.) to fry: **islalaq'alhh** to eat something fried, **lalaq'ata** frying pan

556 **La7lay** a woman's name

557 **Lamas** a man's name

558 **lamatu** domestic sheep

559 **-lancw = -lacw**

560 **lapayaak** rubber gloves

561 **laplit** priest, minister

562 **Laqut** a man's name

563 **7lats** sea cucumber: **7laatsi** dim.

564 **law** loose: **lawlc** it is coming loose, **lawnulitxw!** loosen it a bit!, **lawalaaxttxw!** slacken the line!

565 **-layc** circumstantial suffix (19.14.2)

566 **-layc** tuber(cle), projection (20.2, 20.2.1): **-anlhlayc** ribs, **-al-aaxtlayc** tongue, **nu-...-aaxlayc** chin; heel, **nu-...-iklayc** penis, **-iixwlayc** knee, **-uutslayc** nipple

567 **Layx** Ocean Falls

568 **-lc** inchoative suffix (= **-alc**) (19.16.3): **tmtlhlc** "just getting strong" = adult, grown-up, **tmyalc** "just getting good" = to be in the prime of life, **tsńtsnalc** to have a numb sensation, **nutskwlc** "to become heavy in the water" = to sink

569 **lh-** dualis, ... and company (23.4): **wicanaw ta+lh7na** it is them two, **wicanaw txw ta+lhHank** it was Hank and somebody else, **lhXila Xila** and somebody else

570 **-lh** 1 pl. subj. itr./tr./caus. (14.2, 14.3.1, 14.4.1)

571 **-lh** (dis)connection (18.5, 18.5.1-3)

572 **lha+** = **ilh+** (15.1)

573 **lhaaxta, lhaaxalhta** shoulderblade

574 **lhaclhakway** big sealion

575 **-lhala** petrified suffix common to **skwakwixlhala, t'iclhala, t'ic-t'iixlhalam**

576 **lhalas** boat, canoe: **lhalhlaasi** dim., **Lhalaasik** a man's name, **As-lhalasmc** "canoe carriers" = Carrier natives of Smithers

577 **Lhaluuxmana** a mythical name

578 **lhalya** copper (means of payment, now obsolete): **lhalyalh** piece of copper, **lhalyayanlh** copper-colored cloth, **Lhalyaqs** a woman's name, **Lhalyaaxas** a woman's name

579 **lhaqa** basking shark

580 **lhaq's** edible seaweed

581 **lhawpla** to stack, pile up

582 **lhawps** greedy, stingy: **lhawpsakmtmacw** to begrudge each other

583 **lhay** secondary nominal deictic: increased distance (15.4.1.2)

584 **lhcw** (tr.) to spur, incite, awake somebody: **lhcwtsut** to act on impulse, **lhcwak** (tr.) to remind somebody of what he must do, **lhcwtsinu ska+tl'apilh ska+7ilhtsaylh** I remind you that we will go and pick berries, **lhcwayctu–** to scold, bawl out somebody, **lhiclhicwtmacwilh** we stimulate each other, **lhcwm** to make bustling noises, **slhcwmlh** dried red elderberries (when picking these berries, the women make noise in order to deter bears)

585 ***lhcw** (tr.) to close, cover: **uslhcwits** I will cover it, **nulhcw** (tr.) to shut the window, close the curtains, **nu(nuu)lhcwta** blind, curtain, **nulhcwiixwta** smoke vent, **anulhcwmcwmiiktimut** to mumble, speak unclearly, **lhcwilc** it is getting foggy

586 **lhic** slimy: **nulhi(lh)cmuts** to drool, **nulhicmutsaynicits** I accidentally drooled on it

587 ***lhiixw** treasure: **slhiixw** treasured object, **lhiixwnicits t'ayc** I treasure this

588 **lhima** (tr.) to take something away from somebody: **lhimatst** somebody took it from you, **lhimatss c+7inu** somebody took you away from me

589 ***lhiqw'** = ***lhqw'**: **lhinlhiqw't**, **lhiclhiqw'** to be sobbing, **nulhiqw'miixw** to burp

590 ***lhkw** (tr.) to fill or close a hole: **lhkw** (tr.), **lhkwm** (itr.) to carry by a handle, **lhkwits** I will pick it up (by its handle, or by sticking my finger(s) through its hole), **lhkwmts c+a+sputc** I am carrying eulachons (with a branch stuck through the gills), **anulhkwmuts** (tr.) to carry a fish by the gills, **anulhkwmiixwalstutsakmlhits** I have carried it by (hanging it over) the elbow, **nulhkw** button hole, **lhkwmta**, **nulhkwmankta** buttons, **lhkwmtsut** to button or

zip up, **lhkwm** to plug a hole

591 **lhkw'** big: **lhk'uulh wa+sulhts+ts ala+sulhnu+ts** my house is bigger than yours, **lhkw'anaats** very big, **lhkw'lcanaats** becoming very big, **kulhkw'** having a big penis (/**kulh⌃lhkw'**/), **Lhiclhik'ulhank** name of a site where there are three boulders, **nulhiclhikw'almc** having big breasts, **lhiclhiikwaw smnanaw** they are children of royal descent **lhkw'lc** old: **lh1kw'lcta** village elders

592 *__lhkw'__ care, love: **kulhkw'** "to care very much (about one's possessions)" = to be stingy, a tightwad (/**kulh⌃lhkw'**/), **k'iilhkw'** "to not care (about one's possessions)" = to be generous, unselfish (/**k'iilh⌃lhkw'**/), **wa+lhkw'amktits+ts** my loved ones, **lhkw'm** (tr.), **nulhkw'ikm** (tr.) to love somebody

593 **lhkw'a** to take a shortcut: **lhkw'anu+kw' stcatl'saaxalhnu+ts** you always take a shortcut through the back alley

594 *__lhkw'm__ to pound, bump: **nulhkw'miklxsalh** to bump one's toes on something, **lhkw'mk** to emphasize one's words by pounding the floor with a talking stick, **lhkw'mkaksta** talking stick (miniature totempole used by a speaker in order to emphasize his words)

595 **lhk'** (tr.), **lhk'a** (itr.) to pull off: **lhk'm** to remove stems from fruit, **lhk'tmacw** to have a finger-pulling contest, **anulhk'aaq** the bottom has come off a bottle, **anulhk'ikiixw** the top has come off a bottle, **snulhk'iklxs** "that which serves to pull somebody by the nose" = nose ring (e.g. on a bull), **snulhk'** canyon

596 **lhk'm** to speak: **slhk'msta** language, **axw lhk'maylaycs** he is unable to speak, **nunulhk'malhh** to mutter, mumble

597 *__lhl__ (tr.) to remove: to groom, clean, clip, cut; to quit, stop, leave: **lhliixw** (tr.) to cut somebody's hair, **lh1lhliiqwta** barber scissors, **nulhlxsm** to clean one's nose (/**nu-lhl⌃lxs-m**/), **nulhlals-ikanm** to clean one's ears, **nulh1lhliik** (tr.) to remove the pit(s) from fruit, **lhlus** (tr.) to peel fruit, **lhlulmc** (tr.) to clean the floor, **lhlik** (tr.) to clean the table surface, **lhlaaxla** (tr.) to

clean berries, **axw+7iluk lhltsutaylaycts** I am still unable to keep a clean house, **lhlits tsi+cnasts+tsc** I will leave my wife, **lhlutsm** to stop eating, **alhlalhhim wa+qaaxlamim+ts** people stop drinking (/alh⁻lhl.../)

lhlm to give a feast, potlatch: **nuslhlmsta** building where potlatch is held

598 **lhm** to stand up: **lhmtu-** to erect, stand something up, **lhmtimut** to stand up, rise, **lhmta** corner posts of a house, **silhmak** fish weir (consisting of poles planted across a stream), **Alhmutsamk** "standing in a hole" = Mystery Dancer (/alh⁻lhm.../)

599 **lhmilh** we, us (25.2)

600 **lhmk'mani** weasel

601 **lhmk'mlhp** lodgepole pine: **lhmk'mlhpak** lodgepole pine needles

602 **lhnús** two (26.2): **k'ilhnús** (/k'ilh⁻lhnús/) "lacking two" = eight, **nulhnúslt** to have twins, **snulhnúsltlh** twins, **nulhnúsakmitsut** to work together, **ka+lhnúsanmaaks** at two o'clock (later today), **lhnús-aaxanmalh** (to take) two steps, **lh/lhnúsaaxuts** double-barrelled gun

603 **lhp** (tr.), **lhpa** (itr.) to fill something up: **nulhpik** (tr.) to fill a pot, **nulhpaktulhx!** fill up our containers!

604 **-lhp**, **-alhp** tree, plant; use, function (21.3): **icp'iclhp** crabapple tree, **plhtkŋknlhp** bitter cherry tree, **t'at'kanalhp** yellow pond lily, **aq'miixalhp** cottonwood tree, **stamlhp+7lks?** what is it used for?, what purpose does it serve?, **qmxmtalhp t'ayc** this serves as a shock absorber

605 **lhp'** spongy, springy: **lhp'uulh** dough, yeast bread

606 **lhq** wet: **lhq** (tr.) to dampen something, **lhqm** to soak dried berries, **alhq** cooked elderberries (/alh⁻lhq/), **nulhqutsalh** sleet, **lhqaltwa** rainy season, **lhqaqw's** wet soil, **anulhqmalsiixw** mucus in the posterior nasal cavity

607 **lhqm** to erode, collapse: **lhqmaaxuts** the riverbank is eroding, **nu-lhqmals+kw ti+t'apalst** somebody told me a cave collapsed

608 **lhqw'** to fade: **lhiclhiqw'** it is fading

609 **lhqw'** (tr.) to uproot, dig up: **lhqw'm c+a+7ilk** he is digging for ilk, **lhqw'aynic** (tr.) to accidentally dig something up, **lhiclhiqw'a c+a+sqitilhp** he is digging for roots, **lhqw'aax** (tr.) to pull a tree out, **lhqw'aaxm** to become uprooted, **Lhiqw'alsmc** "people of the bare mountain side" = a former tribal division

610 ***lhqw'** to sob: **nunulhqw'**, **lhiclhiqw'** to be sobbing

611 **lhq'** (tr.), **lhq'a** (itr.) to slap; to slice, cut into slabs: **lhq'us** (tr.) to slap somebody in the face, **lhq'akm** to applaud, **lh(a)q'a** to make a guess in the lahal game, **lhq'm** to be making shingles, **lhq'- ayc** to be chipped, broken off, **lhq'aynic** (tr.) to accidentally chip something

612 **-lhq'** ...fold (20.6.1): **malhq'** single, **lhwaalhq'** double, **asmúslhq'** triple

613 ***lhq'm** (tr.) to strap, secure, fetter: **lhmq'mta** leash, **lhq'maalhta** shoelaces, **alhmq'mtu-** to keep on a leash (/alh⁻lhmq'm-tu-/), **anu- lhq'miiqw** handle (e.g. for bucket or lantern)

614 **lhtn** (tr./itr.) to resist or exert pressure, touch, bump, poke: **lhtnnu ulh+7nts** you bumped into me, **nulhtnalsta** bone implement used to scrape a hide, **lhtnaakts alh+t'ayc** I touch this, **lhtntmacw** to touch each other, **k'ilhtn** he moved around freely (/k'ilh⁻lhtn/), **nulhtnikta** center post, pillar, **nulhtnutsaaxta** housepost
lhtnm "to resist downward pull, conquer gravity" = to climb up a slope: **lhtnm̂tits wa+yaki** I am climbing up the mountain in pursuit of mountain goats

615 **lhts'** (tr.), **lhts'a** (itr.) to hold or press down: **lhts'ma** belt, girdle, **lhts'tsut** to duck, dodge, **anulhts'** "pressed flat" = Indian cheese (sun-cured and compacted cake of fish eggs)
lhts'ancw (tr.) to catch somebody ...ing: **lhts'ancuts** (tr.) to overhear somebody

616 ***lht'** (tr.) to attach to or catch with a hook; to lever, pry off,

pull out: **lht'** (tr.), **lht'a** (itr.) to spike, hang something on a
nail; to pry something off, **nulht'iiqw** (tr.) to hang something (hat
or coat) on a nail or hook, **nulht'uus** (tr.) to hang something (e.g.
picture) on the wall, **nulht'uulhnnak** (tr.) to castrate somebody,
nulht'nlxsaliitstu- to make somebody stick his tongue out (so as to
administer his medication), **lht'aax** (tr.) "to lever the boat" = to
steer a boat or car, **alht'aaxm** to be steering (/alh⁻lht'.../),
lht'aaxta rudder, steering wheel

lht'm to rise, emerge, pop out: **lht'm ti+snx+tc** the sun is rising,
lht'mtinilh the sun is rising in our area, **nulhmt'maaquts wa+sulh
+ts** "the house is popping out of its edges" = it is very crowded in
the house, **nulhmt'maaqws wa+sqaluts** berries are emerging, ripening,
lht'mtimut grasshopper, **Silht'mtimut** a geographical name: Middle
Point, **anulht'muulh** to have a protruding navel, **lht'makts c+ta+
7alhqulhts** "my book popped out of my hand" = my book has disappeared

617 **+lhu, +lhú, +lhuu = +lu, +lú, +luu**

618 **lhuk, lhulhkw** (tr.) to pick up something: **lhulhkwits** I will pick it
up, **alhuclhuk** (/alh⁻lhuc.../) objects that are placed in a mesachie
box, **lhuulhkwa** "to be busy picking up" = to be sexually promiscuous

619 ***lhuku** (tr.) to penetrate a hole: **nulhukwwaax** (tr.) to stick one's
beak into somebody's rectum (an act performed by the **Hawhaw**)

620 **lhukwala** student of supernatural power, shaman-to-be: **lhukwalanic**
(tr.) to allow somebody to obtain supernatural power, **alhukwala**
person with supernatural power, shaman (/alh⁻lhukwala/), **lhukwala-
yamk** (tr.) to derive supernatural power from something or somebody,
alhukwalayxw power song (/alh⁻lhukwala⁻iixw/), **lhukwalatum** he was
given supernatural power, **slhukwala** object filled with supernatural
power, **Alhukwalaakas** a woman's name (/alh⁻lhukwala⁻aakas/)

621 ***lhuk', *lhuuk** to be disinclined, repelled: **lhuk'layc** to have an
aversion to eating, **lhuk'lclayc** to get fed up, bored, **lhuk'laycmim**

nobody likes him, **kanuslhuk'm** having a horrible smell or taste, **nunulhuk'** reluctant to work, lazy, **lhuclhuukliwam** (tr.) to vex, irritate somebody

622 **lhuk'is** toolbox

623 **lhula** ring-finger

624 ***lhulh** informed, having news: **lhulhtu-** to tell somebody the latest, **lhulhtnm** newsreader, **lhulhamktsinu** I have heard a story about you, **alhuulhalus** to be curious, inquisitive (/alh⌃lhuulh-alus/), **alhulhnic** (tr.) to perceive the presence of something or somebody (/alh⌃lhulh-nic/), **lhulhnictsut** to feel a change in oneself, suspect one is ill

625 **lhulhkw = lhuk**

626 **lhulhp** soft, spongy: **lhulhpulmc** muskeg

627 **Lhulhqw'ani** a man's name

628 **lhum** (tr.), **lhuma** (itr.) to sip something: **lhumlhuma** to be taking little sips, **nulhumaaxnm** to have a cup of tea or coffee with somebody, **anulhumuuts** (tr.) to spoon-feed somebody, **anulhumuutsm** to consume liquid food with a spoon

slhum (tr.) to boil down food (e.g. berries, fish) in order to make juice or soup: **nuslhumta** cooking box

629 **lhup** you (pl.) (25.2)

630 ***lhup'** smell, air, breath: **lhup't** it is smelling, **lhunlhup't** to breathe, **lhunlhup'tlxs** to breathe through the nose, **slhup'(t)sta** breath(ing), **k'ink'iŝlhup'(t)stalc** to begin to have trouble breathing, run out of breath

631 ***lhuq'** peeled, skinned: **lhuq'lc** skin is peeling off, **lhuq'alht** inner bark of red cedar

632 **lhuts'** (tr.) to strip, undress: **lhuts'uulh** (tr.) to undress somebody, **lhulhts'uulhm** to get undressed

633 **lhut'** (tr.), **lhut'a** (itr.) to smell something: **lhulht'm** to sniff in, inhale a smell, **lhut'aylayc** to catch a whiff

634 **+lhuu = +lhu**

635 ***lhuuk = *lhuk'**

636 **lhuuxt** poisoned from eating clams caught during a red tide: **slhuuxt** red tide

637 **Lhu7ya** a man's name

638 ***lhwaas** (***lhwaalh** before **tl'** and **lh**) two (26.2.2): **lhwaaslancw** two years, **lhwaaslxs** forty, **lhwaask'mtts ska+7alhits ala+7ats** I will stay here for two days, **lhwaask'mtamts ska+lip'tsutts** I will return in two days, **lhwaalhtl'aputsts snuyamlhts** I sang twice, **lhwaalhq'** double (/**lhwaalh⁻lhq'**/)

639 ***lhx** opposed, away from, other way around, inside out, negative, sinister: **nulhxikam** to turn away or against, **nulhxikam̂tsinu** I turn against you, become your opponent, **lhxusm** to turn one's face away in disgust or disagreement, **lhxiixw** upended, upside down, **alhx** to be quarrelsome with one's spouse (/**alh⁻lhx**/), **(nu)lhxanlh** "turned inside" = self-centered, misanthropic, **nulhxanlhanmikmitsut** to be disgusted with one's situation, to leave in anger or frustration, **lhxanm** to go hunting, **icnulhxlxsanm̲layc** "to continually be missing the terminus" = to be wandering around, **lhxlcts+ts'** "I am becoming ill at ease (estranged) now" = I begin to feel homesick, wish to leave now

*slhx left: **slhxalmc** left breast, **slhxanlhaqw's** left eye, **slhxaak** left-handed, **slhxaakslh** left hand, **slhxaaq** left-legged, **slhxaaqslh** left leg, **slhxaalh** left foot

640 ***lhxw** to be energetic, enthused: **lhxutsmtulhs ska+7aylh c+ts** he enthusiastically approved of our plan to act thus

*lhxus busy, occupied: **slhxus** work, occupation, **kuŝlhxus** to have much work, be very busy

641 ***lhxw** to go through a narrow passage, pass through, escape: **lhxwt** to go through a hole or passage, **lhxwtmmis ti+nutsq+t'ayc** he went through this hole, **lhxwtaycts** I have passed through, **lhxwm** to flee,

escape, **lhxwtm̂tss** he escaped from me

642 **lhxwta** to spit: **nulhxwtaykts** I want to spit, **slhxwta** spittle

643 **+li...** contraction of **+(7)l...** and **+7i...** (28.3.18.5.1, 28.3.24)

644 ***lic** slimy, slippery: **Licimutusayc** a personal name: "sliding on the face of the mountain", **licm** to slip, slide, **nulicmaqw's** knot is slipping, **licmtu-** to make somebody slip, **licm̲lits'nicim** people slip on his body, **anulicmuts** saliva drips from one's mouth, to drool

645 **liclic** ripe, cooked: **alhliclic+ts'** it is already cooked, **liclictu-** to cook something

646 ***licwm** to make noise: **alhlicwm**, **iclicwm**, **liclicwm** to be making noise

647 **-liikw = -likw**

648 **-liits = -lits'**

649 **liixw = lixw**

650 **-lik** body surface, (entire) skin, exterior, appearance (20.2.1): **tsictsik'lik** (tr.) to stab a tree all over, **scwlik** having a dry ("burnt") skin, **qwsm̲lik** to sweat profusely, **stl'mstalikta** appearance, personality, character

-lik-t body, personality (20.2.1), space, volume (20.3.1): **tspliktm** to wipe one's body, **amatlikt** "where body is contained" = coffin, **atmalikt** totally paralyzed, **yalikt** having a good, nice personality, **sclikt** having an angry disposition, **ipliikti** narrowly spaced

651 **-likw**, **-liikw** performer of action (21.2): **tatiixwlikw** caster of spells, witch, **nusxlikw** raider, **qalikw** ill-wisher, **an7aq'ulikw** "he who locks people in" = policeman, **alhxapaliikw** "packer" = horse

652 **likw'** (tr.), **likw'a** (itr.) to roll, turn something over: **likw'm** to be rolling over or down; to spin wool, **nulikw'muulh** car rolls off the road, **uslikw'manalhts c+ti+t'xt** a rock rolled over my feet, **likw'ta** spinning wheel, **alhlik'ulh** (tr.) to roll a cigaret, **nulikw'tsut** to turn around

653 **lik'** (tr.) to fill something: **alhlik'** full, **lik'laycts** my container

is full

654 **lilwi** railroad train: **aslilwi** to go by train

655 **lim** to fall, drop: **limulhiixwts** my hair is falling out, **nulimuts** to drop something from one's mouth

656 **lip'** (tr.) to fold something: **lip'tsut**, **lip'ayc** to return, **lip'-tsutstu-** to return something, **lip'aynic** (tr.) to succeed in making somebody go back, **lip'us** (tr.) to fold a sheet, **lip'alcw** (tr.) to round a corner, **lip'alhm** = **lip'tsut**, **lip'uulhtsut** to draw up one's knees, **slip'nalus(ta)** body joint, **(s)lip'naluslxsak** knuckle, **slip'-akmsta** hinge

657 **lis** (tr.), **lisa** (itr.) to push something: **lisusm** to push the bow of one's boat out, **lisaaxm** to push the stern of one's boat out, **nulis-aaq** (tr.) to push a car, **listsut** "to push oneself" = to fight back, take revenge, **listsutm** (tr.) to take revenge on somebody, **alhlis-aaktmacw**, **lisiiqwaktmacw** to have an arm-wrestling match, **lisalhm** (tr.) to push something with one's foot, **lisaalh** (tr.) to push somebody's foot, **listatsut** to push oneself up, **alhliis** plane (tool)

658 **lisaak** sack

659 **-lit** to make the sound of ... (19.18): **mamawlit** to miaul, **ts'u-ts'uulit** to produce an alveolar click ("tsk tsk!"), **qwaxwqwaxwlit** to caw, croak, **axwlit** to deny, refuse, **waylitm** (tr.) to give somebody permission to do something

660 *****litcw** (tr.) to roll, spin something: **litcwta** spinning wheel, **nu-litcwta** rolling device used for launching a boat, **nulitcwnutsaaq** (tr.) to install a **nulitcwta** under a boat (for launching) or house (for moving), **litcwm** (pl. subject) "to roll out" = to go out en masse to see what is happening

661 **-lits'**, **-liits** sheet, cloth (20.4.1.1), skin, bark, side (20.2.1): **smawlits'** one blanket, **pik'liits** "(having a) shiny surface" = gum boots, **tqw'lits'** (tr.) to singe hairs off a skin, **stpliits** fish scales, **plhtliits** thick bark, **alhxp'lits'** wet all over one's body

lits'-ak back of hand (20.2.1): **squplhlits'ak** (having) hair on the hands

(nu-...)-lits'-alh calf of leg, side of lower leg (20.2.1): **nusp'-lits'alhayc** to get hit on the side of one's lower leg, **sp'liitsalhayc** to get hit on the calf of one's leg, **squplhlits'alh** (having) hair on the calf of the leg or side of the lower leg, **q'awliitsalhm** to wind bandages around one's lower legs

662 **litux** striped: **lituxanlh** striped cloth

663 **-liwa, -liwn-** similar, ...like (18.4): **pcliwa** lovely, pretty, **malhliwa** sort of slow, **paaxûlhlaliwa** fearsome, dangerous, **tsnlhliwa** selfish, self-centered, introverted, **tsaakwliwa** "long-like" = worm, **tsaakwliwni** little worm, **tsakw'liwa** right, correct, **scliwa** ugly-looking, **tl'iliwa** fast in work, **alhkalliwa** handy, adroit, **kw'alhliwa** handy (object)

664 **lixw, liixw** (tr.), **li(i)xwa** (itr.) to chase somebody away: **anulixwaax** (tr.) to chase somebody out of the house

665 **lkw'lulhp** sweet gale

666 **lplii** thin: **nu7lpluutsi** thin layer

667 **-lqs = -lxs**

668 **lq'** (tr.), **lq'm** (itr.) to think of something or somebody: **lq'is +ts'n ilh+stans+7ilh** now her mother came to her mind, **lq'ma+ts' ska+tl'apaw** now they thought of going, **alhlq', iclq'** (tr.) to be thinking of something or somebody, **iclq'its+ma** maybe I will think it over, **iclq'm** to be thinking things over, **lq'aynic** (tr.) to guess something, **slq'** mind, awareness, **aŝlq'** to be sober-minded, level-headed, **nuŝlq'** to be smart, **k'iŝlq'** to lack sense, be stupid

669 **-lq'** around (petrified suffix found in *****tplq'** and *****xlq'**)

670 **lq'llis** giant kelp with herring spawn on it

671 **-lst** rock(s) (20.3.1): **kawlst** to pile rocks on top of something, **qnklst** "rock underneath" = island

672 **-lt** offspring, child(ren) (20.3.1): **nulhnúslt** to have twins, **alh-**

tqw'lt to be holding a baby, **atsiwlt** to be pregnant, **asimlt** to be brooding, hatching

673 ***lu** (tr./itr.) to (cause to) be loose, come off, peel: **lum** to remove the bark from a tree, **lulwits ti+stn+t'ayc** I am peeling this tree, **lulc**, **lulc** bark comes off, **lululiits** (tr.) to peel a tree, **luta** stick used for peeling bark, **Alhlululh** beach across Green Bay

674 **+lu**, **+lú**, **+luu**, **+lhu**, **+lhú**, **+lhuu** still, yet (28.3.9, 28.3.24)

675 **+luks** all along, as expected (28.3.18.2, 28.3.24): **ay+maluks** it must have been the case all along

676 **lulusta** mask: **aslulusta** to wear a mask

677 **luluxwam** to have sexual foreplay

678 **−lun−** reduced form of **−liwn−** (18.4.1): **numutslunitx!** close the door a bit!, **naclunak** to have finished one's work

679 **+luu = +lu**

680 ***lx** to make linear, stretch, pull taut; to jerk or pull down, make jerky motions: **lx** (tr.), **lxa** (itr.) to stretch, extend a rope, **alh-7ic7lxanlh** striped cloth, **ic7lxulmcmayc** running clubmoss; twinflower, **nulxmtnm** to ring a bell, **lxmuuts+kwts'tski ti+7ayuts alh+tu+sulhs t'ax** it seems that a ringing sound came from his house then, **alh7lx** to beat a fast rhythm, **lxaksta** stick for beating time, **lxakmaw** they do a rapid beat, **nulxik** (tr.) to rattle something, **nulxaksta** type of rattle, **Lxulhla** Cannibal (a dance), **lxulhlatimut** to be drunk

681 **−lxs**, **−lqs** nose (20.2.1); point, terminus (20.5.1); multiple of twenty (20.6.1, 26.2.5): **piq'lxs** (having a) flat nose, **talxsayc** to get hit on the nose (/tay⁻lxs−ayc/), **t'kwlxs** to have a nosebleed, **sɫp'lqs**, **sp'lxsnm** to make a phone call, **nutxlxs** (tr.) to sharpen the point of something, **mawlxs** twenty, **lhwaaslxs** forty

   −lxs−ak finger (20.2.1): **mntsklqsakm** to count (on) one's fingers, **smawlqsak** one finger, **alht'tslqsakm** to rap with one's finger, **sp'-llxsakayc** to get hit on the fingers

-lxs-alh toe (20.2.1): **smawlqsalh** one toe, **tclqsalh** (tr.) to cut
somebody's toe off, **sp'llxsakayc** to get hit on the toes

nu-...-lxs-aliits tip of tongue (20.2.1): **nusxwatmlxsaliits** to have
a blister on one's tongue, **nulht'nlxsaliitstu-** to make somebody
stick his tongue out, **nu7iixwlqsaliits** to burn one's tongue

nu-...-lxs-nk tail (20.2.1): **aslqsnk** fish tail, **nutkalqsnkayc** its
tail was shot off, **nutclqsnk** (tr.) to cut an animal's tail off, **nutsatskwlqsnk** "(having a) long tail" = wharf rat

M

682 ***7m** erect: **as7mllxs** pugnosed, **as7m**, **kus7m** to have an erection

683 ***m, *m...a** petrified formative base: **maaxsa** nose, **musa** face, **maka**
testes, **mnlhkwa** hair, **mnk** faeces

684 **+m...** allomorph of **+ma** in enclitic strings (28.3.22.3, 28.3.24)

685 **-m** medium (19.5)

686 **-m** 3 sg. pass. caus. (14.4.3)

687 **-m-, -man(ts)-** 1 sg. obj. caus. (14.4.1)

688 ***ma** one (26.2.2): **maslancwakts sksnmakts** I worked for one year, **malacw** year, **alh+tumalacwa** last year, **kamalacws** next year, **malhq'**
single, **matl'ap** once, **makwtl'uusinaw** they look identical

689 **+ma, +m...** maybe, possibly, likely (28.3.1)

690 **-ma, -mn-** implement (21.2): **sk'ma** comb, **sq'ma** knife used for cutting salmon, **lhts'ma** belt

691 **maask+7iks?** how much?, how many? (25.5): **numaaskaw+ks?** how many are
they?, **maaskulhtucw+lits'?** how much do you charge for it?, **maask-
lancwnu+ks?** how old are you?, **maaskanmaak+7iks?** what time is it?,
ala+ka+maaskaax for a number of days

692 **maaxsa** nose

693 **maaxts** clay: **maaxts** (tr.) to apply clay to something

694 **macsays** husband's brother's wife

695 **macuuli** water hemlock

696 **-macw** reciprocal suffix (see **-tmacw**, **-nmacw**)

697 **maka** testes

698 ***mal** (tr.) to mix something: **maliixw** (tr.) to mix something, **maliixwaqw's** (tr.) to mix paint, **numaliixwikayc** to get mixed up, confused, **numalusayc** to choke

699 **Malasyulh** a man's name

700 ***malh** slow: **malhliwa** sort of slow, sluggish, **mamalhaalhi** walking slowly, **malhuts** eating slowly

701 **mamawlit** to miaul

702 **mamayu** butterfly: **mama7yui** dim.

703 **mamis** blackfly: **mamiisi** dim., **Numamis** Tallio Cannery

704 **man** father: **anusman** having lost one's father, **mantimut** father-in-law or stepfather

705 **-man-**, **-mants-** = **-m-**

706 **maqw'ants** heron

707 **maq'm** to have nothing to eat for a whole day: **ismaq'mlhhts** I had had nothing to eat all day

708 **+mas** always, forever (said naggingly); there is nothing I can do about the situation, I don't care if ... (resignation) (28.3.2)

709 **Masmasalanixw** name of a supernatural being

710 **Masuncw** a personal name

711 **mats** (tr.) to put objects on a string, to thread: **numatstx!** put corks on the line!
*mats (tr.) to line up, align, arrange, spread, cover: **usmatsit** they covered his body, **numatsaax** (tr.) to spread boards on the ground, **numatsik** (tr.) to place boards on the bottom of a canoe, **numatsikta** boards placed on the bottom of a canoe, **kalhmatstsut**

to spread hemlock bows out on the ground for bedding, **matsalh** (tr.) to launch a new canoe

712 **matskin** salmon heart

713 **matskw'** frog, toad: **mʌmnntskw'i** dim., **snknics ti+matskw'** = **p'xwlht**

714 **matsta** side-dish (nuts, dried springsalmon roe)

715 **mats'i** cured salmon roe: **axw is7ismats'its** I never eat **mats'i**

716 ***maw** one (26.2.2): **numaw** one person, **numawta** partner, friend, **nu-mawaakmitsuti** to be alone at work, **mawlxs** twenty, **mawlxsulh** twenty dollars, **mawlxslancwamts** I am twenty years of age

smaw one: **smaŵlh** one dollar, **smawaax** one tree or stick, **smawlqsak** one finger, **smawaaxalh** one day's travel, **smawanmaak** one hour, (it is) one o'clock

717 **maxwat'alaqa** dipper (bird)

718 **mayas** raccoon: **mayaasi** dim.

719 **-mc** population, inhabitant(s), native(s) (21.3): **Talyumc** Tallio native(s), **kanmcnu+ks?** what is your nationality?, **Snutsalaatstmc** name of a (mythical?) village ("place of the dwarf people")

nus-...-mc preoccupied with, always ...ing (19.17.2): **nusts'kmc** always fixing things, adroit person, **nuŝcalimc** morbidly jealous, always suspecting one's spouse of infedility, **nusnaaxwm̂c** professional dancer, **nus7im̂c** preoccupied with sexual intercourse

720 ***mi** wide: **numyuts** having a wide mouth, **numyals** wide room, **miank** wide canoe, **numii(t) ti+nutsq+tc** the hole is wide, **numilcuts** channel opens up; to become increasingly talkative

721 **-mi-** 1 sg. subj. caus. (14.4.2)

722 **Miaysila** a geographical name

723 **micmikalhp** Sitka spruce

724 **micmik'lh** star

725 **mikw'lh** salalberry: **micmikw'lhp** salalberry plant (/...lh⁼lhp/)

726 **mik't** arrowhead

727 **mil, ml** (tr.) to erase something

728 **mila** cane, walking stick: **Asmila** name of a creek

729 **Milha** a type of dance

730 **milicw** bearberry, kinnikinnick: **milmilicwlhp** kinnikinnick plant, **milmilicwlhpaak** false box

731 **miltm** to rise, increase (of water): **numiltm** to overflow, **miltmaqw's** drink spills over

732 **-minilh** 1 pl. pass. caus. (14.4.3)

733 **-minits** 1 sg. pass. caus. (14.4.3)

734 **minnimut** to go into labor: **alhminnimut** to be in labor

735 **-mitsut** reflexive suffix (19.10.2): **numawaakmitsuti** to be alone at work, **t'umitsut, slaxmitsut** to have many relatives, **tsnkwakmitsutts** I can do it myself, **nuscickmitsut** to be sad, **nutl'uk'ikmitsut** to consider oneself superior, be conceited, **alhkaltcwmitsut, alhkw'cw-mitsut** to watch out, be careful, **ixq'nlhamitsut** to be irritated

736 **ml** (tr.) = **mil**

737 **mlk** milk

738 **Mlqis** Alert Bay

739 **-mn-** = **-ma**

740 **mna** child, offspring: **mnamits** I will adopt him, **as7asmnayakaw** they had a child, **mnmnay** doll, **mnmnaalh** animal cub

741 **Mnaakays** the supreme deity

742 **mnk** excrement

743 **mnlh** to pause, interrupt: **mnlhlcakts** the pain is gone from my hand, has subsided, **mymnlhlc** pain comes and goes, **mnlhalusm** (tr.) to have missed somebody, to see somebody again after a long period of separation, **mnlhimut** to have a rest

744 **mnlh** (tr.) to pay somebody: **mnlhayc+ts'** he has been paid now, **mnlh-tsutaw** they draw up a contract

745 **mnlhat** (tr.), **mnlhata** (itr.) to measure: **numnlhat** (tr.) to measure the depth of water, **numnlhatals** (tr.) to measure the height of a room

746 **mnlhkwa** hair of the head: **numnlhkwlalsikan** having hairs in one's ears

747 **mʌmnts** children

748 **mʌmntsa** swamp gooseberry: **mʌmntsalhp** swamp gooseberry plant

749 **mnta** way of going, route, vehicle: **stam+ks ti+ka+mntanu?** how will you be going?, **mʌmnta** path, road, **mʌmnnta** steps, stairway, stepladder, **k'ilhmnta** "having no path" = to wander around

750 **mntcw**, **✝mntacw** (tr.), **mntcwa** (itr.) to dip something up: **mntcuts** (tr.) to dip water, **mntcu(u)tsta** dipping cup, ladle, **usmntacuuts** (tr.) to skim off a liquid

751 **mntsk** (tr.), **mntska**, **mntskm** (itr.) to count: **numntsktanx!** count them!, **mntskulha** to count money

752 **mnts'** yellow, hazel, blond: **mnts'(ulh)iixw** having blond hair, **nu-(mʌ)mnts'ikulhaaqws** having hazel eyes, **mʌmnts'lhp** oceanspray, **smʌmnts'uulhak** catkin, pussy willow

753 **✝mnts'** (tr.) to squeeze something: **mnts'aqw's** (tr.) to squeeze berries so as to extract the juice, **mnts'aqw'saliitsm** (tr.) to crush berries in one's mouth

754 **mnts'lhta** pus: **snumnts'lhtaylh** bloody part of fish backbone

755 **mt** to sit, assume a sitting position: **mtaaxutsayc** to sit around the fire (pl. subject) or at the riverbank, **s7mtsta** seat, chair

756 **-mt** 2 sg. pass. caus. (14.4.3)

757 **mtm** sea urchins; burdocks

758 **-mts** one's (collective) relatives (21.3): **stantanmts** "one's mothers of mothers" = one's mother + maternal grandmother + maternal grandmother's mother etc., **slh7imtsmts** all one's grandchildren, **wa+susqwimtsts** all my younger siblings

759 **mu** fish weir made of cedar sticks

760 **mucwmukwt** bluegrouse: **mucwmuukwti** dim.

761 **mukw** red; dancer's necklace made of cedar bark: **mukusi** "little red face" = newborn baby, **mukwila** boy reaching puberty, **mukwaluuŝlh** red

springsalmon, **Numuukw** name of a former village, **mukwaqw's** brown;
dancer's headband, **numukwikaqw's** having brown eyes, **mukusm** to paint
one's face red, **mucwmukwlclhp** goatsbeard (plant), **mucwmukuulh** gold,
Mucwmukus name of a mountain south of **Nu7ip'utsani**, **mucwmukwaaxakta**
bracelet, **mucwmukwaaxalhta** anklet

762 **-mulh-** 1 pl. obj. caus. (14.4.1); 1 sg./pl. subj. caus. (14.4.2)

763 **mulm** to dive: **mulmtuts+ma ta+7na** maybe I will make him dive, **mulm̂-its** I will dive for it

764 ***muqw'** stale, bland, lacking color or taste: **muq'ulh** food tastes
bland, **muqw'anlh** cloth looks faded, **muqw'alcw** (tr.) to rinse the
soap out of laundered clothes

765 **muqw'lha** louse: **muqw'lhata** flea comb, fine comb, **muqw'lhatim** he has
lice, **mucwmuqw'lhalhp** large-leaved avens

766 **mus** (tr.), **musa** (itr.) to feel, touch something: **musm** to spy, **mus-aynicits** I felt it, **musalcw** to feel around in the water for fish
with a long tapered stick; to spy

767 **mús** four (26.2): **numúsaw** they are four, **músulh** four dollars, **múslxs**
eighty, **músaaqtnaalh wa+qinxts+ts** I have four pairs of shoes

768 **musa** face

769 **musmus** cow, bovine

770 **-mut** reflexive suffix (19.10.3): **q'am̂ut** to bury, attend a funeral,
kulhkam̂ut to pay a prostitute (/q'aw⌃mut/, /kulh-kaw⌃mut/)

771 **Mutana** name of a Rivers Inlet man

772 ***mutsm** mistaken, confused, uncertain: **alhmutsm ka+7axws** maybe it
will not be the case, **mutsmuts** to make a speech error, **mutsmalh** to
go the wrong way, **icmunmutsmalhts** I don't know which way to go, **ic-munmutsmnictsinu** I got you confused with somebody else

773 **muuxwa** to stutter: **mumuuxwa** to stutter repeatedly

774 **muxwlht** to utter a dance-cry: **alhmuxwlhtaykila** somebody who excels
in the art of **muxwlht**

775 **muxwmuxwlht'ulhi(i)kanta** big earring

N

776 **n, in** and (29.3.1)

777 **-n** transitivizer (19.8)

778 **-n-** unintentionally (19.3.1)

779 **na!** there you are! (29.4)

780 **7na** determinative (25.6)

781 ***(7)na** forgotten: **nanic** (tr.), **nunanicikm** (tr.) to forget something or somebody, **nanimut** "to find oneself forgotten" = to mourn, sorrow, **alh7nanic** "forgotten" = **nanimut**

782 **+na** imperative enclitic (28.3.20.5)

783 **naaxwm** to dance: **nacnaaxwm, nusnaaxwm̂c** always dancing, **nunaaxwmals-im** dancing hall, **sinaaxwmiixw** dancer's headdress (made of cedar bark), **nacnaaxwmlhp** trembling aspen

784 ***nac** ready: **nacliwa** ready, finished, **nacliwanicis** he finished (making) it, **alhnacliwa+ts' ti+tii+tc** tea is ready now, **naclunak** work is finished

785 **Nacwtana** a man's name

786 **nalhm** ling cod

787 **-nalus** joint (20.2.1); pieces; (being) between (20.3.1): **tsk'lhp-nalusta** joints of ribs, **slip'nalus** joint, **cm̲nalus** (tr.) to break something into pieces

-nalus-aax crotch (20.2.1): **asnalusaax** crotch

-nalus-aqw's between the eyes, bridge of nose (20.2.1): **asnalus--aqw's, skulhnalusaqw's** bridge of nose

-nalus-lxs-ak joints of fingers; between the fingers (20.2.1): **lip'naluslxsak** joints of fingers, **alhtmpnaluslxsakmits** I have it between my fingers

-nalus-lxs-alh between the toes (20.2.1): **alhtmpnaluslxsalhmits** I have it between my toes

788 **Na7mu** Namu (a geographical name)

789 **nan** grizzly bear: **nan(7)ni** dim., **st'lŝ ti+nan** devil's club berries, **sqalutŝ ti+nan** = **st'lŝ ti+nan**, **nunanta** wild red columbine, **Nanus** a man's name

790 **nanaax** (tr.) to stick something into the ground

791 **nanitkw** digging stick; center of a boil

792 **nap**, ***7nap** (tr.) to take something; to give something to somebody: **nap** what one has, **tmsmaŵlh ti+naps Hank** Hank has only one dollar, **maaskulh+7iks wa+napnu?** how much money have you got?, **napits** I will take it, **naputsm** to help oneself to food, **alh7alh7napits** I will adopt him, **naptsinu c+t'ayc** I will give this to you, **napalimtsk** (tr.) to give out, distribute food, **alh(7)nap** (tr.) to know something, **alhnaputstsant** they know what I said, **napamcw** (tr.) to find out about, learn something, **alhnapamcwaakm** (tr.) to do something expertly, in a habitual way, **napulhlam** (tr.) to make fun of somebody, **napusta** framework of sticks holding smoked salmon; stem of war canoe, **napalitsta** front section of keel

793 **-nap** = **-ap** (14.2)

794 **Naqaqa** a mythical woman's name

795 **naq't** sexually impotent: **kulhnaq'tm** = **naq't**

796 **+nas** imperative enclitic (28.3.20.6)

797 **-naw** = **-aw** (14.2)

798 **Naws** a geographical name

799 **naxnx** mallard duck: **naxnxi**, **naxnaxi** dim.; widgeon

800 **-naxw** = **-axw** (14.2.4)

801 ***(7)nayc** to accompany, be complaisant: **nayctimut** to go along, be obedient, **alh7nayc** to accompany, go with somebody, **alh7naycuts** to join somebody in eating or crying, **alh7naycak** to work with, help somebody

802 **-ncw**, **-ancw** (tr.) = **-nic** (19.13.3): **ts'xancw** to believe somebody, **kañcw** to worry about a missing person, **wañcw** to fail to get, miss

(out on) something, **lhts'ancw** to catch somebody ...ing, **lhts'ancuts** to overhear somebody

803   **nic** (tr.), **nica** (itr.) to saw something: **nicta** saw, **nicuulhalusm** to cut firewood for oneself

804   ***nic** reduced form of **inacw** (23.7): **tunica** yesterday

805   **-nic** (tr.) to accidentally cause something or somebody to (be) ...; to find, consider, think ... is the case (19.13): **t'kwlxsnic** to accidentally give somebody a nosebleed, **sak'amnic** to accidentally hurt somebody, **stnmulhanknic** to cause somebody to have a laughing fit, **nitsmnic** to revive somebody, **tsakw'liwanic** to understand something, **ts'xanic** to believe somebody, **k'axwnic** to consider something not to be the case, **inutnictscw+7iks?** what do you think I am saying?, **acwsnic** to hear something or somebody

806   **nicniq'xm** to have a cramp: **nicniq'xmlxsalhts** I have a cramp in my toes

807   **Nicps** a type of dance

808   **Nictsiqs** a location situated south of **Puuxin**

809   **niixw**, ***niiqw** fire: **niniiixwi** dim., **nuniixwanayc** to have a fire in the corner; to sit beside a fire, **niiqwaliits** to have burnt one's tongue, **niixuts** to have burnt one's mouth, **nuniixwik** steamboat, **siniixw** firewood, **Niixwaltswa** a mythical man's name

810   **nik'** (tr.) to cut something with a blade: **nik'aaxnm** to cut grass, to hay, **nik'iixw** (tr.) to scalp somebody

811   **-nimut** to accidentally cause oneself to (be) ...; to find, consider oneself ... (19.10.6): **tcaakaycnimut** to have cut one's hand by accident, **tsik'aycnimut** to have stabbed oneself by accident, **sak'amnimut** to accidentally hurt oneself, **klhnimut** to (slip and) fall, **kañimut** to accidentally hurt oneself, **q'uxlcnimut** to exhaust oneself, **yalcnimut** to cure oneself, **yanimut** to think highly of oneself, boast, **istsk'nimut** to be lonely, homesick, **nulhnúsiinimutlhts** I thought there were only two of us

812 **niq'x** otter: **niiq'xi** dim.

813 **nist** to snort

814 ***nits** safe, alive: **nitstu-** to save somebody, **nitstimut** to save one-self, **ninits** alive, **nitsm** to hatch, emerge from an egg, **nitsmtnm** to be hatching eggs, **nitsmnic** (tr.) to revive somebody, **Ninitsmlayc** a man's name

815 **-nk** base, bottom: buttocks, small of back, tail; root of plant, stem, base of tree (20.2.1): **ap'lunk**, **ap'lunk** bare, exposed tree roots, **tsiiqnk** (tr.) to dig for roots, **ts'ayxnk** fireweed root, **kulhnk** stem of tree, **mnlhatnk** (tr.) to measure the circumference of a tree's base, **t'xwsususnk** quack grass, **slaq'nk** smoked fish tails, **scimnk** cooked fish tails, **skulhnk** buttocks, **sp'nkayc** to get hit on the buttocks, receive a spanking, **kawnkta** fat around kidneys, **Yank-layc** a man's name: "having a good bottom" = one's canoe pole never slips (on the bottom of the river)
   -nk-aaq-alh hem of dress (20.3.1): **tucnkaaqalh** (tr.) to undo the hem, **stq'nkaaqalh** (tr.) to lower the hem-line

816 ***nm** (tr./itr.) to occupy, cover, fill (up), stop: to spread, ex-pand, swell (up); to be settled, completed, fulfilled; to be full, blocked, stuck, inert; to contain, withhold, suppress, obstruct: **nmaqw'stnmaw** they are spread, scattered all over, **nmtsut** sore is swelling, **alhnm** animal is in his den, **nmlcliwa** to have given up, be resigned, **nmlc+ts'** it (e.g. dance) is over now, **axw nmlcs** he did not complete his term, **axw nmtsuts** it does not stop (e.g. bleed-ing), **nmlcalhts** I cannot walk anymore, my feet are getting numb, **nmnmlcalhts+ts'** I am stuck, cannot move around now, **nmlcuts** to be no longer able to speak, **nmnmuuts** deaf-mute, **nmlxs** (tr.) "to ob-struct somebody's nose" = to smother somebody, **alhnmis ti+s7axxuts +tc** he suppresses his cough, **nmaaxta** beaver dam, **snm** logjam

817 **-nm** caus.-itr. suffix (19.13.2); habitual suffix (19.17.1.2): **acws-nm** to hear, **icaasnm** to search, **anutayaaknm** (to be the) pitcher in

baseball game, **ts'xlh∧lhnuulhnm** to play soccer, **sunp'uulhnm** to play baseball, **alh7ip'ulhnm** to play lahal, **alht'umulhnm** (to be a) leech, **nik'aaxnm** to cut grass, to hay, **nulhumaaxnm** to have a cup of tea or coffee with somebody, **qat'iixwnm** to pick elderberries, **nutsqwilhnm** (to be a) rapist, **sp'lxsnm** to be using the phone

818 -**nmacw** to accidentally ... each other; to find, consider each other ... (19.11.2): **sak'amnmacw**, **kannmacw** to hurt each other accidentally, **pakwnmacw** to catch up with each other, to arrive together, **yanmacw** to like each other, **ts'xanmacw** to believe each other, **anusqwinmacw** to refuse to believe each other

819 -**nmc** = -**nm⌃mc** (19.13.2): **pakwnmc** to catch up, **alh7acwsnmc** to hear, **wannmc** to be late, miss (e.g. the train or a meal)

820 **Nmkis** Nimpkish (a geographical name)

821 ***nmnm** both, double (20.2.7): **nmnmak** both hands, **nmnmiklxs** (both) nostrils, **nmnmaax** both legs, **nmnmalsikan** both ears, **nmnmiixwlayc** both knees, **nmnmikuus** double-bladed axe

822 **n∧nmk'** animal

823 **nmp** (tr.), **nmpa** (itr.) to put something into a container: **alhnmptuts** I have it in a container, **nmpimut** to board a vehicle, **nmpayc** to have boarded a vehicle, **nmplxsakta** thimble, **alhnmpus** to be wearing a mask, **nmpusmaw** they are going to have a mask dance

824 -**nnak** faeces (20.2.1): **qaxnnak** rabbit droppings, **nannnak** grizzly bear's droppings, **tl'mstnnnak** human faeces

825 **ntl'** dark(ness), night: **icntl'** (it is) really dark, **icntl'alhmtsinu** I will pay you a surprise visit tonight, **Icntl'anm** a man's name, **si7ntl'uts** to have supper, **sntl'** night, **asntl'** last night, **alh+ti+ sntl't** tonight, **nukalik ti+sntl'** midnight

826 **nts** I, me (25.2): **nts ti+staltmc** I am the chief

827 **nu-** inside (20.2.2, 20.3.2, 23.6.2); stomach (23.3); in the water (23.6.2); human (23.4, 26.2.1): **nukmats** my stomach aches, **nukw'pt** to be full from eating, **nup'aats** deep water, **nusic** there is blood

in the water, **numaaskaw+ks?** how many are they?, **nut'xúlhaw** they are six in number

828 **-nu** 2 sg. subj. itr. (14.2); 2 sg. obj. tr./caus. (14.3.2, 14.4.2)

829 **Nuakila** name of one of the first (mythical) men

830 **nu7aws** to be stingy with one's food: **nunu7aws** never sharing one's food, **nu7awsmtsinu** I will not share my food with you

831 **-nuc** (recorded in a song) = **-nucw**

832 **nucim** to growl

833 **nucs** quiet, silent: **nucstimut** to keep quiet

834 **-nucw** = **-nic** (19.13.3)

835 **Nuikw'** Noeick (name of a river)

836 **nukakals** flounder

837 **nukum** (tr./itr.) to like, love, desire: **nukumts alh+ts'ayc** I desire her, **nukumtmacw** to love each other

838 **nukwi** sea otter

839 **Nuk'atsu** Ulkatcho (a Carrier village): **Nuk'atsumc** Ulkatcho native

840 **nuk's** (tr.), **nuk'sa** (itr.) to extinguish a fire: **nuk'slc** fire goes out, **nuk'saaxuts** (tr.) to extinguish a cigaret, **nuk'stsut** to turn off the lights in the house

841 **nulaxlx** clear water

842 **nulhilhq** to be frail, sickly

843 ***nulhkw'** (tr.) to pierce, perforate: **nulhkw'm** to knit, make a net, **nulhkw'aqw's** (tr.) to insert sticks into fish heads (prior to barbecuing them), **nulhkw'aqw'sta** sticks used for barbecuing fish heads

844 **Nulht'i** the dwelling place of **Nuakila** and **Nusmata**

845 **-nuli** metathetical variant of **-luni** (18.4.1): **lawnulitxw!** loosen it a bit!, **q'slcnulitxw!** tighten it a bit!, **alhksulhnuli** a bit cheaper, **qiqtnuli** a bit smaller

846 **nulmaax** to turn around and go back, retrace one's steps

847 ***numilik** (tr.) to confuse somebody: **numilikaynictss** he got me confused

848 **numlhak** (tr.) to pay somebody for completing a job

849 **numts'** (tr.) to squeeze out somebody's boil: **Numts'** a geographical name

850 **numus** to be consistent, balanced, evenly distributed: **axw numuŝ s-ka+7astcws** he is not always home, **numustulh+ts' wa+7ulhqnuks+7ats c+ti+smaŵlh ti+t'xt** now we put one rock into each of these buckets

851 **numuts** (tr.) to close the door: **numutslunitx!** close the door a little!, **numutsta** door

852 **nunk'ik** (tr.) to cut something in half: **nunk'ikayc** half-moon

853 **Nunuqw'ays** a geographical name

854 **nup** shirt, dress: **nunupi** dim.

855 **nupalhtcwik** (tr.) to offer advice to somebody: **nupalhtcwiknm** (to be an) advisor, counsellor

856 **nupapayulhaaq** to squat

857 **nupapnt** to boil: **nupapnttxw!** boil it!, **nupapntstuts ti+sq'alh+tc** I am boiling the meat

858 **nupits'tsut** to turn away in disgust

859 **nupq't** to fart: **nupq'talayc** to fart accidentally

860 **nuqaaxp** slough in tidal flats

861 ***nuqatq** (tr.) to cup something with one's hand: **nuqatquts** (tr.) to cover somebody's mouth (e.g. so as to stifle him), **nuqatqalsikanm** to cover one's ears, **nuqaaxtqutsm c+a+qla** he is scooping up water with his hand (and drinking it)

862 **Nuqats'i** a woman's name

863 **Nuqwilhtaaxw** Cape Mudge

864 **nuqw'ɑat** to burp

865 **nuq'ayaaxalh** (tr.) to block somebody's way

866 **nus-...-m = kanus-...-m**

867 **nus(7)alhklhm** seven (26.2)

868 **Nusilawat** a bay north of **Kw'alhna**

869 **nuskum** to start smiling: **anususkum** to be smiling

870 **Nuskut'ini** Nazko Carrier people

871 **nuspkwnuutsta** porch, veranda

872 **Nusqwalhayc** a mythical woman's name

873 **nusq'aaxm** to yell, scream

874 **Nusq'lst** the name of a mountain

875 **nustl'ikw** cover, shelter: **nustl'ikwanm** to take shelter

876 **nustl'p** pool, pond: **Nusmtl'mp** a geographical name

877 **nustq'** (tr.), **nustq'a** (itr.) to patch something, sew together, join something: **nustq'atxw!** tell him to start patching!, **nustq'iktmacw- txw ti+stn+tc!** join the stick to it!

878 ***nustsaax** (tr.) to cover a horizontal surface: **nustsaaxiktx!** put boards over the crosspieces!, **nustsaaxta** sheet, covering, **nustsaax- utsta** tablecloth

879 **Nusxiq'** Nooseseck Bay

880 **nusxl** smart, clever

881 **nusxwaapsta** brooch, safety pin

882 ***nusxwataax** unwilling, reluctant, lazy: **nusxwataaxalh** to not feel like walking, **nusxwataaxak** to not feel like working, **nusxwataaxuts** to not want to eat or talk, **nusxwataaxliwa** generally lazy

883 **nutk'am** to fall over: **nutk'amankiiqw** to fall sideways, **nutk'amaax** to fall backwards

884 **Nutm** a point of land south of Restoration Bay

885 ***nutsik'lam** to turn around: **anutsik'lam(timut)** to turn around, look back (as if expecting something), **icnutsitsk'lamtimut** to constantly be turning around

886 **nutsnm** (tr.) to remember something

887 **nutsunuts** (tr.) to ask somebody's permission, **nutsunutsamktsut** to ask permission to leave, excuse oneself

888 **nut'axwm** to bathe (a Kimsquit word)

889 **nut'qwalm** (tr.) to step over an obstacle: **nut'qwalmik** (tr.) to step over a log

890 **nu7umtaax** to holler

891 **nu7upts** bad smell, stink: **nu7uptstinits** I am overcome by a stench

892 **nux** (fish) caught in a net

893 **Nuxalk** Bella Coola: **Nuxalkmc** Bella Coola native(s), **Nuxalkalas** a beach across **Ista**

894 **nuxwanitsut** whirlpool

895 **Nuxwlst** a valley south of **Yulyulmlh**

896 **nuxwski** soapberries: **nuxwnuxwskilhp** soapberry bush, **nuxwnuxwskyaak** soapberry leaves or branches

897 **nuyulaax** (tr.) to cause to disappear, annihilate something: **nuyulaaxayc ta+7alhqulhhts** my documents have disappeared

898 **nxt** to blow one's nose: **snxt** snot

P

899 **-p** 2 pl. subj. tr./caus. (14.3.1, 14.4.1)

900 **paalhats** potlatch

901 **paaqi7yala** a type of storing box

902 ***paaqu** = **paaxu**

903 **paax**, ***pa(a)q** (tr.), **paaxa** (itr.) to name somebody: **alhpaax** (having been) named, having a name, **alhpaaxtus** he gave him a name, **papqlhis +ts' ta+mans+tx** now he named his father (i.e. mentioned his name), **papqtsuts+ts' c+a+skwatstas** now he mentioned (enumerated) his own names, **paapqa** to make a guess in the lahal game

904 **paaxlh** stern of boat: **paaxlhaaxnu!** be at the stern!

905 **paaxu**, ***paaqu** to be afraid: **pacpaaxu** always afraid, cowardly, **pacpaaqûulhlamtilh** we are going to scare them, **pacpaaquustu-** to scare somebody, **paaxûlhla** strong, heady (said of wine), **paaxûlhlaliwa**

causing fear, terrifying, dangerous

906 **pacw+7iks?** when is it? (25.5): **ala+pacw?** when was it again?, **pacw +lituts' ska+waltulhs?** when will he leave us again?

907 **paktulhk** mesh board used for making nets

908 ***pakw** caught up with: **pakwnic** (tr.) to catch up with somebody, **pakwnmacw** to catch up with each other, arrive together

909 **Pakwani** a mountain at **Kw'alhna**

910 **panya** (tr./itr.) to smoke fish: **nuspanya(a)sta** smokehouse

911 **papink** snake: **papinki** dim., **kulhpapink** there are many snakes around

912 **papnlh** to bark

913 ***paq = paax**

914 ***pats** young, early: **patsilh** young girl's vagina
patsalh to go first, ahead: **patsalhx!** go first!, **patsalhnu stakannu** you are the first one to arrive, **patsalhustuminu** I will serve you the first cup, **wa+patsalh wa+lhk'uulh wa+sulh** the biggest house, **ala+ka+patsalh ska+7ustcws** before he will go in, **panpatsalhx!** be the leader!

915 **pats'** (tr.), **pats'a** (itr.) to pierce, prick something or somebody: **pats'tsinu** I will give you an injection, **pats'ta** hypodermic syringe, **pats'alhta** awl, piercer, **kulhpats'alhta** Scotch thistle

916 **pay** lacking flavor or feeling: bland, tasteless, numb: **payuusi** "to be slightly numb in the face" = drunk, intoxicated

917 **pays** flounder: **papiisi** dim., **paysta** flounder hook

918 **pc** (tr.) to run a wet string between one's thumb and forefinger so as to squeeze the water out of it (= **cp**)

919 ***pc** positive, giving pleasure: nice, enjoyable, entertaining, funny: **pcaqw's** having a pretty color, **pcliwa** lovely, pretty, funny, **pcɬcliwaatimut** comical, clownish, **pculhculhla** happy, feeling fine, **nunupc** active, always busy

920 **Piisla** a stream between the Necleetsconnay and Bella Coola rivers

921 **pik'** bright, brilliant, shiny, sparkling: **pik'anlh** oil pants, **pik'-**

uulh oil coat, **pik'ulhiiqw** southwester (hat), **uspik'uuts** water reflects the sunlight, **spik'** spark, **alhpik'm** sparks are flying, **anupipk'miik** sparks are coming out of the chimney

922 **pilik't** eel, lamprey

923 **piq'** wide, broad: **pipq'aak**, **nupipq'lqs** broad-leaved plantain, **Piq'-ulhla** a man's name, **pipq'uulh** bug characterized by a grey stripe across its body

924 **pisman** to fish with a net

925 **pispis** (tr.) to train, educate somebody: **pispistsut** to study, take lessons, follow a course

926 **pitl'** dirty

927 ***pits'** light, milky, pale: **nupits'** muddy water (beigish in color), **pits'mus** having a pale face

928 **pk'm** mosquito: **pk'mk'mi** dim.

929 ***pl** to have lacking, missing: **plaalh** one-legged, **plalits** toothless
plc** (/pl⌃1c**/) having reached the end, gone, finished: **plcalaaxt** both his parents have died, **nuplcaax** to be extinct, deserted (village, population), **plclxslayc** he cannot speak anymore, **plclxsalhts** I cannot go any further

930 **Plcwlaqs** a woman's name

931 **plht** thick: **nuplhtatlsikan** "thick-eared" = slow learner

932 **plhtkn** bark of bittercherry tree: **plhtkńknlhp** bitter cherry tree

933 **plik** (tr.) to tip, turn over something: **plikm** to capsize, **pliktsut** to play at turning over canoe, **pɬplikusm** to empty one's cup by tipping it over into one's mouth

934 **plki7wa** cedarwood box used for storing food

935 **Plqwit** a personal name

936 **plst** scale of fish

937 **plxani** inner surface of abalone shell, mother-of-pearl: **plxanyuulh** buttons made of **plxani**, **Plxanimc** "Abalone People" (mentioned in a myth), **Plxaniixas** daughter of the chief of the **Plxanimc**

938 **pnaaxta, pnaaxsta** dancer's apron

939 ***pqw'** fine, particled (snow): **spqw'lh** fine snow, blizzard, **icpqw'm wa+suncw** there is a blizzard blowing

940 **ps** (tr.), **psa** (itr.) to shape, mold something

941 ***ps** to blow, hiss: **sps** blizzard coming in from the north-east, **nu-pslitaax** to release a hissing flatus

942 **-ps** constituent of **(nu-...)-alps** (20.2.1)

943 **psayct, spsayct** pitch of fir tree

944 **psc** (tr.) to train, educate somebody: **pscik** (tr.) to scrape roots smooth so as to make them pliable

945 **pscm** to pit-lamp

946 **pskwn** to have a chiefs' meeting (pl. subj.)

947 **pukw's** a mythological ape-like creature

948 ***pulh** to swell, be swollen: **pulhm** it (e.g. dough) is rising
spulh lump: **spulhanalh** lump of ankle, **spulhanak** lump of wrist, **nu-spulhuulhikalhh** Adam's apple, **Spulhus** a man's name

949 **Pulhas** Pootlass (a chief's name)

950 ***pun** to accept, receive: **puntuminu c+t'ayc** I will present this to you, **puñmacw** to exchange gifts

951 **puqw'** ample, loose: **pupqw'aalhts** my shoes are too big

952 **pus** to grow: **pustu-** to raise, bring up somebody, **axw pumpuus** he is not growing, **pusiixw** to bud, sprout, **spus** leaf, **spuustimut** weed, **supuslhp** young willow having light thin bark
pusm to swell, be swollen: **nupusmiilhuts** one's lips are swollen, **nupusmalmcts** my breasts are swollen, **nupusm** to float up, **nupusmutsta** floater line, **anupuspsm** to be floating around

953 **putl'** to come: **putl'm** (tr.) to come to, visit somebody, **putl'tu-** to bring something, **anuputl'uts** saliva comes from one's mouth, **putl'uuts** the river rises, **putl'iixw** to bud, sprout, **putl'aynic** (tr.), **putl'aylayc** (itr.) to get, catch fish or game, **putl's** and, plus (26.2.4, 29.3.2)

954 **Putsla** Mesachie Nose (a point of land notorious for high swells)

955 **putsq'** Indian hellebore

956 **putsut** to swell, rise (of water): **nuputsutik** it is rising (boiling liquid in a pot), **anuputsutik** it keeps rising

957 **puts'tn** bow for shooting arrows

958 **puut** boat: **puutii** dim.

959 **puux** moldy: **puuxlc ti+saplin** bread gets moldy, **spuuxaltswa** grey blueberry (vaccinium ovalifolium)

960 **Puuxin** a point of land situated south of **Yuyupaaxani**

961 **pux** (tr.), **puxa** (itr.) to poke, stir something, rummage, search for something: **puxalus** (tr.) to poke the fire, **puxulmca** to clear the ground, remove rocks from the soil

962 ***pux** hairy, furry: **spux** eagle down, **alhpucwpuxmutsaalh** "having very furry legs" = mature male mountain goat

963 **pu7yaas** Indian tea

964 **p'alc** to come to, wake up: **p'alcalus** to get better, sober up

965 ***p'alu** loosened, freed, elevated, high: **p'alwaax** tree or post is loose, **stip'alwaaq** to have one leg up, **nup'alwaaq** one leg (e.g. of bed or chair) is not level with the others, **p'alulc** to rise, go up, **sp'alu** waist, middle

966 **p'anilhp** green alder, mountain alder

967 **p'as** (tr.) to pay for something: **p'asiltts c+tu+s7alhkultts+txw** I will pay for what I borrowed, **p'asilttuminu** I'll pay for you

968 ***p'a(a)ts** deep: **p'atsuuts** drop-off in sea, **nup'a(a)ts** deep water

969 **p'c** crabapple: **icp'iclhp** crabapple tree

970 **p'iix** (tr.) to apply steam to something: **p'iixm** to be steaming, **nup'iixmaax** exhaust fumes, **icp'iixm** to take a sweat bath, **sp'iix** vapor, steam, **sp'iixutslh** vapor issuing from one's mouth

971 **p'iixla** to drift downstream: **p'iixlayalulhts** the boat is drifting away from me, **p'iixlatimutts ala+7anuxum** I am drifting down the river

972 **p'lha** to wink, blink one eye: **p'lhalha** to blink both eyes

973 **p'lht** warm: **anup'lht** lukewarm, **nup'lhtutstimut** to warm up one's drink

974 **p's** (tr.), **p'sa** (itr.) to bend something: **alhp'sm** it is bent, **p's-tsutx!** bend over!, **axw nup'sms** he does not yield, is adamant

975 **p'ts** (tr.) to hold something under water: **nup'tsiixw** (tr.) to submerge somebody's head

976 **p'ulhkwm** to bubble up: **nunup'ulhkwm** it keeps bubbling up

977 **p'ulhm** (tr./itr.) to go and meet newcomers: **p'ulhmlh** we will go and meet (them), **p'ulhmtsinu** I will go and meet you (there)

978 ***p'uy**, ***p'wi** to tip, fall over: **p'uyaax** tree falls down, **up'wi** to nid-nod

979 **p'wi** halibut: **up'wii** dim., **p'wita** halibut line

980 **p'xwlht** bunchberries (cornus unalaschanensis): **p'xwlhtlhp** bunchberry plant

Q

981 **qa** (tr.) to wish somebody dead: **qalikw** ill-wisher, **qayaynicits** I have brought about his death, **qayutsmtsinu** I wish you would die **nuqaykm** (tr.) to wish, hope, anticipate something: **nuqaykmits ska+ putl's kaynucs** I hope he will come tomorrow, **nuqaykmaynicits ska+ putl's** I anticipated his coming

982 ***qa** to ask, beg: **qaaxayutsmts c+ti+sikalit** I am asking for a cigaret, **qaaxam** (tr./itr.) to ask somebody for something, **usqam** (tr.) to remind somebody of a debt, tell him how much he owes, **qamxamila** term of respect used to address a salmon after catching it

983 **Qaaklis** name of a Rivers Inlet man

984   **Qaali** a personal name

985   **Qaana, Qana** a man's name

986   **Qaap** a woman's name

987   **qaax** salmonberry: **qaaxaaxlhp** salmonberry bush, **qaaxulh** salmonberry juice, **Snuqaax** former village situated below **Snut'li**

988   **qaaxapwala** joist

989   **qaaxatsci** (tr.) to tickle somebody: **nuqaaxatscyaalh** to have ticklish feet

990   **qaaxatscili** swallow

991   **qaaxla** to drink: **qaaxlam** (tr.) to drink something, **qaaxlamim** drink, beverage, liquor, **qaaxlatu-** to give somebody something to drink, **unqaaxlamc** always drinking, drunkard

992   *qaaxp' = *qap'

993   **qaaxqi** unbalanced, (afraid) to lose one's balance: **axw qaaxqis** he does not lose his balance, **k'isqaaxqi** steady, never losing one's balance

994   *qaaxt' = qat'

995   *qalh to be attached to something, to hang (from something): **axw ti+ka+qalhlits'tas** he is not committed to anyone, has unlimited freedom, **qalhqalhm** to be hanging, dangling, **alhqalhm** (tr.) to hang on to, not let go of somebody, **alhqalhm̲likw** person who never leaves his wife out of sight

996   **qalhayu** gaffhook

997   **qalhqa** raspberries: **qalhqalhp** raspberry bush

998   **qalxalulhm** (tr./itr.) to welcome, deliver a speech of welcome: **qalxalulhmlh ulh+lhup = qalxalulhmtulhap** we welcome you

999   **qalxm** to dig for fern roots: **Siqalxm** the month in which people are digging for fern roots

1000 **qama** term of endearment for a grandmother, granny: **ax+ku qamayts** no, (thank you,) my dear, **Qaaqma** a woman's name

1001 **Qamaatslaqs** a man's name

1002 **qamats** dead fern fronds: **Nuqaaxmats** a geographical name

1003 **qamits'a, *qamits'n** to have a communal meal: **nuqamits'naaxnm** entire community is joined in a festive meal

1004 **Qana = Qaana**

1005 **Qanmcsti** a man's name

1006 **Qanxt'u** Deadman's Point

1007 **Qaps7alap'st** name of a Kitlope chief

1008 **qapsmuulhm** to put one's arms around oneself

1009 ***qap', *qaaxp'** (tr.) to adjust, straighten out, tidy up, put away, tuck, fold in: **icqaaxp'tsut** to tidy oneself up, **nuqaaxp'utsm** to wipe one's mouth, **qap'utsm** to put one's food away, **qap'usm** to wipe one's hair from one's face, **qap'tsut** to adjust one's clothes, to tuck in one's shirt, **qap'uulhm** to fold one's arms, **alhqap'uulhlatsut** to put one's arms around oneself

1010 **Qaqaaxs** a man's name

1011 **Qaqatli** a mythical man's name

1012 **Qaqimas** a man's name

1013 **qaqtalhp** ninebark

1014 **Qasana** a mythical man's name

1015 **Qats** a personal name: **Qatsaqw's** a personal name, **Qatsilh** a woman's name

1016 **qatsqilh** ant: **qatsqiiqlhi** dim.

1017 **qatsx** starfish: **qaaqtsxi** dim., **alhqatsx** crossed, crosswise, **qatsxtmacwaak** to cross one's arms, **qatsxtmacwaalh** to cross one's legs

1018 **qat', *qaaxt'** (tr.), **qat'a** (itr.) to press something against oneself, pull towards oneself: **qat'alsikanm** to press one's hand on one's ear, **nuqat'alxm** to put one's hand on one's neck, **nuqat'ikalusm** to fold one's arms, **nuqat'aaxm** to close the door behind oneself, **qaaxt'usm** to jerk one's head back, tilt one's face up, beckon, **qaaxt'usmim c+tx** he was beckoned by him, **nuqat'ikus** (tr.) to strap something around one's forehead, **nuqat'ikusta** headband of packstrap, **qat'ta** trigger of gun, **qat'alusakta** poker, **qat'iixwnm** to be gathering elderberries, **qat'iixwta** type of hook used to gather elderberries, **qat'akm** (tr.) to beckon somebody, **alhqat'iiqw** oar, **alhqat'iiqwnm** to row, **qaaxt'aksta** boards that are attached to the hands and used to propel oneself when swimming

1019   **qaw** (tr.), **qawa** (itr.) to enclose, surround something: **alhqawit wa+ sulh+ts** they are surrounding the house, **anuqawaax** cuddled up in bed with one's lover

1020   **Qawats'i** a geographical name

1021   **qax** rabbit: **qaaxqxi** dim.

1022   **qay** stick used in a gambling game, stake

1023   **qayt** hat: **snuqaqaytiiqw** mushroom

1024   **qiixa, *qiixn** glad, happy: **qiixam** (tr.) to be happy about, enjoy something, **qiixnamk** (tr.) to be proud of something, **sqiixa** "happiness" = Sunday, weekend; week

1025   **qiku, xiku** dragonfly

1026   **qilic** (tr.) to belittle, insult somebody

1027   **qinx** shoe: **qiqnqi** dim.

1028   **qiqipi(i)** small; little children: **nuqiqipalmci** having small breasts

1029   **qiqti** small; little child: **qiqtlqsi** having a small nose, **qiqtalmci** having small breasts, **kulhqiqti** having a small penis, **qiqtaalhi** small vehicle or container

1030   **qism** to avoid contact: **qismak** to refuse to touch something, **qismuts** to refuse to eat something

1031   ***qits'** out of reach, secluded: **qits'an** to spend time in seclusion when having one's first menstrual flow
qits'lc to abhor, avert, evade: **qits'lcuts** to refrain from saying something, **alhqits'lcnicits** I abhor it, cannot stomach it, **nuqits'-lcik** to feel faint, sick to the stomach (from fright), **nuqits'lc-alxi** one's neck shudders, **Qits'lclayc** a man's name

1032   **qla** fresh water: **nuqlaata** water bucket, **nuqlalcalsuts** one's mouth starts watering, **snuqlayalsuts** saliva, **usqlayayc** to crave water, be thirsty, **smqla** to be thirsty, **smqlam** (tr.) to want to drink something, **qlayulh** soup is watery, **qlxlayulmc** soil is wet, **snuqlxlayk** Alaska blueberry

1033 ***qlam** thoughtful, feeling pity, having consideration: **qlamta** pity, consideration, respect, **kulhqlamta** to be very considerate, **k'ilh-qlamta** to have no pity or consideration for anyone, **anuqlamikts alh+tc** I take pity on him, **nuqlamikmtsx!** have pity on me!, help me!

1034 **qlcwila** (tr.) to mix food with grease: **qlcwilatits wa+sqaluts** I am mixing berries with grease

1035 **qlh** (tr.) to touch somebody where it hurts: **qlhaycts** I start hurting again, **qlhaynictscw** you have touched me where it hurts, **alhqlh-tsutts** the pain keeps coming back to me

1036 **qlhm** black cod: **qlhmlhmi** dim.

1037 **qlhpulx** water hemlock

1038 **qlum** blister: **qlxlumalh** to have blistered feet

1039 **qluq's** eye: **qlxluq's** both eyes

1040 **qm** (tr.) to cover, wrap, shelter something: **qmtx ti+st'sals!** wrap the bottle!, **qmta** insulation; armor, **qmxmtsut** to cover oneself, **nu-sqmxmtsut** to build a shelter for oneself

1041 **qmqmi(i)** soft: **snuqmqmani** temple, **snuqmqmikuus** fontanelle, **qmxm** weak, breaking or tearing easily, **qmxmlc** to start decaying

1042 **qnk** deep: **nuqnk** water is deep, **nuqnqnki** water is a bit deep, **Asqnk-uts** name of a dance involving the dead, **qnklst** "deep rocks" = island, **qⁿqnklsti** small island, **Nuqnklstank** Little Mesachie Nose
tqnk (to be) underneath: **tqnkam** to go under something, **tqnkusam** to crawl under something facing up, stick one's face under something, **tqnkus ala+7its'amni+ts** he is under the blankets, **tqnkams**, **tqnkaax-ams** lower jaw, **tqnkiilhuts**, **tqnkanlhaaxuts** lower lip, **tqnqnk** underwear, chemise, **tqnkuulh** underwear, **ustqnkaaq** petticoat

1043 **qpi** thin, narrow: **qpapluulhi** thin string, **nuqpiipqwi** having a small voice, **s(nu)qpɬplxs** a mythical animal with a long snout (mammoth?)

1044 **qp'a** egg: **qp'aap'ayi** dim.

1045 **-qs = -aqs**

1046 **Qtaysalh** a mythical woman's name

1047 **qtl'** to trip, stumble: **qnxntl'ts** I keep tripping

1048 **qts** (tr.) to pass a condition on to somebody: **qtstsinu** I will in-
fect you, you will catch my disease, **qtsaynictscw** you have communi-
cated your illness to me, **qtsuutsaynictscw** you have made me yawn
(eat) too, **qtsikak** (tr.) to lend somebody a hand
qtsamk (tr.), **qtsamka** (itr.) to throw something overboard, cast a
net: **alhqtsamktnm** to have a net in the water, **qtsamkayc** to have
fallen overboard, **qtsamktsut** to jump overboard

1049 **qts'a = xts'a**

1050 **qts'us, xts'us** rack used for drying food

1051 ***qt'** pointed: **qt'aaqlayc** to have a pointed chin

1052 **qulh** (tr.), **qulha** (itr.) to make marks on, write something: **qulhax
ulh+7nts!** write to me!, **alhqulh** written: book, letter, document,
alhqulhuus picture, photograph, **qulhu(u)sm** to apply paint to one's
face, **qulhquulhta** pen, **asqulhquulhtnak** to use a pen, **qulhiixw** (tr.)
to decorate, make designs on a lid, **quulhalus** swamp robin, varied
thrush, **alhqulhqwlhanlh** cloth with a design on it, **anuqulhqwlhaak**
lines in palm of hand, **qulhm** to organize a feast during which all
masks are given away

1053 **qululuuxu** strawberry

1054 **qulun** beaver: **quluni** dim.

1055 **qulutsi** skunk: **quqwluutsî, qwɬqwluutsî** dim.

1056 **quna** thumb: **squnalxsalh** big toe

1057 **qup'** (tr.), **qup'a** (itr.) to punch, hit something with one's fist:
qup'lxs (tr.) to punch somebody on the nose, **nuqup'ikalus** (tr.) to
punch somebody in the chest, **quuxwp'lits'** (tr.) to pummel, beat
somebody up, **quuxwp'ustmacw** to punch each other in the face, **alh-**

qup'a to be beating a drum, **qup'ta** drum, **qup'aaksta** drumstick, **qup'ulhayc** to be knocked down, fall over

1058   **Quqani** a mythical luck-bringing bird

1059   **ququulikn** porpoise

1060   **Ququusxlhm** a man's name

1061   **quts'** (tr.), **quts'a** (itr.) to wash something: **quts'aalhtx!** wash his feet! or wash the car!, **quuxwts'tsut** to wash up, clean oneself, **quts'usm** to wash one's face, **quts'usta** toilet soap, **quts'alhm** to wash one's feet, **quts'ulmcm** to mop the floor, **nuquts'alsm** to wash the walls

1062   **quts'ik** wolverine: **quqwts'iiki** dim.

1063   **quts'ulhkw** western yew

1064   **quuxuux** swan

1065   ***quuxwp'** = **qup'**

1066   ***quuxwts'** = **quts'**

1067   **quuxwwa** salmon milt: **nuquuxwwa** it has milt in it, it is a male fish

1068   **qux** (tr.), **quxa** (itr.) to cover something: **quxtsut** to cover oneself, **quxuulhta** pillowcase, **quxalst** (tr./itr.) to steam-cook something, **quxm** to simmer food (leaving the lid on the pan)

1069   **Quyustitsas** a personal name

1070   **Qwaatsinay** a man's name

1071   **Qwaatswa** name of a Kimsquit woman

1072   **qwaax(w)qwiklhp** mountain ash

1073   **qwaaxwn** youngest sibling: **qwaax(w)qwni** dim., **Nusqwaaxwnmc** a man's name

1074   **qwalas** lizard: **qwaqwlaasi** dim.

1075   **qwals** hemlock needles

1076   **qwanilh** wooden spoon: **qwaqwniilhi, qwnqwniilhi** dim.

1077   **qwaqwaws** sawbill duck: **qwaqwawsi** dim.

1078   **Qwasta** name of a Kimsquit man

1079   **Qwatsilh** a woman's name

1080 **qwaxw** raven: **qwaax(w)qwxwi** dim., **qwaxwqwaxwlit** to caw, **qwaxwaalh** round type of snowshoe

1081 ***qwi** (tr.) to open something: **nuqwitx wa+nulhcwta+ts!** open the curtains!, **nuqwyuts** (tr.) to open a door, **nuqwiixwyutsitx!** open the door a little!, **qwîixw** (tr.) to take the lid off a container, open a can, **qwinqwîiqwta** can opener, **Alhqwyaltwa** a personal name, **Anuqwîktimut** a man's name, **Alhqwyaqw's** a man's name, **Qwyaax** a man's name

1082 ***qwi** untrue, dubious: **qwinic** (tr.) to have doubts about somebody, **qwinictits ska+7alhinaw** I doubt they were there, **nuqwinicutsmts** I deny having said that, **anusqwinictsinu** I do not believe you, **axwtxw anusqwinmacwnu!** let there be no doubt between us!

1083 **Qwikilh** name of a Kimsquit woman

1084 **Qwik'iis** a woman's name

1085 **qwilats** to crush, bruise: **sqwilatslh** fruit juice, wine, **qwilatsaalh** to bruise one's foot, **qwilatsiixwalst** to bruise one's shoulder, **qwilatsiixwlayc** to bruise one's knee

qwilatsm to be bruised: **qwilatsmiixwalst** to have a bruised shoulder, **qwilatsmaak** to have a bruised hand

1086 **Qwinaw** name of a Kimsquit man

1087 **qwit** blue: **qwitaqw's** having a blue color, **itqwitanlh** to wear blue clothes, **nuqwitals** the sky is blue

1088 **qwli** green, yellow: **nuqwlîkaqw's** having green eyes, **sqwli** grassy side of mountain, **nuqwⳑqwli** lemon extract, **snuqwⳑqwlîk** root of western dock, **snuqwⳑqwlials** cascara bark

1089 **qwls** (tr.), **qwlsa** (itr.) to look through one eye, to aim one's gun at something: **nusqwls** one-eyed, always looking through one eye

1090 **qwlxw** (tr.) to hire somebody: **alhqwlxw** hired, **alhqwlxwx alh+7nts!** be my assistant!, **qwlxwayc** to be hired, have a job

1091 ***qwsk** (tr.) to wind string on a spool: **qwskta** spool for net string, **qwskaktsx!** put the string on my spool!

1092 **qwsm** to sweat: **qwsmus** to have a sweating face, **qwsmaalh** to have sweating feet, **qwsm̲lik** to sweat all over one's body

1093 **qwt** crooked: **nuqwt** river is crooked, **nuqwtaalh wa+m̲m̲nta** the path is crooked, **qwtus** carving knife, **qwtulh** cradle

1094 **qwwas** cooked sockeye salmon

1095 **qw'ala** empty, gone: **nuqw'alayk** container is empty, **qw'alayalus** to have no firewood left, **qw'alalaycts c+a+tl'awqw'** I have no tobacco left, **nuqw'alayaax** to have no children, **nunuuqw'ala** to have nothing left, **qw'alayutsts** I have finished eating

1096 **qw'alm** older sibling: **wa+7alqw'alm̂tsts** all my older brothers and sisters, **anusqw'alm** having lost one's older siblings, **sqw'almlxsalh** big toe

1097 **qw'almuulh** (tr.), **qw'almuulha** (itr.) to roast potatoes under sand: **alhqw'almuulh** roasted potatoes, **qw'almuulhnm** to be roasting potatoes (e.g. at a picnic)

1098 **qw'alxs** parsnip: **qw'aqw'lqsi** dim., **nuqw'alqsta** parsnip bed

1099 **Qw'ants** a location at Kimsquit

1100 **Qw'apmay** a personal name

1101 **Qw'apx** a valley at **Talyu**

1102 **qw'aqwina** dogfish: **qw'aaqwinayi** dim.

1103 **qw'asta** mountain goat wool

1104 ***qw'ay** ashes, charred, black(ened): **alhqw'ay** smeared with ashes, **qw'ayusm** to apply charcoal to one's face, **qw'ayaqw's ti+stn+tc** the stick is charred, **Alhqw'ayus** a man's name, **ayqw'ayulhank** "blackened abdomen" = appendicitis, **ayqw'ayulhanktinits** I have appendicitis

1105 **qw'aykila** small red cod

1106 ***qw'i** (tr.) to split, divide, separate something: **ixqw'itmacwaw** they are separating, **axw qw'yaycs ti+slq's** "his mind is not divided" = he is determined, has made up his mind, **alhtamqw'yakm** (tr.) to keep putting things aside, **nuqw'îk** (tr.) to separate, divide in two, **nuqw'îktmacwilh** we will divide it among ourselves, **nuqw'îk-**

tmacwtutilh we will divide it among them

1107 **qw'ilays** young seal

1108 **qw'las** strange, different, other: **aalats'iits+suts' c+ti+qw'las ti+ s7aalats'ii** and now I will tell another story, **qw'laslh** stranger, **Lqw'lasmc** Bella Bella native, **qw'lasalst** to act in an unusual manner, abnormally, **ixw ti+sqw'lasams** he has become very different

1109 **qw'laxw** thimbleberry leaves: **lqw'laxwlhp** thimbleberry bush, **qw'lax-uulh** paper bag

1110 **qw'lh** to laugh: **ilhqw'nlhtimut** to be laughing

1111 **qw'litq** seagull: **lqw'liitqi** dim., **Snuqw'litq** a geographical name, **Qw'litqana** a woman's name, **Nuqw'litqay** a woman's name

1112 **qw'na** pubic hair: **(nu7)nqw'nayalakt** hair in armpit, **nuqw'naykalus** chest hair, **nu7nqw'nayklxs** hair in nostrils

1113 **qw'p** bare, empty: **nuqw'pals** house is empty, **nuqw'piixw** to be bald, **qw'pulhikus** to be balding, have a receding hairline, **qw'pulmc** bare, treeless area, **qw'pɫplcalaaxtlayc** to have no parents, be an orphan, **nuqw'piipqwlhp** pineapple weed, **Qw'pɫplxs** a point of land west of **Nusilawat**

1114 **qw'pm** to be particulate, misty, powdery, dusty: **qw'pmulmc** (there is) dust on the ground or floor, **nuqw'pm** (there is) dust in the water, **qw'pmals ti+smt** snow is blowing around on the mountain side, **sqw'pm** dust, spray, mist

1115 *****qw's** to leak, ooze, flood: **qw'sm wa+suncw+7ats** the world is flooded, **qw'smiixwlaycts** the water comes up to my knees, **qw'st** to leak, ooze

1116 *****qw'wa** (tr.) to impel, urge on: **qw'watsut, qw'watsutamktsut** to persist, persevere, **qw'wata** perseverance

1117 **qw'waax** old mountain goat

1118 **qw'xw** (tr.), **qw'xwa** (itr.) to move something: **qw'xwm** to be moving, to travel, **siqw'xwm** engine, **qw'xwmtimut** automobile, **asqw'xwmtimut** to travel by car, **qw'xwaaxm** to move to another seat, **nunuqw'xwmts** my stomach is growling

1119 **qw'xw** (tr.) to slow down, delay something: **nuqw'xwalh** (tr.) to delay somebody, **nuqw'xwalhayc** to be delayed, **qw'xwɲxwmi** to take one's time, take it easy, **qw'xwmakix!** slow down! (in work), **qw'xwɲxwmutsi** to eat or speak slowly

1120 **Qw'xwnaak** a woman's name

1121 **qxyu** uncommon, unusual, useless: **qixyumts** I am good for nothing

1122 **q'aat** small baited hook

1123 **Q'aku(u)lh** a man's name

1124 **q'akwts** blue lupine: **q'akwtsnk** root of blue lupine

1125 ***q'al** (tr.) to twist, spin something: **alhq'alikw** spun, braided, **anuq'alikwaluulh** type of rope (/...q'al⁻likw.../)

 q'alm to twist, spiral, zigzag (e.g. fish in the water): **Q'alm** a personal name, **alq'almaalh** drill, **anuq'almaalh** drilled hole

1126 **Q'amiix** a geographical name

1127 **q'anas** chiton, periwinkle

1128 **Q'anuukw** a bay in Dean Channel

1129 **q'aq'atsuulh** wild strawberry

1130 **Q'ataxilh** a woman's name

1131 **q'aticts** (tr.), **q'atictsm** (itr.) to steam-cook food: **q'atictstsut** to take a sweat bath

1132 **q'atm** chisel

1133 **q'aw** (tr.) to pack, wrap, store, bury something: **q'aŵtsm** to store one's food, **sq'awals** box used for packing fruit, **awq'awtsut** to pack one's belongings, **q'aŵlh** (tr.) to wrap something up, **q'awiixw** (tr.) to lock a door, **q'awlxsak** (tr.) to bandage somebody's finger, **q'awaalh** (tr.) to bandage somebody's leg, **q'awliitsalhm** to bandage one's lower leg, **q'awim** he was buried, **q'aṁut** to attend a funeral, **alhq'awik** confined to the house, under house arrest

1134 **q'awlhtaqs** grebe, helldiver

1135 **Q'axlhawals** a man's name

1136 **q'ay** poor, pitiful: **nuq'aŷkm** (tr.) to feel sorry for somebody, **nuq'aŷkmitsut** to feel sorry for oneself, be sad

1137 **q'ay** black hawthorn berry: **aq'ilhp** black hawthorn bush

1138 **q'ay** basket made of cedar bark: **q'aq'ayi, aq'ayi, aq'ii** dim.

1139 **q'ilh** (tr.), **q'ilha** (itr.) to scratch something: **nuq'ilhutsa** to be scratching at the door, **q'ilhulhik** (tr.) to scratch somebody's back, **q'ilhtsut** to scratch oneself, **nuq'ilhikaycs+kwts'n s7anayks ska+k'cis** "and then his mind had been scratched as he wanted to see him" = and then he badly wanted to see him, **nuq'ilhanm** (tr.) to ask somebody a favor, **nuq'ilhaaxta** spider

1140 **q'im** filled up: complete, entire, whole; closed, tight: **q'imaw** they are all present, **q'imulhlamim** both his parents are still alive, **Usq'imtnm** name of a location at Kimsquit (a huge boulder with a smooth surface), **q'im** it is sealed, does not leak, **nuq'imlcalhh** one's windpipe gets stopped up, to choke, **snuq'imaax** windowless inner back wall of house

1141 **q'inakwlilh** droning cry

1142 **q'is** stink currant: **inq'islhp** stink currant bush

1143 **q'is** (tr.), **q'isa** (itr.) to singe, burn the surface of something: **q'isits ti+satl'a+tc** I will fire the canoe, **q'isits ti+knum+tc** I will toast the **knum**, **alhq'is** toasted, **q'ism** to toast one's food

1144 **q'itsm** to stink

1145 **q'lax** fence: **Alhq'laxlhh** name of a former village

1146 **q'lhkw** (tr.), **q'lhkwa** (itr.) to fix something up: **q'lhkwaynic** (tr.) to get something done, fixed, **q'lhkwalus** (tr.) to build a fire, **q'lhkwatu-** to help, do something for somebody, **q'lhkwakm** (tr.) to repair something, **q'lhkwtsut** to get dressed, **q'lhkwta** clothes, **nusq'lhkwta** suitcase, **sq'lhkw** what one has (on) or uses: belongings, tools, clothes, **sq'lhkwĺkwliwa** belongings, **sq'lhkwak** tools

1147 **q'lhp** balsam fir: **q'lhpnk** balsam root

1148 **q'lm** to stagger: **iclq'lm** to stagger repeatedly

1149 **q'ls** cottonwood cambium

1150 **q'lscw** rope: **lq'lscwi** dim.

1151 **q'lst** (tr.), **q'lstm** (itr.) to steam-cook something: **q'lsttsut** to take a sweat bath

1152 ***q'lu** (tr.) to stick one's finger into something: **q'lûlhaqw'sm** to stick one's finger into one's eye, **nuq'lualhhm** to stick one's finger into one's throat

1153 **q'luk** barbecued salmon

1154 **q'lum** to go up, climb: **q'lumliitsayc** to have climbed a tree

1155 **q'm** (tr.), ***q'm** (itr.) to step (on something): **q'mtx!** step on it!, **q'malustx!** step on the fire!, **ixq'm** to walk, travel on foot, **ic7ixq'mtimut** to be walking around, **ixq'mayctu-** to help, enable somebody to walk, **ic7ixq'muustu-** to walk around holding a child so as to pacify it

1156 ***q'm** (tr.) to scorch, toast something: **q'muulh** (tr.) to toast something, **q'muulhutsm** to toast one's food, **q'muulhutsta** toaster, **q'mlc** to get scorched, **sq'mlhh** charred, charcoal

1157 ***q'mstcw** (tr.) to start working on something, get something ready, complete something: **axw alhq'mstcws** it has not been started on yet, **alhq'mstcw stl'mstas** "he is a complete(d) person" = he holds a high position, is a dignitary, **nuq'mstcwiixw** (tr.) to (start) mend(ing) something, **q'mstcwliwatsut** to prepare oneself, get ready for an occasion, **q'mstcutsayc+ts'** "what he says is complete now" = he is making sense now, **axw alhq'mstcutsaynicits** I cannot make sense of what he is saying, **alhq'mstcutstimut** to be speaking half-sensibly, be mumbling

1158 ***q'nlha** vexed, irritated: **alhq'nlha** fed up, **alh7alhq'nlhaatu-** to annoy somebody, **alhq'nlhamuutstsinu** I do not like what you are saying, **ixq'nlhaatnm** to be annoying people, **ixq'nlhalcaw** they got fed up, **ixq'nlhamitsut** to be cranky, irritable

1159 ***q'p** dull: **q'puts** having a dull edge, **nuq'plxs** having a dull point

1160 **q'pst** (tr.), **q'pstm** (itr.) to taste something: **q'pstalayc** he had a taste, **q'pstaynicits** I had a taste of it, **alhq'pstayc** tasty

1161 **q's** tight, firm; to ... solidly, thoroughly, to be very ...; to be rough, violent: **q'slctu-** to tighten something; to hug somebody, **q'slcnulitu-** to tighten something a little, **nuq'saqw's** knot is tight; to gaze, stare, **nuq's** water is flowing fast, **nuq'slcik** to sob, **axwtxw q'snu ska+7alh7alh7aynu!** don't overdo it!, **q'slits'** to be busy, **q'slits'lhts s7ilhtsaylhts** I have been busy picking berries, **q'slits'amktsut** to have a busy or hard time, to suffer, **q's skmalaycs** he is very ill, **q'silh ŝt'saaxilh** we salt it thoroughly, **q'suslmclhp = alhaaq'likw**, **nunuq'sm** (tr.) to bawl out, scold somebody, **q'sakm** (tr.) to beat somebody up, **isq'isaakm** (tr.) to handle something roughly, **axwtxw q'snu ska+7isq'isaakmicw!** don't handle it too roughly!

1162 **q'tsiixwalh** to trip over something

1163 **q'tsm** to creak, make a sharp or metallic sound: **q'tsⱴtsm** it is creaking (e.g. a falling tree), **q'tsⱴtsmllxsak** to make one's fingers creak, **nuq'tsmtsmiiknm** to be playing the trumpet

1164 **q'um**, *⁺uqw'm** high, large: **alhq'um alh+7nts** he is higher (in rank) than I am, **alhq'umlhtuts ta+tl'aplhtuts ulh+7inu alh+t'ayc** I have given you more than him, **umq'um** large waves, swells, **q'umik** hunchbacked, **Q'umtswa** a personal name, **Uqw'mikmc** a man's name

1165 **Q'umaanakwla** a chief's name

1166 **Q'umk'ut's** name of a former village

1167 **q'umniqw'** skull

1168 **q'umsciwa** whiteman: **q'umsciwni** dim., **q'umsciwaalhh** cat

1169 **Q'umukwa** a marine supernatural being; a man's name

1170 **Q'umuus** Comox

1171 **q'up** (tr.), *⁺uqw'p** (tr.), **q'upa** (itr.) to treat something with, expose something to smoke: **q'upm** to emit smoke, **nuq'upmaax** exhaust fumes, **q'upmiixw wa+sulh+ts** there is smoke rising from the chimney of the house, **sq'up** smoke, **nusq'upiixw** smoke coming from chimney, **nusuqw'p(s)ta** tobacco pipe, **nusuqw'p(s)tam** to smoke tobacco, **anu-suqw'p(s)tamiknuɬa?** do you want to smoke?, **nusq'upta** stovepipe, **kuŝq'uptnm** to create a smudge

1172 **Q'uqwayaytxw** name of a Heiltsuk village

1173 **Q'usalq** a geographical name

1174 **q'ux** filled to capacity, unable to contain more: **q'uxtsɬmas tiɬs-7alhps** "I am always full as an eater" = I never eat much, **q'ux tiɬ lhalasɬtc** the canoe is full to the brim, **q'uxliwa** to be fully occupied, not find the time or energy to do what one is asked to do, **q'uxlc** tired, **q'uxlcnimut** to exhaust oneself

1175 **q'ux** (tr.) to invite somebody, **uq'x** (tr.) to call somebody: **q'ux-tinilh** somebody invited us, **q'uxayc** to have been invited, **q'uxlikw** inviting people, **nusq'uxlikwsta** building where feasts are held, **Sq'uxlikwana** a woman's name, **icuq'xtmacwaw** they called each other

1176 **q'x** rank, rancid

1177 **q'x** (tr.), **q'xa** (itr.) to carve something: **alhq'x** carved, **q'xuusnm** to be carving a face (in rock)

1178 **q'xnxna** berries of false Solomon's seal or star-flowered Solomon's seal: **q'xnxnalhp** false or star-flowered Solomon's seal

1179 **q'xtis** fish weir made of rocks

S

1180 **s-** connector-nominalizer (23.4, 23.9 ff.)

1181 **ɬs...** enclitical element (28.3.22.4, 28.3.24)

1182 **-s** 3 sg. subj. itr./tr./caus. (14.2, 14.2.3, 14.3.1, 14.4.1)

1183 **saaxwan** tidal flats: **Saaxwan** a girl's name

1184 **sacwa** dipnet (used at sea): **sacwam** to fish with a dipnet

1185 **sakwm** bracken fern: **sakwmlhp** bracken fern (plant and leaves), **sac-sakwmlhp** bracken fern plants, **sacsakwmlhpnk** bracken fern root

1186 ***sak'** (tr./itr.) to spread (something): **sak'ak** to raise and spread one's arms, **sak'ak c+a+mⁿmnts+ts** the children are out of his control, he cannot keep them together, **sak'akim** his arms were spread apart, **nusak'ak** (tr.) to try to pry somebody's hand open, **sak'alhim** his legs were spread apart

1187 ***sak'a** "to go for it": to move straight ahead, do something without delay, immediately, straight through, all the way: **sak'ayalh** to walk right in, **sak'ayalh usaqw'sam** he went right down to the bottom of the river, **nusak'ayaaxtimut** to enter and leave again right away, to walk right through a house, **nusak'ayustus** he killed him with one shot, **nusak'a** to go from house to house (begging)

1188 **sak'am** to be injured: **sak'amak** to have an injured hand, **sak'amnic** (tr.) to injure somebody, **sak'amnmacw** to injure each other, **sak'amnimut** to injure oneself

1189 **sak'ima** twine, string

1190 **sala** cellar, root house

1191 **Salhya** Tallio Point (a geographical name)

1192 **sa7lkuus** a type of crab

1193 **salmamktsut** "to sell oneself, make oneself available commercially" = (to be a) prostitute

1194 **Salmt** a geographical name

1195 **samlh** sockeye salmon: **samlhtam** sockeye season

1196 **saplin** flour, bread: **nusaplinta** flour sack, **tamsaplin** to bake bread

1197 **saqwaaksta** axe made of **sqwalst**

1198 **saqw'** holding much, insatiable: **nusasqw'iiklayc** to take a long time urinating, **saqw'tnulhikim** it takes a while to fill it

1199 **sasa** suckling: **Nusasayk** a woman's name

1200 **sast** to move house: **sasaast** it is moving

1201 **satic** chum, partner: **saticmtmacwaw** they have a very close friend-
ship, are intimate friends

1202 **Satskw** Chatscah (a geographical name)

1203 **Satsk'ayxw** a mountain near Burnt Bridge

1204 **satsqwla** log used as raft: **satsqwlam** to use a log-raft, **aŝatsqwlam-
lhtxw!** let's go rafting!

1205 **sats'alan** echo: **sats'alanlh** echo (when heard), **sats'alanlhaycts** I
heard my echo

1206 **sats'm** old springsalmon: **Nusats'm** Noosatsum Mountain

1207 **sawa, sawsawa** pillow, cushion

1208 **sawanaaxkw** raft: **sawanaaxkwit ta+satl'anaw+txw** they made a raft
with their canoes (by tying them together and putting boards over
them)

1209 **Saycnaas** a man's name

1210 **s7ayk's** grave: **nus7ayk'sta** graveyard

1211 **s7ayk'sa7na** caterpillar that develops into tiger swallowtail

1212 **s7aylh** waste, leftover: **s7ayutslh** leftover food, scraps

1213 **s7aym** (tr.), **s7aymis** (to) always (...) (29.2.1): **s7aymits sksnmakts**
I always work, **s7aymip ska+7alhkaltcwmitsutap!** always be careful,
folks!, **s7aymtx ska+yayaatwiinu!** be happy always!, **s7aymistxw!** =
s7aymtx!, **xlhalhhts s7aymis** I am always hungry

1214 **s7ayt** year: **alh+ti+s7ayt** (in, during) this year

1215 **s7ayulh, S7ayulh** thunder, Thunderbird: **s7ay7ayulhm** (there is a)
thunderstorm, **s7ay7ayulhmtinilh** we had a thunderstorm

1216 **Say7walus** Siwallace (a family name)

1217 **sc** bad: **scm** to be gravely ill, **sctu-** to forbid, prevent somebody
from doing something, **nuscm** (tr.) to hate somebody, **kanuŝcm** having
a bad odor or flavor, **sclayc** to have bad luck, **scliwa** clumsy, **sclikt** angry, **sclcliktm** to leave in anger, **nuscliktik** = **sclikt**, **sc-
liktnic** (tr.) to anger somebody, **nusclits'** ugly, **scanm** to wear out,
deteriorate, **scali** jealous, **nuŝcalimc** given to jealousy, **scanktimut**

envious, **scaltwa** bad weather, **scak** witch, **nuscaaksta** mesachie box, **nuscaakstatim** a spell has been placed on him, he is bewitched, **scaqw's** having an ugly color; to have poor vision, **nuscickmitsut** to feel sorry for oneself, be sad, **scuutsm** (tr.) to swear at somebody, **nuscmankamk** (tr.) to crave something (food), **sculhla** to disallow, not give consent, **sculhlamim+kwalukw' c+7ilh+stans+7ilh ula+7anaykmtis ska+7umats ska+talawss** his mother repeatedly discouraged him to marry the ones he wanted to marry, **scuukstu-** to beat a team (in a game or race)

1218 **scimnk** cooked fish tails: **iŝcimnkulh** to eat stew made of fish tails

1219 **sclhh** afterbirth

1220 **scnts** transsexual, hermaphrodite: **nuscntsaax** cowardly, **scńcntslhp** old willow having dark (greyish) thick bark

1221 **sculm = scwilm**

1222 **scw** to leak: **nuscwaax** pot or boat leaks, **nuscwaaxik** roof leaks

1223 **scw** (tr.), **scwa** (itr.) to burn something: **sicsicwits+alu** I keep trying to burn it, **scwaak** (tr.) to burn somebody's hand, **scwm** to burn, be on fire, **scwńcwm** lightning, **scwmta** gunpowder, **nuscwmiklaycts** I got my pot burnt, **ascwmalus** to suffer from indigestion, heartburn, **siscwmtn̲mak** kindling

1224 **Scwacwilk** name of a former village

1225 **scwilm, sculm** salmon roe

1226 **scwpanilh** deer: **scwpapniilhi** dim.

1227 ***scwtl'** to be inadequate: **scwtl'alh** to not get somewhere in time, **scwtl'iiqwalhmtsinu** "I missed you by a toe" = I could not jump as far as you, **nuscwtl'aax** to fail to make it to the bathroom in time, be incontinent, dirty oneself, **anuscwńcwntl' alh+ta+qaaxlamim+t'axw** he did not have enough to drink of that

1228 **si-** paraphrasing suffix (23.4, 23.10): **si7aŝtnak** crutches, **siscwmtn̲mak** kindling, **sisikyumaaxalits** molar, **sinuxi** lamp, **siniixw** firewood, **sinaaxwmiixw** dancer's headdress

1229 **sic** blood: **nusisciik** blood vessel, **siculh** water mixed with blood

1230 **s7ickw'cw** bushtail rat: **s7ickw'cwi** dim.

1231 **Sicmana** a woman's name

1232 **si7ik'lh** spouse

1233 **siiscmi** type of moss (mnium affine)

1234 ***sikw'ik** (tr.) to line things up: **asikw'ikaw** they are lined up, **asikw'ikulh ti+lhts'ma** (it is a) cartridge belt, **nusikw'ikta** quiver for arrows

1235 **sik'm** (there is a) noise

1236 **sik's** trap, snare

1237 **silin** kidney: **sislini** dim.

1238 **Silyas** a personal name

1239 **sim** limbs of red cedar

1240 **Sinalh** a geographical name

1241 ***sipi = *tsipi = *tipi: sipyaaqts squts'alhmts** I am washing (my) one leg

1242 **siqw'yuuslh** chickadee

1243 **Siqyulc** name of a month (around April)

1244 **siq'aax** fish that is about to die (after spawning)

1245 **Sisaalhmc** Sechelt native(s)

1246 **Sisawk, Susawk** higher class dance: **Sisawkiixw** higher class song

1247 **Sisinay** a woman's nickname

1248 **sisksum** aunt

1249 **sisk'uulh** (tr.) to peel a fruit

1250 **sissi** uncle

1251 **Sistulhila** a man's name

1252 **Sisyulh** mythical double-headed sea serpent

1253 **sitaaxsu** catfish

1254 **sits'm** sheet: leather; paper money: **ik'axw ti+ka+sits'mts** I have no money, **sits'maalh** moccasins, **uŝits'maakam c+a+ts'up'akt** he put on leather gloves

1255 **sityaax** steering fin

1256 **s7ixwalhkw** charcoal fire, glowing embers: **s7ixwalhkulhuus** glowing, red-hot

1257 **skalkw** porcupine: **skaklkwi** dim.

1258 ***ski** to knead, massage: **skim** (tr.) to massage somebody, **siki**, **skim-likw** masseur, **skimaaxutsis ti+squlh+tc wa+sxiximuuts+ts** the bee massages the flowers, **Anuskimalhnm** a personal name

1259 **skip'** carrots: **skiikp'i** dim., **nuskip'ta** carrot garden

1260 **skli** supernatural being that decides when one is going to die

1261 **skma** moose: **smkmayi** dim.

1262 **sksi** in-laws

1263 **sktsulhk** heart: **sktsulhktinits** my heart is troubling me

1264 **skulukt** canoe pole

1265 **skupik** rosehip: **skukwpiklhp** rosebush

1266 **skwakwixlhala** bluebird

1267 **skwatiwa** imaginary monster, bogeyman

1268 **skwatsta**, ***skwats** name: **skwatstatsinu** I will give you a name, **skwa-kwatstimut** nickname

1269 **skwlatn** ptarmigan

1270 **skwp** (tr.) to moisten, spray water on something: **skwpanlh** (tr.) to spray water on somebody's shirt, **askwpapayaalhi** April shower, light rain, **skwpay** inner bark of fir tree

1271 **skwtsals** cheek: **skwtsatslsi** dim., **skwtsatsls** both cheeks, **skwtsuus-als = skwtsals**

1272 **skwts'** wrinkled: **skwts'us** (having) a wrinkled face

1273 **skw'** (tr.), **skw'a** (itr.) to undo, untie something: **skw'alaaxt(n)** (tr.) to untie a boat, **skw'm** to come loose, **skw'ayc** to have come loose, **skw'iixw** (tr.) to open a lock, **nuskw'maqw'sanilhayc** one's hip is dislocated

1274 **skw'anik's** black twinberry: **sakw'nik'slhp** black twinberry bush

1275 **skw'wams = kw'wams**

1276 **skw'yan** knee: **sikw'yan** both knees, **sikw'yanaaxikus** to kneel

1277 **sk'** (tr.), **sk'a** (itr.) to scrape, card, rake, comb something: **sk'-iixw** (tr.) to comb somebody's hair, **sk'iixwm** to comb one's hair, **sk'ma** comb, **sk'ulmcta**, **sk'mnulmcta** rake

1278 **sk'alhutslayc** eyelashes

1279 **sk'amtsk** a mythical fish-like monster

1280 **sk'aptsanilh** posterior abdominal fin

1281 **sk'awlht** dead alder tree

1282 **sk'c** black: **sk'cus** negro, **sk'caqw's** black soil

1283 ***sk'ik** (tr.?) to spread (something): **sk'ikmtu-** to unfurl, spread something out

1284 **sk'ilcts** golden-eye duck

1285 **sk'inwas** cloud

1286 **sk'l** cold: **sk'l** (tr.) to cool something off, **sk'laltwa** (it is) cold weather, cold season, **nusk'luts** (it is) cold weather, **sk'luulhm** to cool off (food), **sk'laaxutsm** to cool one's drink, **nusk'lctu-** to cool something, put something into a cooler (/...sk'l⌃lc.../)

1287 **sk'llatap** unidentified small seafish

1288 **sk'st** charcoal

1289 **sk'stlits'** skin

1290 **sk'ult** porcupine quill

1291 **Sk'yaax** a geographical name

1292 **sl** (tr.), **sla** (itr.) to slice something, cut boards: **slulhuus** (tr.) to plane sticks for eulachon net, **Aslslik** a personal name

1293 **slaax**, ***slalhx = slax**

1294 **slalimts** great-grandchild: **wa+slalimtsmtsts+ts** all my great-grand-children

1295 **slalimtskak** cone of fir or pine tree

1296 **-slancw = -lacw**

1297 **slaq'k** sliced and smoked salmon: **slaq'nk** smoked salmon tails

1298 **slaws** grass

1299 **slax, sláx, slaax, *slalhx** much, many (26.3.1): **slaxulh** expensive, **slaxmitsut** having many relatives, **is7iŝlaax** to eat much, **Nuslaxm** name of a mountain, **axw slalhxiinaw** they were not many, **nuslalhxaax** clubmoss

1300 **slaylhxuts** to misbehave, be obstinate: **kuŝlaylhxuts** never following people's advice, always misbehaving

1301 **-slh** characteristic, typical (of ...) (18.7): **slt'liislh** horsefly, **tsitstumnalŝlh** night moth, **ts'aaqaluuŝlh** white springsalmon, **skakp'ayslh** small biting fly that abounds during the **kap'ay** run, **slhxankslh** left side of the body, **skw'pankslh** right side of the body

1302 **slh7imts** grandchild: **wa+slh7imtsmtsts+ts** all my grandchildren

1303 **slhip'nakt** branch: **slhip'naakti** dim.

1304 **slhq'** barbecued and dried springsalmon

1305 **slhq'an** collar: **slhanq'an** necklace

1306 **slhul** sliver: **slhulxsakaycts** I have a sliver in my finger, **slhulxsalhaycts** I have a sliver in my toe (/slhul⌃lxs.../), **aslhulakaycts** I have a sliver in my hand

1307 ***slhulhani** cover, shelter: **slhulhanim** to camouflage oneself, make use of a blind when hunting, **nuslhulhani(m)ta** blind, shelter used by a hunter to conceal himself

1308 **slic** slime: **slictinits** I have tuberculosis

1309 **sliixw** salmon head stew: **tamsliixw** to prepare **sliixw**

1310 **slilhqwamams** fish cheeks

1311 **sliq'uts** saliva: **nusliq'uts** to drool

1312 **slis** gall

1313 **slk'laaxt** crystal; icicle

1314 **Sl7lapa** a geographical name

1315 **slqw'** to find: **slqw'amk** (tr.) to find something

1316 **slucta** crosspiece of canoe

1317 **sluq'** eulachon grease

1318 **sm-** already, right away, from the very beginning (23.5)

1319 **sma** myth(ical), legend(ary): **smsma** (to tell a) myth, legend, **smsma-yuus** (tr.) to tell somebody a myth or legend (the listener is the grammatical object), **smayusta** myth, **smalhh** myth(ical being), story, **smalhham** to become a myth, legendary, **Nusmata** name of one of the first men, **Smayana** a woman's name, **Nusmalhhixwayc** a mountain

1320 **smak** to prepare eulachon grease: **nusmaaksta** eulachon box

1321 ***smam** to be in constant motion: **smamiiqw** to work without interruption, **icsmmam**, **icsamam** to sway back and forth

1322 **smamatstnak**, **smamatstnalhp** fir cone: **smḁmntstnaaki** dim.

1323 **smatmc** friend, relative: **smatic** = **smatmc**

1324 **smaw** one (see ***maw**)

1325 **Smawn** the father of **Lhaluuxmana**

1326 **smicmixwts** thrush

1327 **smiks** mussel: **sḁsmiiksi** dim.

1328 **smlhk** fish, salmon: **sḁsmlhki** dim., **sḁsmlhkuts** to talk about fish

1329 **smt** mountain: **sḁsmmti** dim.

1330 **sm7ulha** to do something right away, take immediate action: **sm7ulha+kw t'ax ulh+ta+puts'tns+tx ska+t'ksnis** right away he went for his bow and shot him, **sm7ulha+kw'its'ik t'ax s7alha7itimutis c+a+s-tl'yuks wa+kw'ntas** and right away he did what he had said he would do

1331 **snaax** slave: **snaax** (tr.) to enslave somebody

1332 **snanik** pitch, gum: **snaniklhp** pitchwood, **nusnanikaalhaycts** I have gum on my shoes

1333 **sniniq'** a mythical ape-like creature

1334 **sninya** earthquake: **sninyatim Nuxalkmc** the Bella Coolas suffered an earthquake

1335 **snqw's** (tr.) to be very angry with somebody

1336 **snx** sun: **snxaalh** sunbeam, **sḁsnxaalh** northern lights, **Snxlhh** the name of a former village (now graveyard site), **Asnxik** a man's name, **snxana** cricket, **Snxana** a woman's name, **Snxakila** a woman's name

1337 **spakwank** ray, skate

1338 **Spanyant'u** a woman's name

1339 **spatl'tn** (tr.) to put roofing on a house: **spatl'tnta** roofing material, shingles, **nuspatl'tnuutsta** porch, **Spanpatl'tnayc** a man's name

1340 **spikw'** groundhog: **spiipkw'i** dim., **spikw'anlh** blanket made out of
groundhog pelts

1341 **splilh** vagina: **splilhta** opening of the world, beginning of creation

1342 **sputc** eulachon: **spuuptci** dim., **sputcm** (it is the) eulachon season

1343 **spyu** auklet

1344 **sp'** (tr.), **sp'a** (itr.) to hit something with a stick: **sp'lxsnm** "to
hit the end" = to apply the Morse key, cable a telegram, use the
telephone (the latter meaning now prevails), **sp'(ulh)iixwta** war
club, salmon club, **sp'alustnm**, **sap'lusm**, **sap'a** to be splitting
wood, **sunp'uulhnm** to play baseball, **nusp'uts** "hit in the mouth" =
good at dancing, **sp'aknm** to hit the branches of a fruit-bearing
tree so as to shake the fruit off

1345 **sp'u** to fart: **nuŝp'u** farting all the time

1346 ***sqa** (see **asqa**, **usqa**)

1347 **sqala** red huckleberry: **sqaaxlalhp** red huckleberry bush, **Nusqala** a
river east of Kimsquit

1348 **sqaluts** mountain bilberry; any fruit: **sqalutŝ ti+nan** devil's club
berries, **sqalutŝ ti+nutsakwaax** queenscap, **aŝqalutsak** branch bearing
fruit, **sqaaxlutslhp** mountain bilberry bush

1349 **sqapts** old springsalmon: **sqanqptŝlh** tiger swallowtail

1350 **sqili** woman of slave ancestry

1351 **sqitilhp** root

1352 **sqma** chest

1353 **sqts'** sand, gravel: **sqts'ats'ls** gravelly mountain side, **nusqnxnts'-
ta** gizzard

1354 **squlh** bee, wasp: **squulhqwlhi** dim., **nusqulhta** beehive

1355 ***squm** (tr.?) to spread, open up (something): **nusqumalhhik** (tr.) to spread-eagle and disembowel somebody (a type of capital punishment), **Squmalh** Thorson Creek

1356 ***squp** hair: **squpaqw's** eyebrows, **squputs** beard, whiskers, **aŝquputs** "bearded" = grey cod

*squplh superfluous hair: **squplhlits'alh** hair on lower leg, **squplhlits'ak** hair on lower arm or hand, **squplhalakt** armpit hair, **squplhaak** hair on arm, **squplhiklxs** hairs in nose, **squplhikals** hairs in ear, **squplhikaluus** hair on chest, **squplhikalh** hair on shin, **squplhutsak** hair on lower arm, **squplhulhiik** hair on back, **squplhaalh** hair on leg

1357 **squsa** left-over food that one takes home

1358 **squts'** sack made of cedar bark

1359 **Sqwaamismc** Squamish native(s)

1360 **sqwaax(w)qwa** bullhead

1361 **sqwal** love song: **sqwalxwalm** to sing a love song

1362 **sqwalst** type of rock out of which axes were made (described as having a pale green color): **sqwalstulh** a piece of **sqwalst**

1363 **sqwinacw** flesh of crushed eulachons

1364 **sqwlh** fishbone: **nusqwlhalhh** to have a fishbone (stuck) in one's throat, **sqwlhan** collarbone, **sqwlhik** dorsal fin

1365 **sqwlitq** dried up rotten fish (such as found on river banks)

1366 **sqwsn** loon: **sqwsnsni** dim.

1367 **sqwtsilh** posterior abdominal fin

1368 **sqw'** to fly, jump: **sqw'tum tpyaaxam** he was flown across, **sicsiqw'** to be flying or jumping, **sicsiiqw** airplane, **Nunusqw'aaxuts** a geographical name: Jump Across, **Nusqw'ikulh** a man's name

sqw'm to be startled: **ka+sqw'm+ma alh+7nts** I think he will be startled to see me, **sqw'mtu-** to intentionally startle somebody, **sqw'm̲nic** (tr.) to unintentionally startle somebody, **sṃqw'mtimut** to be skittish, **sṃqw'mtnm** always startling people, **sqw'maaknictss** "it startled my hand" = I quickly withdrew my hand from it

1369 **sqw'alhkw** ashes: **nusqw'aalhkwta** ashtray

1370 **sqw'alm** edible male fern root: **sqw'aaqw'lmi** dim., **sqw'aqw'lmlhp**, **sqw'almiixw** fern plant

1371 **sqw'ayxlhh** ashes

1372 **sqw'xwlun** kneecap

1373 **sq'** (tr.), **sq'a** (itr.) to tear, cut something open: **nusq'** (tr.) to cut an animal's belly open (before skinning it), **nusq'** the sky opens up, the clouds disappear, **asq'** cut, wound, **sq'ma** knife used for cutting salmon, **smq'mni** small salmon knife, **kuŝq'** "all cut up, torn apart" = tired from walking

1374 **sq'alh** flesh, meat

1375 **sq'alh** it has stopped raining

1376 ***sq'amta** greed, avarice: **nuŝq'amta** given to greed, **k'iŝq'amta** "to lack avarice" = to be generous

1377 ***sq'atc** nails: **sq'atciixwak** fingernails, **sq'atciixwalh** toenails

1378 **sq'im** scar: **sq'imus** having a scar on one's face, **sq'imlc+ts'** a scar has formed, it has healed

1379 **sq'sk** saskatoon berry: **sq'sklhp** saskatoon berry bush

1380 **sq'talhp** douglas maple

1381 **sq'usa** knothole

1382 **-st-** causative suffix (14.4.1.1, 19.12)

1383 **-sta** = **-ta**

1384 **stakaw** sister-in-law

1385 **staltmc** chief: **staltmctimut** would-be chief, **stataltmc** dignitaries

1386 **stam+ks?** what is it? (25.5, 25.5.5): **ti+stam** something

1387 **stam-** together with (23.6.2)

1388 **stan** mother: **stantanmts** "one's mothers of mothers" = one's mother + maternal grandmother + maternal grandmother's mother etc., **anuŝtan** having lost one's mother, **stantimut** mother-in-law, stepmother

1389 ***stap** steep: **stapals** steep mountain side, **stapik** steep roof, **statputs** steep shore

1390 **staq'** to contact, touch, grab: **staq'akayc** to grab hold of a branch (e.g. when near drowning), **staq'alhayc** one's feet have touched bottom, to reach shallow water

1391 **stcus** opponent: **stcusm** (tr.) to play against somebody, **stcusmtmacw** to have a contest

1392 **stcw** (see **astcw, ustcw**)

1393 **-stcw = -tcw**

1394 **stcwts'** cottonwood buds

1395 **sti-** asymmetrical (23.2): **stikits'ank** lopsided, **sti7atmnus** to be paralyzed at one side, **astistnmaaq** having one stiff leg, **stits'y-alsm** to wink, blink one eye, **stistnaaq** having one wooden leg, **sti-mukuulhals** having a port-wine mark on one cheek, **stiktl'aatl'qi** having one leg shorter than the other

1396 **stilwa** fat floating on top of jarred or canned fish

1397 **stits', nustits'** watery excrements

1398 **stlkw'a** jellyfish: **stɪ́tlkw'i** dim.

1399 **stl'axt** caribou: **stl'actl'aaxti** dim.

1400 **stl'cw** to act properly, behave well: **nûstl'cw** well-behaved, **alh-tamstl'cw** (tr.) to tell somebody how to act, give advice

1401 **stl'kw** wart: **stl'kwapsm** (having a) wart on one's neck, **stl'kusals** (having a) wart on one's cheek, **stl'kuutsalmc** nipple

1402 **stl'mstayts'** cranberry

1403 **-stmacw** causative reciprocal suffix (19.12.4)

1404 **stn** tree, pole, stick: **stntni** dim., **stnaalh** wooden spoon, **stnaax** timber, **si7aŝtnak** crutches

1405 **-stn- = -tn-**

1406 **stnm** stiff: **astistnmaaq** having one stiff leg, **anustnmikak** having a stiff upper arm or elbow, **stnmanlh** stiff clothes, **stnmulhank** "hav-a stiff belly" = to have a laughing fit, "laugh one's head off", **aŝtnmaalh** to wear stiff shoes

1407 **stqw** mud: **nustqw** muddy creek, **nustqwaqw's** muddy water, **nustqwaalh-**

qwlhayc to have mud on one's shoes

1408 **stq'** (tr.) to add to something: **stq'tx!** add to it!, **stq'aaxtx!** put more (meat) in the stew!, **stq'alusits** I will put more wood on the fire, **stq'ulhits** I will add (a tea bag, spice) to it (tea, soup), I will strengthen its flavor

1409 **sts** (tr.) to spread something (mass or substance) evenly over a surface: **stsits wa+nuxwski+ts** I will spread the soapberries out (on a board, floor, or table), **stsulmc** (tr.) to dampen the floor with a mop, **stsiliktmtu–** to spread rocks in a pit

stslh frost; laxative: **stslhulmc** frost on the ground, dew, **stslhlc-ulmc** dew is forming, **nustslhlc** the window is fogging up; thin ice is forming on water surface

1410 **Stsalh** Necleetsconnay Basin: **tcastsalh** wind blowing from the north

1411 ***stsay** which is of interest: curiosity, news, information: **kaŝtsay-ulh** (tr.) to ask somebody something, to seek information from somebody, **kaŝtsayulhtx!** ask him!, **axwtxw asqw'mnu ala+kaŝtsayulhts ulh+7inu!** don't be alarmed at what I will ask you!, **kaŝtsatsyulhm** to be nosy, inquisitive, **stsayulhayc** to have news, **astsayulhm** to bring news, report something, **anustsayanm** (tr./itr.) to pay attention, listen to somebody, **anustsayanmtsx!** listen to me!

1412 **stsicalt** bridge

1413 **stsli** (tr.) to keep caught fish alive on a line in the water

1414 **stsĺtsli, astsĺtsli** bush of dwarf blueberry

1415 **stsuc** film, thin layer: **uŝtsucuutsayc ti+qla** there is a thin film (e.g. of oil) on the water surface

stsucm fish breaks the surface, jumps: **stsuctsucm** fish are jumping

1416 **stsulhk** words of a song, lyrics: **stsulhkt+7it!** make words to it!, apply words to the melody!, **sktsulhkm** to use words in a song

1417 **stsumay** ice or snow floating on the river is clustering, river is gradually freezing over

1418 **stsunxwa** tear stains: **stsunxwayuts** to have a tear-stained face

1419 **stsutswanyulhiixw** to have dandruff

1420 **sts'** to disperse, scatter, spray: **sts'aak** something is sprayed on one's hand, **asts'alh** waterfall, **asts'alhts'lh** heavy rainfall, **sts'-iixwalstutsakts** (I fell into a puddle and) water splashed up from my elbows, **sts'ints'ikalh** water splashes up from under one's lower legs, **iŝts'uuts** to chatter, ramble, **sts'ta** stick used for beating a fast rhythm, **nusts'** food or drink enters one's nasal cavity, **nu-slts'llxs** water enters one's nose

1421 ***sts'ap** (tr.) to subdue somebody: **sts'apayc** to submit, resign one-self, **sts'apaynicits+ts'** I have subdued her now

1422 **sts'ayuts, asts'ayuts** arrow used for hunting grouse

1423 **sts'icin** skein holding fish roe together; greaves, cracklings

1424 **sts'iknulh** half-decayed tree stump

1425 **sts'its'xwatwalalhp** waxberry

1426 **sts'ix** sand, gravel: **sts'ixaqw's** sandy soil, **sts'ixikalh** sandbar in river, **sts'ixuts** sandbar in ocean

1427 **Sts'kiilh** name of a former village

1428 ***sts'l** rough, thorny, prickly: **sts'ltculh** having a rough surface, rasp, **slts'l** porcupine quills, **aŝlts'lus** to have porcupine quills stuck in one's face, **kuŝlts'l** Scotch thistle, **Slts'lani** son of Por-cupine and Raven

1429 **sts'mas** devilfish: **smts'maasi** dim.

1430 **sts'piilh** unidentified bird

1431 **sts'q** animal fat: **(nu)sts'qiiqkalh** marrow

1432 **sts'qaaxqa** wren

1433 **sts'qwasma** red face paint (a mixture of goat fat and clay or iron rust): **sts'qwasmayaqw's, sts'xwasmayuus = sts'qwasma**

1434 **sts'qyaaxaksta** tree stump

1435 **sts'up** to itch: **sts'upak** to have an itchy hand, **sts'upanm** to start itching

1436 **sts'uuxin** brains

1437 -stu- = -tu-

1438 **stulkw** dolphin: **stutulkwi** dim.

1439 **stup** stove

1440 **stuq'** snag: **stuq'tsut, stuq'aycnimut** to get tangled up in a net, **astuq'** snagged, **stuq'layc** to get snagged, **astuq'aqw's** knot in wood

1441 **stuu(a)** store

1442 **Stwic** Stuie (a geographical name): **Stwicmc** Stuie native(s)

1443 -stxw = -txw

1444 **st'ala** hemlock bark: **sat'lalhp** western hemlock

1445 **st'a7m** to be in contact with the floor, lie or be flat: **st'a7mtuts ula+kulhulmc+ts** I laid it down on the floor, **st'a7mulhank** to lie flat on one's stomach, **st'a7mus** having a flat face, **nust'a7miklqs** having a flat nose, **St'a7muus** a man's name

1446 **st'anikw** boil, carbuncle

1447 **st'awlht** whetstone: **st'awlhulh** (tr.) to sharpen a tool

1448 **st'axw** hard, difficult: **st'axwaalh ti+snxaalh+tc** the sunlight is too bright, **st'axwanaats** very difficult

1449 **st'cwm** mat, mattress: **st'cwmcwmi** dim., **nust'cwmikta** table cloth, **nust'cwmaaqutsta** napkin, **kalhst'cwmta** cedar bark used for mattress, **nust'cwmaaxta** bark on top of which **kalhst'cwmta** is placed, **st'cwm-ulmc** floor, **st'cwmulmcta** floor covering, linoleum, **nust'cwmaalhta** floormat, **anust'cwmaaxmis ilh ta+lhalya+tx** she had the copper for a cushion

1450 **st'ls** highbush cranberry: **slt'lslhp** cranberry bush, **st'lŝ ti+nan** = **sqalutŝ ti+nan**, **slt'lsanilh** lymph nodes in groin

1451 **st'n** nits

1452 **st'uc(w)si** swell, big wave: **st'uut'cwsî** dim.

1453 **st'umts'a** ripe crabapple

1454 **st'win** hide: **st'winlits'** bark, **nust'winuulhnnak** scrotum

1455 **+su** surprise (28.3.8, 28.3.24)

1456 **suca, *sucn** hand, lower arm: **wa+sucsucats+7ats** both my hands, **sucn-**

ayc to have hands

1457 +suks impatience (28.3.18.3)

1458 sukwa sugar: nusukwaata sugar bowl

1459 sukwwaat cat's cradle: sukwwaatm to play cat's cradle

1460 *sukw' = *suk'

1461 sukw'ptus mountain lion: sukw'ptuusi dim.

1462 *suk', *sukw' wind blows: asuk' wind, asuk'(m)tinilh we are having wind, nusuk'tsut storm, nusuk'aax to follow the wind (in sailboat), suk'ta sail, suk'tnulh tent, nususkw'iiqw brome grass, pussy toes, sweet cicely

1463 sulh house: suuslhi dim., suulh root house (a Kimsquit word), tam-sulh to build a house, tamsulhtu- to build a house for somebody

1464 sulicts victuals, food-to-go: sulicts (tr.) to give somebody food to take with him, sulictstsutts I will bring my own food, asulicts-ts I have brought my own food along, nusuliictsta provision box, lunch box

1465 s7ulm stakes used in the lahal game

1466 sulut sea, inlet: susluuti dim.

1467 sum pants: suusumi dim.

1468 sum (tr.), suma (itr.) to lap, sip something: sumsuma to be sipping

1469 Sumxulh a village in the Rivers Inlet area

1470 Sunats a man's name

1471 suncw universe, world, sky, weather: ya ti+suncw it is a nice day, the weather is nice, susuncw moonlight, suncwt day, alh+ti+suncwt today, Suncwana a woman's name, Suncwakila a man's name

1472 s7unkwtsta human body: s7unkwtstalh human corpse

1473 sunq'uts to yawn

1474 supt to whistle: sunsupt to be whistling, nusuptaqw'snm swamp robin

1475 Suqw' a personal name

1476 *suqw', *suq'u hump, lump: suqw'(w)alakt lump on tree; lymph nodes in armpit, nusuqw'ik, nusuqw'wiik old humpback salmon

1477 **suq'** (tr.), **suq'a** (itr.) to peel, skin, remove the bark of something: **alhkuŝuq'** circumcised, **suq'm** to peel a tree, **suq'ulhiixwayc** to have been scalped

1478 ***suq'u** = ***suqw'**

1479 **suq'uuxin** tadpole

1480 **Susawk** = **Sisawk**

1481 **susqwi(i)** = **suuxi**

1482 **susu** berry sauce made by boiling dried berry cake in water

1483 **Sutaalhh** a woman's name

1484 **sutk** winter: **sustkanmi** late fall, autumn

1485 **Sutslhmc** Kimsquit native(s)

1486 **+suts'** again (unexpectedly) (28.3.21, 28.3.24)

1487 **suts'm** pimple

1488 **suts'mus** barnacle

1489 **suuxi**, **susqwi(i)** younger sibling: **anuŝuuxi** deprived of, having lost one's younger sibling(s), **wa+susqwimtsts** all my younger siblings, **susqwimtmacwaw** they are siblings

1490 **Swak'c** a mountain at Kimsquit

1491 **swalut**, ***swal** (tr.) to leave somebody behind, by himself: **swalutaycilh ulh+7inu** we are longing for you, **nuswalutaaxnm** to stay in (and look after) somebody's house, **swalaaxm** to be left behind

1492 **swanalhkw** green algae, aquatic moss

1493 **sx** (tr.), **sxa** (itr.) to plane, scrape something: **sxm** to scrape off the inner bark of the western hemlock, **sxta** plane, scraper, **sxalsta** scraper used to remove fat from a hide, **nusxilh** (tr.) to scrape out the bloody part of fish, **sxaaxutsm** to shave oneself, **nusxik** (tr.) to scrape the bottom of a pot, **sxik** (tr.) to scrape the surface of something, **sxuulh** (tr.) to peel fruit, **nusx** (tr.) to raid a village, **Sxulmcnm** name of a month, **sxalc** rockslide or snowslide, **nusxalctu-** to make something slide

1494 **sxan** lover, sweetheart: **sxaxni** dim., **sxaxnmtmacwaw** they are lovers,

wa+sxaxamtsts+ts all my sweethearts

1495 **sxayaxw** taboo: **sxaxyaxwii** girl who has her first menstrual period

1496 **sxiilhla** boastful song used by chiefs (e.g. on war expeditions or at potlatches)

1497 **sxitsta** bed: **sxiixtstni, sxinxiitstni** dim., **ya ti+sxitstas** "his bed is good" = he is successful, has good luck (e.g. in hunting)

1498 **sxp** (tr.), **sxpa** (itr.) to tie something up: **sxpayc** he has been tied up, **sxɯxmpit** they were tying him up, **anusxpikuulh** a type of hammer

1499 **sxp'ik, sxp'iip'k** spine: **uŝxp'aax** small of the back

1500 **sxtl'ik** fish backbone: **sxtl'ikm** to prepare fish backbone for consumption

1501 **sxts** thimbleberry and salmonberry sprouts

1502 **sxwat** sphere, globe, bulb: **sxwatilh** urine bladder, **sxwaxwtaaxlhp** hollow-stemmed umbel

*sxwatmlxs (having a) blister: **sxwatmlxsak** to have a blister on one's hand, **sxwatmlxsaliits** to have a blister on one's tongue

1503 **sxwaxwa** mud: **sxwaxwayanmtimut** to change oneself into mud (done by Raven in a story), **nusxwaxwa** mudpool

1504 **sxwayxw** (tr.) to wash somebody's head

1505 **sxwilh** arrogant, conceited: **sxwilhxwiilhliwa** sort of conceited, making the impression of being conceited

1506 **sxwlxwli** mole (animal)

1507 **sxwnata** nickname: **sxwnatatsut** to give oneself a nickname

1508 **syut** powerful, supernatural phenomenon: supernatural being; killerwhale; song; a type of musical instrument (horn): **Syut** a point of land, **syuyuuti, sisyuuti** small killerwhale, **kuŝyut** lower class dance, **kuŝyutiixw** lower class song, **Syutakila** a man's name

T

1509 **t-** locative prefix (23.6.1)

1510 **t-** reduced non-female article (15.4.1.1, 15.4.1.2, 15.4.1.3.1)

1511 **-t** 3 pl. subj. tr./caus. (14.3.1, 14.4.1)

1512 **-t** tr. participial suffix (sg. obj.) (14.3.1.1)

1513 **-t** formative suffix (22.3)

1514 **-t-** intentionally (19.3.1)

1515 **-t-** causative suffix (14.4.1.1)

1516 **ta+** indefinite article, non-fem. remote sg./pl. (15.1)

1517 **-ta, -tn-, -sta, -stn-** tool, implement (21.2): **tcutsta** table knife, **qulhquulhta** pencil, **nusuqw'p(s)ta** tobacco pipe, **at'aaksta** paint brush, **qup'aaksta** drumstick, **paysta** flounder hook, **nicta** saw, **asnictnak** to use a saw

1518 **taala** money: **nutaalaata** wallet, **kulhtaala** rich

1519 **takan** to arrive: **nutakan** tide is going out, **anutakananm** the tide is low, **nutakanalsikan** to have an earache, **nutatkanikuulh** to be ripe

1520 **takws** willow grouse: **taatkwsi** dim.

1521 **takwta** medical doctor

1522 **talaws** to get married: **talawsmis** he married, wed her, **alhtalaws** married, **unusitalawsmtus** he sent her somewhere to get married

1523 **Talyu** Tallio (a geographical name): **Talyumc** Tallio native(s)

1524 **tam-** iterative (23.5)

1525 **tam-** to make, construct (23.2): **tam7akw'na** to make a war canoe, **tamsulh** to build a house, **tamsulhtuminu** I will build you a house, **tamts'la** to make a basket, **tamqnk** (tr.) "to make somebody low" = to ridicule somebody, **tam7ulx** (tr.) "to make somebody (look) silly" = to fool, cheat somebody

1526 **-tam** the time of ... (21.3): **kap'aytam** season of the humpback salmon, **nukalikutstam** lunchtime

1527 **-tan** tr./caus. participial suffix (pl. obj.) (14.3.1.1, 14.4.1.1)

1528 **tanaps** turnips

1529 **tanksta, *tankstn** ear: **tankstni** dim., **tatanksta** both ears

1530 ***tap** (tr.) to spread, open, expose something: **tapus** (tr.) to spread out a sheet or blanket, **tapalhutstx!** open the door wide, all the way!, **anutapalhuts** the door is wide open, **stantapilhm** "exposing one's genitalia" = bat (animal), **kulhtap** (tr.) "to expose somebody to much" = to lavishly give money to somebody, shower somebody with money

tapa to meet one's obligations, return somebody's belongings: **tapa** dowry, **tapatutis** he returned the things on their behalf, **tapanm** to visit a sick person

1531 **-tap** 2 pl. pass. tr./caus. (14.3.3, 14.4.3)

1532 **taqw'lh** downstream area (23.6.1)

1533 ***taq'** thick, dense: **taq'aax** dense foliage or bush, **taq'aqw's** clustered branches

1534 **tas** (tr.), **tasa** (itr.) to poke, push, bump, hit something: **nutasaqw'stx!** poke the fire!, **nutasalsta** tanning stick, **tastmacwaycaw** they bumped into each other, **tasulmc** (tr.) to clear land with a bulldozer

tas blunt arrow used to stun birds with

1535 **tata** daddy (term of endearment): **Taataw!** Oh God! (exclamation used to address the supreme deity)

1536 **tatiixw** (tr.) to cast a spell on somebody: **tatiixwlikw** witch, black magician, **alhtatiixw** bewitched, under a spell, **snutatiiqw** thimbleberry

1537 ***tats'** (tr.) to press, put one's hand down on something: **tats'aak** (tr.) to place one's hand on somebody else's hand, **tats'alxi** (tr.) to place one's hand on somebody's neck, **tantats'** (tr.) to press the eulachons down when making **sluq'**

1538 **Ta7wisilaqs** a woman's name

1539 **(+)tax** interrogative form of **(+)tx** (15.4.1.1)

1540 **-taxw, -twaxw** caus. imp. pl. (14.4.1.1)

1541 **tay** boy (term of address): **Taylh** a man's name, **Statikw** a man's name

1542 **tay** (tr.) to hit, pound something: **taym** (tr.) to pound cedar or hemlock bark so as to make it soft, **taytaymlhh** a type of **lhalya** (said to be hammered out of a fish), **nutaŷkalus** (tr.) to hit some-body in the chest, **anutayaaknm** pitcher in baseball, **tayulhiixwayc** to have been hit on the head, **tayaaqalitsayc** to have been hit on the teeth, **talxsayc** to have been hit on the nose (/tay⁻lxs-ayc/), **alhtaya** to call out the words of a song, announce the lyrics

      tayamk (tr.) to throw away, discard something: **tayamkiixwmts** I threw my hat away, **ictatyamkis** he kept throwing it away (e.g. a bug that would not leave him alone)

1543 **Tayaqwila** a man's name

1544 **taynacw** the morning past (23.7): **alh+taynacw** this morning (said later in the day)

1545 **tc** (tr.), **tca** (itr.) to cut something with a knife: **tcalustu-** to cut up meat, **tciikanim** his ear was cut off, **tcutsm** to cut one's food, **tcutsta** table knife, **tcaakaycnimut** to accidentally get one's hand cut

1546 **tc-** locative prefix (23.6.1): **tctl'uk'ams** upper jaw, **tctl'uk'iilh-uts** upper lip, **ala+nutctl'uk'als+ts** upstairs, **wa+tcamatlhh** where one comes or originates from, **wa+tcamatlhhalh** where one has (re-cently) come from, **tcatl'sikus** back room, kitchen, **tcatl'saax** out-side back of the house, back porch, **tcats'aaxlh** south-east wind, **tcastsalh** north-east wind, **tcalsqalh** wesł wind, **tcitskwaaxalh** to stand on the other side of the river, **tcucwnikwlh** south wind, **Nutc-iictskwani** Necleetsconnay River

1547 **(+)tc** definite (article), non-fem. close sg. (15.4.1.1)

1548 **tcalh-** locative prefix complex (23.6.1)

1549 **tcńcni** owl

1550 **tcu-**, **tcul(h)-** directional prefix complex (23.6.1, 29.2.2): **tcul-atl'suuts** tide is coming in, **tculsqamus** facing towards the channel

1551 **tcukawk** to go down towards the riverbank

1552 **tcul(h)-** = **tcu-**

1553 **tculh7aylikt** as long as one ...s: **tculh7ayliktaw ska+7alhinaw ala+7ats** as long as they will be here

1554 **-tcw**, **-stcw** caus. participial suffix (sg. obj.) (14.4.1.1)

1555 ***ti** hard, firm, steady: **tyak** to hold something firmly, **tyaqw's** wood is hard to split, **tyalh** to stand firm, **tiliwatxw!** steady it!, **tyaaxik** flat roof, **tyaaxam** to steady one's boat, **tyaax ti+lhalas+tc** the boat is steady

*tilc to come to a stop, settle: **tilculh** the slide has subsided, **tilcalhts** my feet hit something, something prevented me from sliding further down, **tilcuulh**, **tilcalaaxt** the anchor holds

1556 **ti+** indefinite article, non-fem. close sg. (15.1)

1557 **ti-** bound non-fem. article (16.4.4, 25.3, 25.5.2)

1558 **-ti-** 3 pl. obj. tr./caus. (14.3.1, 14.4.1)

1559 **tic** non-fem. sg. identifier (25.3)

1560 **(+)tic** interrogative form of **(+)tc** (15.4.1.1)

1561 **tic-** to catch (23.2): **ticmawlxsts c+a+smlhk** I caught twenty fish, **tick'acw** he caught nothing at all

1562 **tictik'** piece of wood used for kindling

1563 **tictsa**, ***tictsn** tongue: **nutictsnalsiixw** uvula

1564 **tictsamulh** red-hot rocks

1565 ***tictsn** = **tictsa**

1566 **tii** tea: **istiialus** to want to drink tea, **nustiista** teapot

1567 **tiilh** (tr.), **tiilha** (itr.) to bait a line or trap: **tiilhm** (tr.) to use something for bait, **tiilh** bait

1568 **tiixw** (tr.) to hit something with a hammer: **nutiixw** (tr.) to drive in a plug or dowel, **nutiixwta** plug, dowel, **tiixwaqw's** (tr.), **tiixwaqw'sa** (itr.) to drive in a nail, **tiixwaqw'sta** nail, spike, **tic-**

tiixwm to drive poles for an eulachon net, **alhtiixw** eulachon net, **tiixwama** sledgehammer, **anutiixw** tanning frame, **nutiixwalsta** tanning stick, **tiixwm** (tr.) to spread rumors about somebody

1569 **tiltilit** eagle is calling

1570 **-tim** 3 pl. pass. tr./caus. (14.3.3, 14.4.3)

1571 **-timut** to purposely cause oneself to (be) ... (19.10.5): **spuustimut** weed, **mantimut** father-in-law, stepfather, **tupmaaktimut** to apply soap to one's hands, **staltmctimut** would-be chief

1572 **-tinilh** 1 pl. pass. tr. (14.3.3)

1573 **-tinits** 1 sg. pass. tr. (14.3.3)

1574 ***tip** (tr.) to show, reveal, make visible: **tipmaqw'sm** (tr.) to catch a glimpse of something, **ictiptsuut+mas ulh+7nts** he is forever showing off to me

stip understudy, double (in movies): **stiiplh** shadow, projection, picture, **stiiplhtinilh** they are taking our picture, they are filming us, **nustipusta** mirror

1575 ***tipi** single, mono-, having one ...: **tipyaaq** one-legged, **tipyaaqts alh+ti+lhalas+tc** with one foot I am standing on the boat, **tipîkus** single-bladed axe, **tipyaakmi** (tr.) to hold something with one hand

1576 **tiq'** (tr.), **tiq'a** (itr.) to sew, stitch something: **tiq'tmacwtu-** to join, sew things together, **nutiq'ik** (tr.) to sew things together, **tiq'anlhm** to sew one's clothes, **tictiiqta** thread, yarn, **titq'uulhta** paper

1577 **tka** (tr.), **tkaya** (itr.) to shoot something with a gun: **tkata** gun, **tkatsuut** to shoot oneself, **nutkalqsnkayc** its tail has been shot off

1578 **tkw** dirty: **tkusnu** your face is dirty, **tkwakwaknu** your hands are dirty, **tkulh ti+stup+tc** the stove is dirty, **nutkwik ta+satl'a+tx** the canoe's interior was dirty, **nustkwmals** there a smell of dirt in the house

1579 **tkw'** (tr.) to dig something up: **tkw'm** to dig for edible roots

1580 **tk'** sticky: **tk'us** to have a sticky face

1581 ***tk'ilh** nearby, at this side: **tsi+tk'ilhank+tsc** the girl on this side, **tk'ilhaaxutsalh** to stand on this side of the river

1582 **tlh** strong: **nutlh** (there is a) strong current, **tlhmlhm** to be show-ing off one's strength, **tlhulh** vehicle is fast, **s(nu)tlhuulhikak** biceps, **stlhuulhlits'alh** muscle of lower leg, calf, **kûstlhuulhlits'** hefty, muscular

1583 **tlhmas** Indian paint

1584 **tlkw** (tr.), **tlkwm** (itr.) to swallow something: **t*tllkw** pill

1585 **tlqw'** (tr.), **tlqw'm** (itr.) to swallow something

1586 **t*tlkw** slippery

1587 **tl'a** black bear: **aatl'ayi**, **tl'aatl'ayi** dim., **tl'ata** deadfall for bear, **tl'ayanlh** coat or blanket made of bear hide

1588 **Tl'aaqwaylh** a woman's name

1589 **tl'aaqwitkw** red cod

1590 **tl'aaqw'** = **tl'awqw'**

1591 **tl'aayaqm** song sung in order to shame one's deserting spouse

1592 **tl'akix!** come on!: **tl'aki+7it lhk'mnu!** come on, speak!, **tl'akinaw +7it!** come on, folks!

1593 **tl'akwani** elbow

1594 **Tl'alamin** Clellamin (a chief's name)

1595 **tl'a7laya**, **tl'a7yala** beads

1596 **tl'alh** (tr.), **tl'alha** (itr.) to dry something: **tl'alhm** to dry meat or berries, **tl'alhama** clothesline

1597 **tl'alhix!** come here!, come on!: **tl'alhanix nulhumaaxnmnu c+a+tii!** come on, have some tea!, **tl'alhaninaxw!** come on, folks!, **tl'alhtxw!** give it to me!

1598 **tl'amk** (tr.), **tl'amkm** (itr.) to bring somebody something that needs repairing: **tl'amktsinu c+t'ayc** I have brought this for you to fix, **tl'amktsut** to visit a doctor for a medical check-up

1599 **tl'ap** to go, start (going): **tl'apm** (tr.) to go towards somebody, **tl'aputs** to start eating, talking, or crying, **tl'apak** to start a manual activity, **tl'apliwam** (tr.) to try something, **tl'apamk** (tr.) to get, catch something

1600 **-tl'ap** times (20.6.1): **matl'ap** once, **lhwaalhtl'ap** twice

1601 **Tl'aqwakila** a man's name

1602 **Tl'aqwamuut** a chief's name

1603 **Tl'aqwmayqs** the name of a supernatural child

1604 **tl'aqw't** douglas fir bark (peeled off): **stl'aqw'tlits'** douglas fir bark (still on tree), **tl'actl'aqw'lhp** douglas fir

1605 **tl'aq'an** snail: **tl'aatl'q'ani** dim.

1606 **tl'awqw'**, **tl'aaqw'** tobacco

1607 **tl'axw** hard, stiff: **nutl'axwals** fat inside hide that is hard to remove, **tl'axwaqw's** wood is hard to split, **tl'axulmc** ground is hard (to dig into), **tl'axwaalh** dress shoes

1608 **tl'a7yala** = **tl'a7laya**

1609 **tl'i** fast, quick: **tl'its sputl'ts** I came quickly, **tl'iliwa** fast worker, **tl'yalh** to walk fast, **tl'yaktimut** to hurry in work, **tl'yuts** to eat fast, **itl'yaalhtmacw** to have a race, **imtl'imtmacw** to have a canoe race, **nutl'îk** to think quickly, be intelligent, **tl'îkm** to run, **tl'îkmtimut** to be on the run, escape, **ictl'îkm** to participate in a race, **tl'ictl'îktnmnaw** they are having a race, **Ustl'îkmanay** a man's name

1610 **tl'ima**, ***tl'imn** sinew, tendon: **stl'imnalaaxalht** Achilles' tendon

1611 **tl'ina** eulachon grease

1612 **tl'iq'lhkn** dwarf blueberry: **tl'intl'iq'lhknlhp** dwarf blueberry bush

1613 **Tl'itsaplilhana** the name of one of nine supernatural siblings

1614 **tl'ixin** sealion: **tl'iitl'xini** dim.

1615 **Tl'knii** a location near **Qw'ants**

1616 **tl'kw** (tr.), **tl'kwa** (itr.) to gather tiny objects: **ictl'ikwats** I am going around picking up little things, **tl'kwanlh** (tr.) to remove lint from clothes

1617 **tl'l** (tr.) to cover something with a sheet: **tl'lusta**, **alhtl'lus**

curtain, **ustl'lits** I'll cover it over, **nutl'l** canyon, **Nutl'l** Kimsquit, **nu7lt'lii** small canyon, **Snutl'lalh** a geographical name, **Alh-
ltl'liiqw** hot springs situated south-west of **Scwacwilk**

stl'luts (tr.), **stl'lutsm** (itr.) to put eulachons into a bin: **s-
tl'luts**, **nustl'luutsta** eulachon bin

1618 **tl'lh** dry: **nutl'lh** shallow water, **tl'lhaltwa** dry season, **tl'lhulh**
reef, **tl'lhuuslc** fish is drying up, **nutl'lhlcmim** he is withering,
becoming lifeless, **nutl'lhalhh** to have a dry throat, **Nutl'lhiixw**
Burnt Bridge

1619 **tl'lhax!** come on: **tl'lhanaxw uq'xip lha+7na!** come on, folks, call
her!

1620 ***tl'ms** to dream, have a vision, be inspired, aware, human: **mtl'msila** to have a nightmare, be restless in one's sleep, **stl'ms** love
charm, **smtl'msim** she was made to fall in love with somebody, **nustl'msak** to make use of a **stl'ms**

tl'msta, ***tl'mstn** human, person: **tl'mstnamtimut** to become a person,
tl'mstaliwa well-to-do, self-sufficient, **stl'mstalikta** body, appearance, personality, **stl'mstanalus** mortal, truly human, civilized

1621 **tl'p** (tr.), **tl'pa** (itr.) to pinch, snap, cut something off; to stop
something (short): **nutl'p** (tr.) to pinch somebody, **tl'palqi** (tr.)
to cut somebody's hair (in the neck), **tl'pa** to cut a dress to size,
tl'piipqwalhm to trim one's toenails, **alhtl'palitstmacw** "cut into
teeth (so as to fit) together" = log cabin, **Alhtl'paaxulmc** a point
of land across **Alhku**, **Tl'pipkalh** a geographical name, **axw tl'ptsuts**
it does not cease, **nutl'pikalhm** to stop walking, **nutl'pikakm** to
stop working

1622 **tl'pa** fish spear with three prongs: **tl'paapay** dim., **tl'pa** (tr.) to
spear fish with a **tl'pa**

1623 **tl'panta** head of penis

1624 ***tl'q** to stick up or out, protrude: **tl'qalii(c)tsm** to stick one's
tongue out, **tl'qulh** hill, mound, **tl'qlculhtu-** to pile things up,

tl'qmulh it is over-priced, **alhtl'qmulh** to overtop, be higher, **Anu-tl'qmiixwana** a woman's name

tl'qmtu- to extend something to somebody, to present: **tl'qmtuminu c+t'ayc** I give this to you, **tl'qmlhtums c+ta+ts'lhtaatalhs** he has given me his umbrella, **nutl'qmalhhiituminu c+t'ayc** I give this to you to eat

1625 ***tl'ql(a)** (tr.) to scoop, bail something: **nutl'ql**, **nutl'qlayulh** (tr.) to bail a canoe, **(nu)tl'qlayulhta** bailer, **(nu)tl'qltsut** to abandon ship

1626 **tl'tuu!** expression of irritation: darn it!, damn it!

1627 **tl'uk'** high; moon, month: **tl'uk'ikus** high riverbank, **nutl'uk'ikmitsut** high-handed, arrogant, **tl'uk'uuts** the water is high, **ala+nu-tctl'uk'als+ts** upstairs, **utl'uk'** upwards, **tl'uk'uts** to boast, brag, **alh+ta+patsalh ta+tl'uk'+tx** last month

1628 **tl'ulay** basket made of birch bark

1629 **tl'upana** cormorant: **tl'upanii** dim.

1630 ***tl'x** to rattle, crackle, burst, sparkle: **stl'x** spark, **stl'xusmalh** it is hailing, **stl'xλxlxsm** woodpecker, **alhtl'xmaaqalitsts** my teeth chatter, **nutl'xm** it (e.g. bottle) is cracked, **nutl'xmik** it (e.g. balloon) has burst, **anutl'xmikiiqwalitstimut** to bust something between one's teeth, **S7anutl'xmulhlalt** Happy Boy Dance

1631 **tl'xa** having holes, meshes: **tl'xaaxay** open-work weaving, meshwork, **tl'xayalxi** having bald patches in one's hair, **tl'xalcalus ti+sq'lhkw** clothing is wearing out, becomes holey

1632 **Tl'xus** Sliammon

1633 ***tl'xwi** (tr.) to break something off: **tl'xwîixw** (tr.), **tl'xwîixwa** (itr.) to break off a fish head, **tl'xwîixw** its neck is broken, **nutl'xwyalitsts** I have broken a tooth

1634 **Tl'xwtsaytxw** Kitlope

1635 **tl'xwtsn** onions: **tl'xwtsńtsni** dim., **tl'xwtsńtsnlhp** onion plant, **tl'xwtsniixw** onion leaves

1636   **tl'yuk** to talk, discuss, argue: **wic ats wa+stl'yukts** this is what I am talking about, **nustl'yukaw** they talk too much, **tl'yukamk** (tr.) to talk about, discuss something, **nu7itl'yukiiknm** to be talking on the phone, **itl'yukmtmacw** to have an argument, **itl'yuktimut** to grumble, mutter, **nu7itl'yukalpsm** to mumble

1637   **tm-** just, only (23.5): **tmlimlhaw** they just dropped down, **tm7axtsmlclhts** I just had to go to bed, **tmsc** weak, **tmtlhlc** grown, adult, **tmyalc** in the prime of life

1638   **-tmacw** to consciously (be) ... (to) each other (19.11.1, 19.12.4): **nukumtmacw** to desire each other, **saticmtmacwaw** they are intimate friends, **alhpstmacw** to eat together, **pacpaaquustmacw** to be afraid of each other, **alhk'ilhtmacw** to wait for each other

1639   **tmcw** river: **wa+tmcw+ts** the river, **wa+tmcuks+ts** the rivers

1640   **tmkwa** cured salmon roe

1641   **tmp** (tr.), **tmpa** (itr.) to insert something: **tmptx t'ayc!** put this into your mouth!, **alhtmpaaxalitsmits** I have it between my teeth, **alhtmpnaluslxsalhmits** I have it between my toes, **tmplxsanilhmtx!** put it in your pocket!

1642   **-tn-** = **-ta**

1643   **-tnm** caus.-itr. suffix (19.12.3); habitual suffix (19.17.1.1): **pustnm** to raise, bring up, be a parent or guardian, **scuukstnm** to win a contest (pl. subject), **nitstnm** to hatch an egg, **alhlxwtnm** to be a newsreader, show the news, **lhulhtnm** to have news, be a newsreader, **ksnmaktnm** to have work for somebody, be an employer, **alhpstnm** "to feed everyone" = to give a feast, banquet, **alhwnts'tnm** to be a murderer, **nukaliilhtnm** (= **nukaliilhnm**) to play at ring-throwing, **nukw'plcutstnm** to analyze, interpret (a text)

       -tnmc = /-tnm$\pm$mc/ (19.12.3): **kw'alhtnmcts** I am raising a child, **(a)alats'tnmc** to tell on somebody, **alhk'ilhtnm** to be waiting for somebody

1644   **tntn** bell, alarm, siren

1645   ***tp** spot(ted), dot(ted): **alhtpanlh** dotted shirt
stp spot, freckle: **stpuusps** having a freckled face, **stpuulhals** having a freckle on one's cheek, **nustpalsaaqws** having a cataract

1646   ***tp** (tr.) to spread, put something onto a frame: **tpik** (tr.), **tpika** (itr.) to stretch a hide on a frame, **tpiksta** frame used for drying hides, **tputsta** stick used for drying eulachons, **nutputslxsta** stick used for drying salmon, **tpiixw** (tr.) to cover, close a container, **tpiixw** cover, lid

1647   ***tpi** next, adjacent, (a)side, half: **nutpîik** next room, **nutpîixw** next door, next house, **inulhtxw ti+nutpîk+tc!** you have the other half!, **tpyalus** one side of one's chest, **ti+tpyusts+t'ayc** this one that is next to me, **tpyankus** other side of hill, **tpyaaxuts** other side of river, across the channel, **tpyams** one side of jaw, **tpyaaxam** to cross a river or road, **itpyaalh** fifteen

1648   ***tplq'** (tr.) to turn something inside out: **nutplq'** (tr.), **nutplq'a** (itr.) to turn something inside out, **alhtplq'ak** to have shingles, herpes zoster

1649   **tqan** deaf, unable to understand: **tqants alh+ti+slhk'mstanu+tc** I do not understand your language, **tqants ala+kstucw+ts** I do not understand what you are doing, **tqan ti+wats' inu!** you are a dumb dog!

1650   ***tqm** to have something sticky on oneself: **tqmalh** to have stepped into something sticky, have sticky soles, **tqmalhts ala+sxwaxwa** there is mud on my shoes, **tqmakts ala+mnk** there is excrement on my hands

1651   **tqwlc** to get spoiled

1652   **tqwm** (tr.), **tqwma** (itr.) to hang something over something: **alhtqwm** hanging, **anutqwmik** to hang draped over something, **tqwmiixwayctu-** to hang something over a bar or line, **nutqwmaqw'sayctu-** to hang something on a branch, **nutqwmiktsut** to swing or climb over an obstacle

1653   **tqwntl'** hither, this way (23.6.1, 29.2.2): **putl's tqwntl'** he came this way, **utqwntl'** = **tqwntl'**

1654   **tqw'** (tr.), **tqw'a** (itr.) to remove fur from a hide: **tqw'lits'** (tr.) to singe hairs off a skin, **tqw'iixwts** my hair is falling out

1655   **tqw'** (tr.) to lift, hold something up: **alhtqw'ltnu+a?** are you holding the baby?, **tqw'amkaalhtmacw** to cross one's legs, **tqw'amkaalhits tsc** I placed my leg over her, **tqw'amkaalhmts ulh+tsc** I am placing my leg over her

1656   **tq'** to arrive by boat, land alongshore: **tq'aw+alhu** they made an attempt to land, **ax+ku tq'aqw'sts alh+tc** "my eyes did not land alongside him, you see" = you see, I am not surprised at what he did; I knew what he was up to, **stq'ta** port, harbor, **nutq'ankis t'ax ta+ 7apsulh+tx** he moored his boat alongside, touched at the village

1657   **tq'lha**, ***tq'lhn** knife: **tq'lhaalhay** dim., **astq'lhnakts stcits** I use a knife to cut it

1658   **ts–** reduced fem. article (15.4.1.1, 15.4.1.2, 15.4.1.3.1)

1659   **(+)ts** definite (article), close pl. (15.4.1.1)

1660   **–ts** 1 sg. subj. itr./tr./caus. (14.2, 14.3.1, 14.4.1)

1661   **–ts** allomorph of **–uts** (9.2.4): **kwntsis c+a+qla** he will bring him water, **sulicts** "selected food" = victuals, food-to-go, **q'aticts** (tr.) to steam-cook food, **watstum+ks?** what is his name?

1662   **–ts–**, **–tsan–** 1 sg. obj. tr. (14.3.1)

1663   **tsaatsaws** church

1664   **tsaatsi** a little bit: **alhpsx c+a+tsaatsi!** eat a bit!, **tsaatsilhtuts ta+tl'aplhtuts ulh+7inu alh+t'ayc** I have given you less than him, **tsaatsyuulhi** cheap

1665   **tsaatsti(i)** youth, youngster: **tsaatstluninu+ts'** you are looking young yet, **alhtamtsaatstlci ti+lhkw'lcam+t'ayc** he looks younger as he grows older

1666   **tsaaxa**, ***tsaaxn** (tr.) to chase somebody out: **ik'axw tsaaxnaynicits** I cannot get rid of him

1667   **tsakw** long: **stsakw** length, **tsakwaax** tall tree, **tsactsakwaax** tall trees, **tsactsakwalh** (to be a) tall (person), **nutsatskwalsikan** "having long ears" = curious, inquisitive, **tsakwaalh** butcher knife, **tsaakwliwa** worm, **nutsatskwlqsnk** wharfrat, **nutsakwaax** wolf

1668 **tsakw'** straight: **nutsakw'** straight river or channel, **tsakw'alxi** having lank hair, **tsakw'liwa** right, correct, **tsakw'liwanic** (tr.) to understand somebody rightly, get his meaning, **tsakw'** (tr.), **tsakw'a** (itr.) to straighten, stretch something, **tsakw'ayc** "strung out" = not having eaten for a long time, hungry, **alhtsatskw'anktmacw** to lie side by side

1669 **tsalaatsti** young people, adolescents: **snutsalaatst** dwarf, pygmy

1670 **tsalh** lake: **tsatsaalhi** dim.

1671 **tsaltcw** bark of red cedar

1672 **tsan** harpoon

1673 **-tsan- = -ts-**

1674 **tsap** bone: **tsaptinits** I have arthritis, **stsapankiixw** lateral aspect of the skull, **tsapiixw** steelhead trout

1675 ***tsatsaslhq'** so many (26.3.9): **tsatsaslhq' wa+7its'amni wa+s-7uskwtl'tinits ŝk'lcts+7iluk** no matter how many blankets they piled on me, I was still cold, **tsatsaslhq'uulhamts** I wrapped myself in so many blankets

1676 **tsatsa7yayu, *tsatsa7yaw** shotgun pellets: **nutsatsa7yawik** shotgun

1677 **tsatstawlhp** red cedar: **tsatstawlhpaak** cedar boughs

1678 **Tsawat** a geographical name

1679 **tsaxwm, *tsaxw** to wade: **Stsaxwmsta** "ford" = the name of a river, **Stsatsxwan** Tatsquan Creek

1680 **tsay** to stop, finish; all (26.3.5): **tsayuts** to finish talking or eating, **tsayak** to stop working, **tsayalh** to stop walking, **k'axw alh-tsayakms** it is unfinished, **wa+tsay wa+nⱦnmk'** all animals, **ala+tsay kulhulmc** in all countries
*tsalc (/*tsay⌐lc/) to change one's mind, give up: **tsalcakm** (tr.) to give up one's job, drop one's work

1681 **tsay** girl (term of address): **Stsaylh** a woman's name, **Stsayliwa** a woman's name

1682 **tsa7yamuus** red, yellow, and pink Indian paint brush (plant)

1683 **(+)tsc** definite (article), fem. close sg. (15.4.1.1)

1684 **tscm** to disappear: **nutscmaax** to disappear behind something

1685 **tscw** dark: **nutscwaltwa** the sky is dark, it is a dark day, **nutscwals** it is dark in the house, **Nutscwani** name of a small bay

1686 **tscwi** sufficient, adequate, just enough: **axw tscwis** it is not enough, will not do, **tscwinaw+ts'** there are enough people (in here) now, **tscwicwyuulhi** medium-sized, **nutscwyusnicit uuxnk** they figured it was deep enough, **istscwimits sksnmakts** I have done enough work

1687 **tscwyakm** (tr.) to reach for something

1688 ***tsi** (tr.) to cause something to move forward or protrude: **tsitsyutsms s7alh7alhtsims** "he makes his voice ring out as he talks" = he speaks resonantly, **anutsyalsikanm** to perk one's ears, **tsyalhm** to stretch one's legs, **tsyakm** to reach out, **tsyakm** (tr.) to pass something on, **tsyus** (tr.) to hand somebody something, **tsyusim t'ayc c+ti+...** a ... was handed to him, **tsyaaxm** "to move one's leg forward" = to take a step

1689 **tsi+** indefinite article, fem. close sg. (15.1)

1690 **tsi-** bound fem. article (16.4.4, 25.3, 25.5.2)

1691 **(+)tsi** interrogative form of **(+)ts** (15.4.1.1)

1692 **-tsi-** 1 sg. subj. tr. (14.3.2)

1693 **tsic** fem. sg. identifier (25.3)

1694 **(+)tsic** interrogative form of **(+)tsc** (15.4.1.1)

1695 **tsictsik** wagon, railway train: **astsictsik** to travel by wagon or railway train

1696 ***tsiiq = tsiix**

1697 **Tsiis** a personal name

1698 **tsiix, *tsiiq** (tr.), **tsiixa** (itr.) to dig for something: **anutsiixlh** hole dug in the ground, **tsiixm** to dig clams, **tsiiqnk** (tr.) to dig up roots

1699 **tsiixwt** wedge

1700 **tsikw** (tr.) to move something: **tsikwm** to be moving, **axw tsictsikw-aycts** I cannot move, **tsikwalhm** to start walking, **nutsictsikwmuulh-ikalhh** one's Adam's apple is moving

1701 **tsik'** (tr.), **tsik'a** (itr.) to poke, stab something: **tsik'alus** (tr.) to poke the fire, **tsik'alusta** poker, **tsik'aycnimut** to get oneself stabbed, **nutsik'alsta** implement used for fleshing a hide, **tsik'aax-alitsm** to use a toothpick, **tsintsik'uutsta** fork

1702 **tsim** to get hit, bumped: **tsimlxs** to bump one's nose, **tsimak** to bump one's arm, **tsimaalh** to bump one's leg, **nutsimikulhaqw's** to get hit in, bump one's eye, **Tsimlayc** a man's name

1703 **tsimani** horseclam

1704 **tsimilt** draw in mountain, gully

1705 **tsipa** subterranean shelter, kickwillie house

1706 ***tsipi** single, mono-, having one ...: **tsipyulhaaqws** having one eye, **tsipyaaq** one-legged, **tsipyuulhnnak** having one testis, **tsipyaakmits s7apcwits** I lift it with one hand

1707 **tsipsc** fisher (animal): **tsiitspsci** dim., **Tsipscaaxuts** the name of a creek

1708 **tsiqw'** (tr.), **tsiqw'a** (itr.) to bust, break, smash something: **alh-tsiqw'** broken, smashed up, **tsiqw'alus** (tr.), **tsiqw'alustu-** to smash something up, **tsiqw'aalh** (tr.) to break a cup, **nutsiqw'** (tr.) to break a window, **nutsiqw'aqw's** (tr.) to break someone's spectacles, **nutsiqw'aaq** (tr.) to break a pot or saucer, **anutsiq'uuts** the top of a bottle is smashed, **anutsiqw'aaq** the bottom of a bottle is smash-ed, **alhtsiqw'als** bottle is cracked

1709 **tsitstsip** bird (large): **tsitstsipii** bird (of average size), **tsits-tsiipi** small bird

1710 **tsituma**, ***tsitum(n)** to sleep: **tsitumlc** to fall asleep, **stsitumlcta** sleeping pill, **tsitstumnalŝlh** night moth

1711 **tsix** new, fresh: **tsixaalh** new shoes or vehicle, **tsixuulh** new house, **tsixanlh** new clothes, **tsitsxuulh** fresh berries

1712 **+tsk(i)** somehow, wh...ever (28.3.5)

1713 **tsklh** term used to address little girls

1714 **tskw** heavy: **nutskwlc** to sink in water, **tskwaltwa** "heavy sky" = (it is) very cloudy, **tskwalhkwalh** to walk with heavy steps, **tskusta** sinkerline

1715 **tskwm** (tr.) to draw, pull something out

1716 **tskw'm** (tr.), **tskw'ma** (itr.) to pull something out: **tskw'maak** (tr.) to fillet fish, **tskw'maax** (tr.) to pull a pole out of the ground, **tskw'maaqalits** (tr.) to extract somebody's tooth

1717 ***tsk'** pointed, sharp, stinging: **tsk'm(aliits)** hot-tasting, spicy, **stsk'** sliver of fir bark, **tsk'lhp** ribs, **tsk'alhkw** devil's club, **is-tsk'nimut** "to find oneself panging intensely" = to be lonesome, homesick

1718 **tslh** (tr.), **tslha** (itr.) to break or pull something off: **tslhalaaxt** (tr.) to break a rope, **tslhm** to gather seaweed, **tslhlits'** (tr.) to pluck a bird, **tslhalha** to pull hairs out, **tslhiixw** (tr.) to remove weeds, **nutslhik** (tr.) to break something in half, **nutslhulhaaxank**, **nutslhaaxulhank** the bottom has come off a bottle, **tslhlayc** "to have broken (the string)" = to win a race, **tslh(t)nm** = **tslhlayc**

1719 **tsl(7)lik** coyote

1720 **tsɪ́tsluksi** youngsters

1721 ***tsn** self (25.7): **alh+tsnlh** to, for oneself, **alh+ti+stsnlhs+tc** by himself, **tsnlhakmtx!** do it by yourself!, **tsnlhliwa** introverted, not paying attention, clumsy, **tsnlhakmitsut** to do something "just for the heck of it", not control one's actions, commit an offense, **tsn-kwakmitsutts s7alhpsts** I am eating by myself, **alh+ti+stsnkwaw+tc**, **alh+ti+stsnlhaw+tc** by themselves

1722 **tsna** stinging nettle: **tsɪ́tsnay** dim., **tsɪ́tsnalc** to have a tingling sensation, "pins and needles", **tsɪ́tsnalcakts** my hand is tingling

1723 **tsp** (tr.), **tspa** (itr.) to wipe something: **nutspik** (tr.) to wipe a pot clean, **tspusm** to wipe one's face, **tspaalhta** doormat

1724 **tsq** (tr.), **tsqa** (itr.) to make a hole, opening in something: **nutsq** hole, **tsqta** chisel, **tsqm** to open one's mouth, **nutsqalsikan** to have a pierced ear, **nutsqaaq** needle, **stsqaaq** anus, **stsqiklxs** nostrils, **Stsqiklxs** a point of land

1725 **tsqw** (tr.) to begin doing something: **tsqwistxw!** let him start on it!, **tsqwakm** to begin a manual activity, **tsqwalhm** to start walking, **tsqutsm** to start talking or eating, **axw anutsqwilhs** she has not been deflowered, she is a virgin

1726 ***tsqw** wet: **tsqwanlh** wet clothes, **tsqwaltwa**, **tsqwaltm** wet season

1727 **tsq'** (tr.), **tsq'a** (itr.) to grab, pull, tear (at) something: **alh-tsq'** torn, ripped, **nutsq'iiktx t'ayc c+ka+sqaluts!** grab this (bowl) for (putting) berries (in)!

1728 **tsq'm** to curl up, shrink: **alhtsmq'mulhiiqw**, **alhtsmq'malqi** having curly hair

1729 **tst!**, **tsst!**, **hatst!**, **hatsst!** calling attention: hey!, pst! (29.4)

1730 **-tst** 2 sg. pass. tr. (14.3.3)

1731 **tsum** to make a rustling sound: **anutsum** water is boiling in kettle, sizzling, **alhtsumalh** to make a crackling sound when treading on frost, **alhtsumaak wa+stn+ts** the wind whistles in the trees, **alh-tsumals ti+smt+tc** the wind is howling around the mountain, **alhtsum-alits ti+lhalas+tc** the water is splashing softly around the bow of the boat, **Tsumuulh** a former village

1732 **tsumtsumis** horsetail, scouring rush

1733 **tsuntsupt** to whistle

1734 **tsup** (tr.), **tsupa** (itr.), **tsupm** (itr.) to pound cedar bark so as to soften it

tsupts (tr.) "to fill an orifice with soft material" = to plug, cork something: **nutsupts** (tr.) to plug a hole, **nutsuptsta** plug, **nu-tsuptsalsikanaycts** my ears are plugged

1735 **tsupinaalh** shinbone

1736 **tsut** to say: **tsutm** (tr.) to tell somebody something, **nutsutik** to think, **nutsutikm** (tr.) to think of somebody

1737 **-tsut, -tsuut** reflexive suffix (19.10.1): **p'stsut** to bend over, **lip'tsut** to return, come back, **tkatsuut** to shoot oneself, **tuk'tsut** to stretch oneself

1738 **tsutsa, *tsutstn** mouth: **tsuutstni** dim.

1739 **Tsuusila** a small bay

1740 **-tsuut = -tsut**

1741 **-tswa** formative suffix (22.2)

1742 **Tswaakilakw** a man's name

1743 **Tswaast** one of Raven's female Crow relatives

1744 ***tsx** (tr.), **tsxm** (itr.) to drip on something: **tsxtinilh** our house is leaky, **stsx** trickle(s), drop(s), **tsxmaax** water is dripping from the roof, **anutsxmiklxs** to have a running nose

1745 **tsyap** loincloth: **ustsyapaaqta** skirt

1746 **+ts'(n), *+ts'i** now, already (28.3.6)

1747 **Ts'aamas** Victoria

1748 **ts'aaqaluuŝlh** white springsalmon: **ts'ats'qalusuulh** golden form of soapberry; pale form of any berry

1749 **ts'aaxwm** red clouds at sunset

1750 **ts'acam** fermented, sour-tasting

1751 **+ts'akw** optative (28.3.7)

1752 **ts'alh** rockweed: **Ats'alhani** a geographical name

1753 **ts'ap'ax** bough tips of red or yellow cedar

1754 **ts'awikalh** long snowshoes

1755 **Ts'awlhmim** a former village

1756 **(+)ts'ayc** demonstrative, fem. close sg. (15.4.1.1)

1757 **ts'ayx** fireweed: **ts'ayxnk** fireweed root

1758 **Ts'ayxlilh** a man's name

1759 **ts'cm** to drip: **ts'c̲m̲nicis wa+sic+ts alh+ti+7alhqulhts+tc** he let the

blood drip on my book, **ts'cmus** to drool, **ts'cmcmalh** raindrops are
falling

1760 ***ts'i** (tr.?) to close one's eye(s), wink: **stits'yalsm** to blink one
eye, **its'yalsmtss** she winks at me, **ts'imuus** to close one's eyes for
a moment

1761 ***+ts'i = +ts'(n)**

1762 **ts'icw** (tr.), **ts'icwa** (itr.) to grate, scour something: **ts'icwta**
sandpaper; unbranched horsetail, **sts'icts'icwtalhp** scouring rush,
horsetail

1763 **ts'ícw** five (26.2)

1764 **ts'ikm** dirty: **nuts'ikmaqw's** water is dirty, **sts'icts'ikmlhp** lamb's
quarters

1765 **ts'ikwa**, ***ts'ikwn** clam: **ts'iits'kwni** dim., **ts'ikwnals** "with a clam-
-like surface" = drinking cup, **Ts'ikwa7ya** a man's name

1766 **ts'ikw'its'** sea urchins

1767 **ts'ima**, ***ts'imn** guts, intestines: **snuts'imnaax** rectum

1768 **Ts'ipasa** the name of a Kitkatla chief

1769 **ts'ipscili**, ***ts'pscili** wild blue currants, black garden currants:
ts'ints'ipscililhp, **ts'psciclilhp** currant plant

1770 **Ts'iqwi** Restoration Bay

1771 **ts'it** call of the **kwakwas** announcing a death

1772 **ts'ix** (tr.) to burn, scald something: **ts'ixliitsayc** to have burnt
one's skin, **ts'ixaakayc** to have burnt one's hand, **nuts'ix** (tr.),
nuts'ixa (itr.) to refine eulachon grease

1773 **ts'k** (tr.) to fix, prepare something: **alhts'k** fixed, **nuts'k** (tr.)
to string up, prepare a hide, **nuLs'kta** tanning stick, **k'ists'kaak**
to be clumsy, **k'ists'kuuts** to mispronounce, **nusts'kmc** handy, dex-
terous, **nuts'kik** (tr.) to divide something in two, **Nuts'kusa** a woman's name

ts'kta "doings": event, happening, circumstance(s): **stam+ks wa+
ts'ktanu?** how are you doing?, **iclq'ms ula+ka+ts'ktas** he was think-

ing of what to do next, thinking ahead

1774 **ts'klákt** ten (26.2)

1775 **ts'kt** to arrive: **ts'ktulh** to arrive by boat, **ts'ktmim** "it has come to him" = he is ready to start dancing, **ts'ktakmim** he was beset, attacked, **alhts'ktiilh** to be closely related

1776 **ts'la**, ***ts'ln** basket: **asts'layak, asts'lnak** to have, use a basket, **Asts'lniiklh** a mountain in the **Talyu** region

1777 **ts'lh** (tr.), **ts'lha** (itr.) to shelter, cover, shade something: **nuts'lhaax** shade in the bush, **nuts'lhals** the sun is covered by the clouds, **ts'lhtaata** umbrella

1778 **ts'lkt** bald eagle: **lts'lkti** dim.

1779 ***ts'ln** = **ts'la**

1780 **ts'ls** to be mistaken, confused

1781 **ts'm** forefinger

1782 **ts'mtaaq** smoked eulachons

1783 **ts'n** tidal lagoon

1784 **+ts'n** = **+ts'(n)**

1785 **ts'p** stuck, blocked

1786 ***ts'pscili** = **ts'ipscili**

1787 **ts'qamin** mountain jack

1788 **Ts'qwikaaya** the name of a Kitlope chief

1789 **ts's** loud, noisy

1790 **ts'u** grey: **ts'waaxuts** having a grey beard, **nuts'wikulhaqw's** having grey eyes, **ts'wiixw** having grey hair, **ts'ulciixw** one's hair is greying, **suts'wakt** old man's beard lichen, **sts'waktaak** lung lichen

1791 ***ts'u** to suck: **ts'uts'uulit** to produce an alveolar click **ts'um** (tr.) to suck on something: **ts'umuus** (tr.) to kiss somebody, **ts'umaak** (tr.) to kiss somebody's hand, **ts'umnk** (tr.) to suck on a (cooked) fish tail

1792 **ts'ulapla** quiver for arrows

1793 **ts'umlc** half-smoked fish: **ts'umlctu-** to half-smoke fish, **ts'umlcuus** surface of half-smoked fish

1794 **Ts'umqlaqs** a woman's name

1795 **ts'upilhm** to scratch one's private's parts

1796 **ts'up'akt** glove, mitten

1797 **ts'usm** dusk: **usts'usmi** early evening, **ts'usmtim** they were overtaken by the darkness

1798 **ts'uts'qw**, ***ts'uux** having sores: **ts'uuxlc** to develop sores

1799 ***ts'x(a)** real, true, credible: **ts'xlh** true, **ts'xlhuts** to tell the truth, be right, **ts'xmayc** to be really the case, **ts'xanic**, **ts'xancw** (tr.) to believe somebody, **ts'xancwikmits s7atmas** I was convinced he was dead, **ts'xanmacw** to believe each other, **ts'xanmacwayctimut** to see if something is true, verify something

1800 **ts'xlhm** to fall in the water, drown: **ts'xlhmkw** drowned

1801 **ts'xlhn** (tr.), **ts'xlhna** (itr.) to kick something/somebody: **ts'xlhńlhnim** he was kicked repeatedly, **ka+t͟mnuts'xlhnaaxmlhts** I will just push ("kick") off my boat, **ts'xlhńlhnuulhnm** to play soccer

1802 **ts'xw** white: **nuts'xulhaax** white-tailed deer, **ts'xwaluûŝlh** white springsalmon

1803 **ts'xwtalhp** red willow, red-osier dogwood

1804 **ts'yaaxw** flicker (bird): **nuts'yaaxwanim** whirlwind, **its'yaaxwlhp** yarrow, Queen Anne's lace

1805 **ts'yawlh** sack made of sealion's stomach or bladder

1806 **tts** term used to address little boys

1807 **tu+** indefinite article, remote pl. (15.1)

1808 **tu-...-a** last, previous (23.7)

1809 **-tu-**, **-stu-** to purposely cause something or somebody to (be) ... (14.4, 19.12)

1810 **+tu** really, indeed (28.3.3)

1811 **tuc** (tr.), **tuca** (itr.) to unwind, unravel something: **tucayc+ts'** it is unraveled now, **istuc** (tr.), **istuca** (itr.) to butcher fish

1812 **+tuks?** wh... exactly? (28.3.18.4)

1813   **tuk'**, ***tukw'** (tr.), **tuk'a** (itr.) to stretch something: **tuk'm** to become sprained, **tuk'maaxalh** to sprain one's ankle, **nututkw'mik** to sprain one's back, **tuk'anilhm** to dislocate one's hip, **tuk'usm** (tr.) "to extend one's face towards somebody" = to pay somebody a visit

1814   **-tulh-** 1 pl. obj. tr. (14.3.1); 1 sg./pl. subj. tr. (14.3.2)

1815   **tultaya** mountain trout

1816   **tulu**, **tuulu** to manage, succeed, win: **axw tu(u)luts ska+k'cits** I can not see him, **tulwamktsut** to successfully complete something, **tulumits** I defeated him

1817   **tum** (tr.) to impale, poke something with a stick: **tumutsit ti+numutsta+tc** they ram the door, **anutumuts** spear, **tutmuulh** (tr.) to roast mountain goat fat on a stick

    tum to protrude: **alhtumikusts** I have a lump on my forehead

1818   **tums** woman's breast: **tumstu-** to give somebody the breast, **tumstnm** to be giving a child the breast, **tums** (tr./itr.) to suck on something, **kulhtums** (tr.) to perform fellatio on somebody

1819   ***tup** foam, bubbles, specks: **tupm** to bubble up, froth, **nutupm** to foam, **nutupmik** it is bubbling in the pot, **nunutuupm** carbonated beverage, beer, **stuplh** bubbles, foam, **tutup** trout

1820   **tupa**, **tuupa** navel

1821   **tuts** (tr.) to wet, soak something: **tutstsut** to get oneself wet, walk in water, **tutsm** to soak dried fish, **stutsm** dried fish that has been soaked, **tamstutsmts** I will prepare some **stutsm**

1822   **tutu-** to prepare, work on something (23.2)

1823   **tutustiq'** flying squirrel

1824   **+tuu** exactly, just, even, too (28.3.4)

1825   **tuulu** = **tulu**

1826   **tuupa** = **tupa**

1827   **(+)tux(w)** interrogative form of **(+)txw** (15.4.1.1)

1828   **twa**, ***tw(i)n** to ask, beg: **twax ulh+ts!** go and ask them!, **tutwayutsm** to ask for food, **Tutwayuus** name of a mask, **st/tw(i)niitscw!** "your (turn to be) begging me!" = thank you!, **st⫫tw(i)nakmtscw!** thank you for your help! (29.4)

1829 **Twalalh7it** a supernatural mountain goat hunter

1830 **-twaxw = -taxw**

1831 ***twin** to be(come) visible: **stwin** grave marker, memorial pole, **twin-aalh** footprint, **nutwinuts** whistle used in a **Sisawk** dance, **twinm** to emerge, show up from behind something, **twinmuts** to reveal, report something to the police, **twinmtu-** to show something

1832 ***tw(i)n = twa**

1833 **tx** (tr.), **txa** (itr.) to carve something with an adze: **txta** adze, **nutxlxs** (tr.) to sharpen the point of something with an adze

1834 **tx-** locative prefix (23.6.1): **ti+txaqw'lhankiixws ti+smt** lower side of mountain

1835 **(+)tx** definite (article), non-fem. remote sg. (15.4.1.1)

1836 **txu-** directional prefix complex (23.6.1): **nutxuuxnkalh** road is going down, descending

1837 **(+)txw** definite (article), remote pl. (15.4.1.1)

1838 **-txw, -stxw** caus. imp. sg. (sg. obj.) (14.4.1.1, 19.12)

1839 **txwnayaax** across the river (29.2.2): **tayamkits txwnayaaxutsam** I threw it across the river

1840 **t'aaxw** (tr.), **t'aaxwa** (itr.), **t'aaxwm** (itr.) to lick something

1841 **t'akw** sanitary towel

1842 **t'amas** cockle: **t'at'maasi** dim., **nut'amasikta** scraper used to smooth the inside of a canoe

1843 **T'ants'ni** Carrier native(s) from Anahim Lake

1844 **t'apalst** cave: **Nut'apalstuts** a geographical name

1845 **t'as** wren

1846 **t'at'kanalhp** yellow pond lily

1847 **(+)t'ax** demonstrative, non-fem. remote sg. (15.4.1.1)

1848 **(+)t'axw** demonstrative, remote pl. (15.4.1.1)

1849 **t'aws** wet, damp: **t'awsulmc** wet ground, dew

1850 **(+)t'ayc** demonstrative, non-fem. close sg. (15.4.1.1)

1851 **t'cw** (tr.), **t'cwa** (itr.) to brush, sweep something: **t'cwanlhta** clothes-brush, **nut'cwalsm** to sweep the house, **t'culmcm** to sweep the floor, **t'c(unc)ulmcta** broom

1852 **t'iclhala** robin: **t'ict'iclhalayi** dim., **t'iclhalayulh** robin's egg, **sqaluts̓ ti+t'iclhala = skw'anik's**

1853 **t'ict'iixlhalam** to hop on one leg

1854 **t'in** small dorsal fin; clitoris: **snut'inalhh, snut'inalsiixw** uvula, **St'inayalh** name of a mountain

1855 ***t'ka** (tr.) to move something up and down: **t'kayxwm** to nod in approval, **alht'kalqsakm** to drum with one's fingers (on the table)

1856 **t'ksn** (tr.), **t'ksna** (itr.) to shoot something: **t'ksn(i)mta** arrow, **ast'ksnimtnak** to shoot with bow and arrow, **nut'ksnimta** quiver for arrows

1857 **t'kw** to bleed: **nut'kulhaqw'sts** my eye is bleeding, **t'kwlxs** to have a nosebleed, **t'kuskwstalhp** Indian hemp, spreading dogbane

1858 ***t'kwi** chipped: **st'kwiilhh** chip, **alht'kwi** it is chipped, **nut'kwyuuts+ma ti+mntcuutsta+t'ayc** this dipping cup may be chipped

1859 **t'li** dog salmon: **lt'li** dim., **t'lianm** dog salmon season, **slt'liislh** horsefly, **Snut'li** name of a former village

1860 **t'miixw** tree stump drifting in the water

1861 **t'niixulh** tumpline

1862 **t'nxw** head: **t'ft'nqwi** dim., **t'nxwlh** skull, **ist'nxulh** to eat salmon head stew

1863 ***t'q** to be in close contact, adhere to a surface: to come close; to stick, be pasted on; to be spread over a surface: **t'qalc** to get stuck; to float towards the shore, **t'qmuuts** high tide, **t'q** (tr.), **t'qa** (itr.) to stick, paste something, **t'qaakta** bandage for hand, **t'qalc** (tr.) = **t'q** (tr.), **nut'qan** (tr.) to affix a postal stamp, **nut'qanta** postal stamp, **alht'qalcanlh** many little objects are stuck to a net or cloth, **t'qusqwsi** "little thing sticking to the face" =

gnat, no-see-um, **t'qus** (tr.), **t'qm** (itr.) to spread berries out to dry, **alht'q** crushed berries that are going to be spread out and dried, **t'qim wa+st'ala+7ats** this hemlock bark is spread out to dry, **nut'q1qlqsaki** chickweed

1864 **-t'q** span, distance measured between spread thumb and middle finger (20.6.1): **mat'q** one span, **lhwaast'q** two spans, **múst'q** four spans, **ma(n)maat'qa** inchworm

1865 **t'qwl** (tr.), **t'qwla** (itr.) to braid, weave something: **t'qwlus** (tr.) to snare an animal, **t'qwlusta** snare, trap

1866 **t'qwm** rotten: **t'qwmlc** to rot

1867 **t's** salty: **nut's** salty water, **t'sulh** salty food, **t'stu-** to salt something, **st's** salt, **st'saax** (tr.) to put salt in food, **st'sals** "with a salt-like surface" = glass bottle

1868 **t'ts** (tr.), **t'tsa** (itr.) to knock on, strike (and break) something: **t'tsiixwlayc** (tr.) to knock somebody on the knee, **alht'tslqsakm** to rap with one's fingers, **nut'tsayc** to knock on a window, **alht'ts-lits'** branded, tattooed, **nut'tsik** (tr.) to bust an egg, **nut'tsmiik-nicis ta+nusximta+tx** he shattered the crystal

t'tsuulh (tr.) to light, set fire to something: **t'tsuulhalus** (tr.) to light the oven, **nut'tsuulhiiqw** (tr.) to light something with a match, **nut'tsuulhiiquts** (tr.) to light somebody's cigaret

1869 ***t'u** more than sufficient, extra, numerous: **t'umitsut** having many relatives, **t'ulcaaxlaycts** I put a little too much (e.g. water) in the container, **nut'wiik** container is full, **T'waax** a geographical name

1870 **t'uka**, ***t'ukwa**, ***t'ukwn** mink: **t'uut'kwni** dim., **t'ut'kwayana+mats' ka+7aluuxalhilh** it looks like our offspring will now be replaced by minks

1871 **t'um** (tr.), **t'uma** (itr.) to suck something: **alht'umapsm** having a small bruise, "hicky" in the neck (caused by lover's sucking), **alh-ut'mapsm** having several "hickies", **alht'umlqsakm** to suck on one's

finger, **t'umutsm** to smirk, simper, **alht'umuulhnm** (to be a) leech
t'uma, ***t'umn** stuck, jammed: **t'umnalhts** my foot is stuck

1872 ***t'up(i)** (tr.) to break, split something: **nut'upik** (tr.), **nut'upika**
(itr.) to split a rock in half, **nut'uplxs** tip is broken off, **t'upy-
alqi** handle is broken off, **t'upnklhh** "split bottom" = Raven's canoe
in the beginning of time

1873 **t'upilhts** sealice

1874 **t'upiwas** fawn

1875 **T'uqwtaqs** Small Mouth Bay

1876 ***t'uuts** to get diverted, sidetracked: **t'uutsutsliwaᵻmastuu tiᵻs-
7aalats'ii** he always changes a story in the middle, never tells a
story to the end, **T'uuts** a woman's name

1877 **t'xt** rock, stone: **t'xtuulh** sinker, anchor, **snut'xtiitk** stone, seed
of fruit, **t'xtulmc** rocky soil, **Sit'xt** a geographical name

1878 **t'xúlh** six (26.2)

1879 **t'xwsus** clover rhizomes: **t'xwsuslhp** clover plant, **t'xwsususiixw**
clover leaves, **t'xwsususnk** quack grass

U

1880 **u-** directional prefix (23.6.1)

1881 **-uks, -uk's** plural suffix (18.2, 18.2.1-5)

1882 ***ukw'p** to lower oneself, crouch: **icukw'plc** (tr.) to stalk, sneak up
on somebody

1883 **-uk's** = **-uks**

1884 **uk'uk'** skunk cabbage: **uk'uk'nk** skunk cabbage root

1885 **uk'um** to groan (e.g. when carrying a heavy load): **ukw'k'umaax** sound
caused by somebody walking on swampy ground

1886 ***ul** (tr.) to come close to, reach the end of something; to bring something out or forth: **alh7ulik(us)** (tr.) to stay with, keep somebody company, **alh7ul** to be unable to contain oneself any longer, **alh7ults ska+7aaxqats** I am almost wetting myself, have an urgent need to urinate, **alh7ulcilhts** (/alh-7ul⁻lc-ilh-ts/) = **alh7ults ska+ 7aaxqats, ulamktx!** bring it out!, show it!, **ulamcwits ulh+ts wa+ 7its'amni+ts** I give them the blankets that I made, **anu7ulaaxits ska+wlis wa+qla+ts ulh+tc** I will persuade him into spilling the water on him, **nu7ulaaxayc** to have reached a dead end, **nu7ulaaxta** dead end, **Anûlikutsayc** "the one who waits at the door" = the name of a mythical woman (/a-nu⁻7ul.../), **s7ulus** stakes used in gambling game

1887 **-ul** formative suffix (22.3)

1888 ***ula** thither, over there (23.6.1, 29.2.2): **ixq'maw tcula** they walked that way

1889 **ula+** = **ulh∔wa+** (16.3)

1890 ***ulatl's** towards the Interior (23.6.1, 29.2.2.1): **tl'apaw tculatl's** or **tculatl'saw** they went to the Interior

1891 **ulh+, úlh+** (going) towards (16.1, 16.4.2, 23.6.1)

1892 **-ulh, -uulh** (capable of) containing something, to have bulk, be inflated: (1) human body, (2) ball (egg, moon); rock (metal, money), (3) large container, vessel: vehicle, car; house, (4) clothes, garment, hat, (5) food contained in cup or bowl (soup or beverage) (20.2.1, 20.3.1, 20.4.1, 20.4.1.1): **qapsmuulhm** to put one's arms around oneself, **plhtuulh** obese, **pipq'uulh** bug having a grey stripe across its body, **yalquulh** ball, **sunp'uulhnm** to play baseball, **k'aqasulh** crow's egg, **qwaxulh** raven's egg, **kasmiûlh** golden eagle's egg, **smaŵlhtxw ti+ka+lalaq'aticw!** fry one egg!, **pusulh** the moon is waxing, **piq'uulh ti+t'xt** it is a flat rock, **sk'culh** black rock, **mucwmukuulh** gold, **t'xtuulh** sinkerline with anchor, **mawlxsulh** twenty dollars, **t'xúlhulh** six dollars, **mntskulha** to be counting money, **tlhulh** fast vehicle, **tmsculh** slow vehicle, **pik'uulh** shiny car,

quts'uulhis ti+qw'xwmtimuts he is washing his car, **lhk'uulh wa+sulh
+ts** the house is big, **músulh wa+sulh** there are four houses, **at'-
uulhits wa+sulh+ts** I am painting the house, **lhulhts'uulhm** to get
undressed, **ksuulhm** to take one's trousers off, **pik'uulh** oil coat,
tqnkuulh underwear, **músulh wa+qayt** there are four hats, **maaskulh
+7iks wa+qaytnu?** how many hats have you got?, **piq'uulh wa+qayt+7ats**
these are wide hats, **muq'ulh** bland food, **t'sulh** salty food, **ist'nxulh** to eat salmon head stew, **k'iptulh** elderberry wine, **nuxwskyulh**
soapberry wine

nu-...-ulh belly, abdomen (20.2.1): **nutayulhayc** to have been hit in
the belly

nu-...-ulh-aax base, seat, posterior (20.2.1): **asulhaaxs ti+quna**
base of the thumb, **nucwpulhaaq** diaper is coming off; to slip off
one's chair, **nu7ilulhaaqta** diaper, **nupapayulhaaq** to squat

nu-...-ulh-aax-ank button (20.3.1): **nutslhulhaaxank** button has come
off

-ulh-als cheek (20.2.1): **stpuulhals** to have a freckle on one's
cheek, **sp'ulhalsayc** to have been hit on the cheek

nu-...-uulh-an side of face, temple (20.2.1): **skulhuulhan, asuulhan**
temple, **nusxuulhanm** to shave one's sideburns

nu-...-ulh-an-alh anklebone (20.2.1): **nut'tsulhanalhm** to knock on
one's ankle, **nusp'ulhanalhayc** to have been hit on the ankle

(nu-...)-ulh-ank belly, abdomen (20.2.1): **tlhulhank** to have strong
abdominal muscles, **tsitsk'ulhank** (tr.) to stab somebody in the belly, **(nu)sp'ulhankayc** to have been hit in the belly, **st'a7mulhank** to
lie flat on one's stomach

nu-...-ulh-aqw's eye, glasses (20.2.1, 20.5.1): **nutayulhaqw'sayc** to
have been hit in the eye, **nut'kulhaqw's** to have a bleeding eye,
tsipyulhaaqws having one eye, one-eyed, **nutspulhplhaqw'sm** to wipe
one's glasses

-ulh-iixw head, hair, hat (20.2.1, 20.5.1): **tayulhiixwayc** to have been hit on the head, **sk'stlits'ulhiixw** skin of fish head, **mnts'-ulhiixw** to have blond hair, **ts'xulhiixw** to have white hair, **alhtsm-q'mulhiixw (-iiqw)** to have curly hair, **pik'ulhiiqw** oil hat, south-wester, **ksulhiiqwm** to take one's hat off, **tayamkulhiixwlhim c+ta+ qaytlhs** somebody has thrown his hat away

-ulh-iixw-layc knee (20.2.1): **sp'ulhiixwlaycayc** to have been hit on the knee, **kwlhulhiixwlayc** to have a cracked kneecap

(nu-...)-ulh-ik back (20.2.1): **kulhulhik** back, **squplhulhiik** hair on the back, **tsik'ulhik** (tr.) to stab somebody in the back, **sp'ulhik-ayc** to have been hit on the back, **nutsⱥtsnalculhik** to have "pins and needles" sensation in one's back

-ulh-ik-ak back of hand; upper arm (20.2.1): **sp'ulhikakayc** to have been hit on the back of one's hand, **kmayulhikak** the back of one's hand hurts, **stlhuulhikak** biceps

-ulh-ik-alh top of foot (20.2.1): **sp'ulhikalhayc** to have been hit on one's foot

nu-...-uulh-ik-alhh throat (20.2.1): **nutsictsikwmuulhikalhh** one's throat is moving, **nuspulhuulhikalhh** Adam's apple, **nusp'uulhikalhh--ayc** to have been hit on the throat, **asuulhikalhh** throat

-ulh-ik-us forehead (20.2.1): **tayulhikusayc** to have been hit on the forehead

-uulh-lits' muscle (20.2.1): **kuŝtlhuulhlits'** to be muscular

(nu-...)-uulh-lits'-alh calf of leg (20.2.1): **stlhuulhlits'alh** calf muscle, **sxuulhliitsalhm** to shave one's calves, **nicniq'xmuulhliits-alh** to have a cramp in the calf, **nutsⱥtsnalcuulhlits'alh** to have "pins and needles" sensation in the calf

nu-...-uulh-nnak testicles, scrotum (20.2.1): **nutcuulhnnak** (tr.) to castrate somebody, **nusp'uulhnnakayc** to have been hit in the testi-cles, **nucwilmuulhnnak** to have an itchy scrotum, **nmnmuulhnnak** both testicles, **tsipyuulhnnak** to have one testicle

-ulh-us joint, connection; surface of rock or metal: **skw'mulhuusayc**

one's shoulder is dislocated, **alh7umatalhuss ti+qla+tc** where the
water pipe joins the main pipe, **s7ixwalhkulhuus** to be red-hot, **Yayuulhus** a location at Kimsquit characterized by the presence of
small pretty pebbles

1893 ***ulha** dependable, responsible: **alh7ulhats ulh+7inu** I depend on you,
alh7ulhamim people depend on him, **ulhalxstu-** to hold responsible,
blame, accuse somebody

1894 **-ulhla**, **-uulhla** bulk, total(ity), appearance, character, behavior
(20.3.1): **q'imulhlamim** both his parents are still alive, **nukalikuulhla** half moon, **nukalikuulhlatut snûlikit** they half-emptied it
(the bottle) (/s-nu⌒wl.../), **in7ip'uulhla** catcher in baseball game,
sculhla to refuse, not give permission, **sculhlas ulh+tx ska+...** he
did not give him permission to ..., **yayulhlamim** he is allowed (to
...), **alhqap'uulhlatsut** to put one's arms around oneself, **statalt-
mcuulhlaliwanaw** they look like dignitaries, **napulhlam** (tr.) to make
fun of somebody, **kwmuulhla** to be fat, obese, **ayulhla** to be cranky,
ill-natured, **pculhculhla** happy, easygoing, **paaxûlhlaliwa** scary,
dangerous, **pacpaaqûulhlam** (tr.) to scare somebody, **Lxulhla** Cannibal, **Piq'ulhla** a man's name

1895 **ulhqn** pail, bucket

1896 **ulhtsax!** go ahead!: **ulhtsa(y)naxw!** go ahead, folks!

1897 ***uli** hither, over here (23.6.1, 29.2.2): **ixq'maw tculi** they walked
this way

1898 **ulic** (tr.), **ulica** (itr.) to choose something: **ulicutsm** to choose
food, decide what one is going to eat, **ulicatimutts c+ti+ka+kwtmts**
I keep myself busy looking for a potential husband, **sulicts** food-
-to-go, victuals

1899 **-ulits'**, **-uli(i)ts** (through a) hole; clothing (20.3.1): **t'umuulits**
gun barrel, **kw'pupliits tiixwaqw'sta+7ats** these spikes are straight
("go straight through a hole"), **cnasuliits** lady's wear, **s7imlk-
uliitsta ti+nup** it is a man's shirt, **si7axtsuliits** nightshirt, pa-

jamas, **s7ixqlmuliitsta** bathing suit, **kululits'tumx!** lend me your clothes!, **xtl'ulits'ta** object used in a "washing ceremony" (cleansing ritual, during which amends are made for a wrongdoing)

1900 **-ulmc** land, ground, floor (20.3.1): **piq'ulmc** wide country, **puxulmc** (tr.) to remove rocks from the soil, **tculmcta** plough, **tkulmc** the floor is dirty, **t'culmcm** to sweep the floor, **t'c(unc)ulmcta** broom

1901 ***ulq = *ulx**

1902 ***ulsqa** towards the west (23.6.1): **tculsqa(m)** to go towards the west

1903 ***ulx, *ulq** to be dizzy, silly, foolish, mischievous, criminal: **ulxanm** to faint, **ul7ulxanm** to keep fainting, **ulxanmus** to be drunk, **ulxusi** to be slightly intoxicated, **ulxliwa, u(7)lqliwa** crazy, silly, stupid, **tam7ulx** (tr.) to fool, cheat somebody, **tam7ulqliwa** (tr.) to make a fool out of somebody, **Ulx** a dance

ulx (tr./itr.) to steal (something): **ulxayc ti+slq's tc** his mind has been stolen, **nus7ulxmc** to be given to stealing, **ulxiixw** (tr.) to steal somebody's hat, **ulxiixwlhtinits+ma c+ta+qaytlhts** somebody must have stolen my hat, **nu7ulxuts** (tr.) to steal somebody's food, **ulxalstn** (tr.) to rob somebody

1904 **ulxlh** (to be) going up the river (23.6.1, 29.2.2.1): **tl'apaw ulxlh** or **ulxlhaw** they went up the river

1905 **um** to get off, disembark (car, boat, airplane): **umtu-** to let somebody off a car or boat, **umalulhtu-** to unload a boat, **nu7umiktu-** to remove something from a box, **Nu7umuutsi** a geographical name

1906 **umat** where something (somebody) is taken (going) to (23.6.1): **ula+ 7umataw+tsk** wherever they are going to, **k'ilh7umatliwa** not knowing where to go, **tu+7umatstus tu+ways+txw** the place he had taken the cohoes to, **umatulmc** beams supporting the floor, girders, **umatalaalh** threshold

1907 **Umc7it** a man's name

1908 **Umtl'um** Deep Bay (south of **Scwacwilk**)

1909 **Umq'umklika** a man's name

1910   ***un** (tr.) to subject something to strain, pressure: **anu7unlaycts** I am in a rush to eat, **unaakm** to stretch out one's hands with the palms turned up, **nu7unaakm** to train, exercise, **nunu7untsut** to exercise oneself

1911   **un–** to have a predilection for, be fond of (23.2)

1912   **un–** waist, middle, small of back (23.3)

1913   **unikw, unnikw** towards the west: **k'c unikw** he looked towards the west, **unikwlhaw** they are from the west, **Unikwak** a man's name, **Unikulh** a man's name

1914   **unus(i)–...–m** to go somewhere with a purpose (23.2)

1915   **upk** (tr.) to send, dispatch something: **upkamk** (tr.) to go to the post office and mail something out

1916   **uqw'** to drift downstream (23.6.1)

1917   ***uqw'm = q'um**

1918   ***uqw'p = q'up**

1919   **Uqw'smay** a mythical woman's name

1920   **Uqw'wani** name of a mountain

1921   **uq'al** cinquefoil roots: **uq'q'allhp** cinquefoil plant, **uq'q'aliixw** cinquefoil leaves

1922   **uq'uuni** throat

1923   **uq'x** (tr.) (see 1175)

1924   ***us** directional basis (23.6.1): **usutsaaxam** to go under the house, **usaqw'sam** to dive to the bottom of the river

1925   **us–** to long for, crave (23.2)

1926   **us–** top surface, **us–...–uuts** surface of liquid (23.6.2)

1927   **us–...–aax** buttocks (23.3)

1928   **us–...–am** to don, put on (23.2)

1929   **–us, –uus** surface, outer appearance: face, looks (20.2.1); cover, blanket (20.3.1): **putl'us** one's face emerges from the water, **mukusm** to paint one's face red, **alhtcutl'uk'us** to lie face up, **makwtl'uusinaw** they look alike, **tqnkus ala+7its'amni+ts** he is under the blan–

kets, **tapus** (tr.) to spread out a blanket

-us-als cheek (20.3.1): **sp'usalsayc** to have been hit on the cheek

-us-ilh private parts: **uts'usilh** region above private parts

1930 **usmacmiksm** fat has come to the surface, is floating on top (of jarred fish)

1931 **Usnaaxwlh** name of a creek

1932 **usp'us** lungs

1933 **usqa**, ***usqn** (to be) going outside (23.6.1, 29.2.2.1): **tl'apaw usqa** or **usqanaw** they went out, **usqatu-** to let somebody out, **alh7usqayxw-alh** to have turned-out feet, **usqalits'** to have smallpox, **nu7usqa** to give birth, **nu7usqnamkim** he was born, **nu7usqatnm** to be a midwife, **snu7usqaalhi** newborn baby

1934 **ustam⧾ks?** where is he going? (23.6.1, 25.5)

1935 **ustcw** (to be) going inside (23.6.1, 29.2.2.1): **tl'apaw ustcw** or **ustcwaw** they went in, **ustcwtu-** to let somebody in, **ustcwayc** to have come in, **nu7ustcwmtinilh c⧾a⧾7an7aq'ulikw** the police entered our house, **alh7ustcwiixwalh** to have pigeon feet

1936 **usukw'lt** blackcap berry: **usukw'ltlh** blackcap berry jam, **usukw'ltlhp** blackcap berry bush

1937 **usxlh** (tr.) to bring out, produce, exhibit something: **un7usxlh** to always show off

1938 **utl'uk'** upwards (23.6.1, 29.2.2): **k'cx utl'uk'!** look up!

1939 **utqwntl'** = **tqwntl'**

1940 **-uts**, **-uuts** orifice: oral, mouth, speech, eating, food (20.2.1, 20.5.1); rim (knife), beach, tide, ocean, river, water (20.5.1): **tsputsm** to wipe one's mouth, **squputs** beard, whiskers, **anupusmuuts** to have a swollen mouth, **anuputl'uts** water is coming out of one's mouth, **alhnaputstsant** they know what I said, **numilcuts** to become increasingly talkative; channel opens up, **malhuts** to eat slowly, **tcutsta** table knife, **mntcu(u)tsta** dipping cup, **q'puts** dull knife, **k'apatuts** sharp knife, **kulhuuts** beach, shore, **statputs**, **ilhmuuts** steep shore, **sts'ixuts** sandbar in sea, **putl'uuts** river rises, **tcul-atl'suuts** tide comes in, **t'qmuuts** high tide, **p'atsuuts** drop-off in sea, **tpyuts** other side of river, **snupapntuuts** bubbles in water, **us-pik'uuts** water surface is shiny, reflects the sunlight

nu-...-uts flat layer (20.3.1); weather (20.3.1); door (20.4.1.1, 20.5.1): **nu7lpluutsi** thin(ly) layer(ed), **nuplhtuts ti+st'cwᶄcwm+tc** the mattress is thick, **nusk'luts** weather is cold, **nukwluts** weather is warm, **numyuuts ti+numutsta+tc** the door is open, **nuqwyuts** (tr.) to open the door, **nuq'ilhutsa** to be scratching at the door

nu-...-uts-aax under house or floor (20.3.1); buttocks (20.2.1): **nulhtnutsaaxta** housepost, **asutsaax** to be under the house, **usutsaax-am** to go under the house, **asutsaaq** buttocks, **nukᶇkmayutsaaq** one's buttocks are hurting

-uts-ak forearm (20.2.1): **skulhutsak** forearm, **squplhutsak** hair on forearm, **tcutsakaycts** my forearm is cut

-uts-alh lower leg (20.2.1): **stputsalh** having a freckle on one's lower leg

(nu-...)-uuts-almc nipple (20.2.1): **stl'kuutsalmc** nipple, **nukmay-uutsalmcts** my nipple hurts

-uuts-layc nipple (20.2.1): **skulhuutslayc** nipple

1941 **utsi(i)** having a certain (limited) size, having reached a limit: **utsii c+t'axw** that is all, the end (of a story), **utsinaw+tuu c+a+wats'+ts** they have exactly the same size as dogs, **utsitimutiinaw s7issutaw** they are rowing at full capacity

1942 **⁺uts'** top, upper: **uts'alulh** mountain top, **uts'aak** top surface of leaf, **uts'aax** small of back, **uts'ik** table top, **uts'ikaaxuts** upper lip, **uts'ikalh** shin, **uts'usilh** region above private parts

1943 **ut'ak** to vomit: **alh7ut'akalus** to want to vomit

1944 **ut'ikalh** instep, flap of moccasin

1945 **ut'itk** third oldest sibling

1946 **ut'p** rotten wood: **ut'plc** wood is starting to rot

1947 **ut'pi(i)** widgeon

1948 **Ut'u7wa** a man's name

1949 **-uulh = -ulh**

1950 **-uulhla = -ulhla**

1951 **uuqwat = huuqwat**

1952 **-uus = -us**

1953 **-uuts = -uts**

1954 **uuxi** to display jealousy towards one's younger sibling

1955 **uuxnk** downwards (23.6.1, 29.2.2): **tl'apaw uuxnk** they went down, **uuxnki** a little further down

1956 ***uxw** (tr.) to cause something to come down: **uxwayc** to come down, descend, **uxwilh** (tr.) to pull somebody's pants down, **uxwilhayc** his pants have come down, **uxwm** to have a miscarriage

1957 **Uy(7)yu** a man's name

W

1958 **wa+** indefinite article, close pl. (15.1)

1959 **wa+ks?, wal+...?** who is it? (25.5, 25.5.1, 25.5.4, 25.5.5): **wa(1)ts +7iks?** who am I?, **walnaw+7isuks?** who are they then?, **alhk'yuktsant swats** they know who I am, **walh+7iks?** whose is it?, **ti+ka+wa c+7inu** somebody like you

1960 **Waakas** a chief's name

1961 **waats** clock: **waatsaaqakta** wrist watch

1962 **Wacwwas** a village at Kwatna Inlet

1963 **wakayak** to overdo: **wakayakiilhnu+ma** you may have overdone it

1964 **wal** (tr.) to leave somebody: **alhwaltuminu** I am leaving you behind, **nûalalhtsinu** I am falling behind you, cannot keep up with you, **alh-**

walm to bequeath, **Siwalusim** "where the canoes were left" = a geographical name

1965 **wal+...?** = **wa+ks?**

1966 **walasya** lynx: **walaasyayi** dim.

1967 **waltstum+ks?** = **watstum+ks?**

1968 ***wan** to miss, be late: **wañcwits ti+mntalhts+alu** I missed my transport, **wannmc** to miss, be late for a meal

1969 **Wanqlhh** the name of a Kitlope woman

1970 **Wanukw** Rivers Inlet

1971 **wapat** (tr.) to turn something sideways, cause to be transverse: **anûapatilh** having a transverse vagina (said about Japanese women), **alhwapattsut ala+sxitsta+ts** he is lying across the bed, **icwappattsut** to constantly turn one's head, look to and fro (as birds do), **wapataaxta** drying frame

1972 **Wasila** a man's name

1973 **wastu+** and so (28.2.3): **wastu+7alh7ay+tuya** and so he was really like that, you see, **wastu+7alh7ay+kwtuya ti+ts'xw alh+tu+7asiixw** and so it is said that there was a white thing near the smokevent, you see

1974 **Watcii** a man's name

1975 **watstum+ks?, waltstum+ks?** what is his name? (25.5, 25.5.4): **wa(l)-tstumt+7iks?** what is your name?, **watstutim+ks wa+7alhpus+7ats ala+ tsalh+7ats?** what does one call these plants that grow around the lakes?

1976 **wats', *wnts'** dog: **wᴧwnts'i** dim., **snûats'ams** eyetooth, **snûats'** butterball duck, **Snûats'** name of a little creek

1977 **Wawalis** the name of a famous shaman

1978 **wawslc** jumpy, skittish, nervous: **Wawsaqw'slayc** a man's name

1979 **Waxit** a personal name

1980 **waxtsya** cape, garment; corona around the moon

1981 **waxwaxtsya** great-grandchildren

1982 **way!**, **wii!** well!, okay!, now then! (29.4): **way ustcwnu!** come on in!, **way∓7isu!**, **way+nisu!** repeat it!, **waynaw+7isu!**, **waynaw+nisu!** repeat it, folks!, **way∓7ilhú!** wait a while!, **waynaw+7ilhú** wait a while, folks! (28.3.20.2, 28.3.20.3), **waylit** to agree, consent, **waylitmtsinu** I agree with you, you have my permission

1983 **wayc** new, recent: **wayclh** to be a newcomer, **nûayclh** fresh (food), **waycis+kw s7atmas ta+tl'msta+tx** they say that the man had recently died, **ala+waycii scwpakmis** he finally let him go

1984 **Waylhmkilakw** a man's name

1985 **ways** coho salmon: **wawiisi** dim., **waystam** coho season, **nûaysaax** Coho Creek

1986 **wi-** bound pl. article (16.4.4, 25.3, 25.5.2)

1987 **wic** pl. identifier (25.3): **wic s...** because ..., **wic txw s...** that is when ..., **wic ts si...** that is why ... (25.3.2)

1988 **wii = way**

1989 ***wiiq**, ***wiix** (tr.) to pry something open: **wiiqamsa** to be prying traps open, **nûiixalhhm** to open one's mouth wide, **nûiixuts** (tr.) to pry somebody's mouth open, **nûiixakayc** one's hand has been pried open

1990 **Wiiqa7ay** a personal name

1991 **wiisxw!** = **wisxw!**

1992 ***wiix** = ***wiiq**

1993 **wika(1)+ks?** where is it? (25.5.2, 25.5.4, 25.5.5): **wika+ks wa+tc-amatlhhnu?**, **wikalhhnu+ks?** where are you from?, **wika+ks wa+tcamat-lhhalhnu?**, **wikalhhalhnu+ks?** where did you come from?, **wika+ks si-tl'apamkicw?** where did you obtain it?, **ala+wika(1)** somewhere

1994 **Wikat** a legendary man's name

1995 **wik'** (tr.) to cut wood into shingles: **nûik'uts** to have chapped lips

1996 ***wik'** (tr.) to shake, wiggle something back and forth, cause something to squeak rhythmically: **nûik'utstx!** shake the door!, **alhwik'm** it is shaking, squeaking, **alhwik'miiqw** tree is shaking back and forth, **alhwik'mtimut, alhwik'tsut** to rock back and forth, **nûik'aax** to wiggle one's posterior

1997 **Wik'inxw** Oweekano, Rivers Inlet native(s)

1998 **wilc** to have something in one's way, be obstructed: **alhwilcts alh⁺ t'ayc** this is pressing against me, **nûilcalhts** I feel something under my foot

1999 **Wilhpun** a woman's name

2000 **wilhwilh** mica

2001 **win** (tr.), **wina** (itr.) to wage war against a community: **wintmacwaw** they are waging war against each other

2002 ***win** (tr.) to poke, skewer something: **winwin** (tr.) to dig for clover roots, **winaaxit wa⁺7alh7ikwit⁺7ats** they skewer their barbecue

2003 **winusm** to lower one's face, bend over: **winusmaylayc** to fall forward

2004 **winwints** sandpiper

2005 **Wismkilakw** daughter-in-law of **Smawn**

2006 **wisxw!, wísxw!, wiisxw!** yes indeed! (29.4)

2007 **witl'ax** horn, antler

2008 **Wits'lks** a man's name

2009 **Wit'aalaw** name of a Kimsquit man

2010 **wl** (tr.), **wla** (itr.) to pour, spill a liquid: **wlaax** (tr.) to pour a liquid, **alhwlalh** it is raining, **alhwlalhmtinilh** we are having rain, **nuswlaasta** kitchen sink, **swlwlaax** big waves, swells, **kuŝwlwlaax** there are many swells

2011 **wĺwlkatsut** to limp

2012 **wlxlha** lame

2013 **wnts'** (tr.), **wnts'm** (itr.) to beat (to death), kill somebody: **ta⁺ 7alhwnts's⁺tx** the one he killed, **nûnts'ikmim** somebody wanted to kill him, **wńwnts'm** to be in a killing mood, **alhwnts'tnm** murderer

2014 ***wnts' = wats'**

2015 **wnts'lht** (tr./itr.) to fish for halibut

X

2016 -**x** sg. imperative (14.2.4, 14.3.1.1, 14.4.1.1)

2017 **xaatcsya** to sneeze: **xanxaatcsya** to sneeze repeatedly

2018 **Xa7isla** Haisla, Kitimat people

2019 **xala** lady fern, spiny wood fern, sword fern: **xaaxlay** dim., **Xala** a man's name

2020 **Xalika** a man's name

2021 ***xam** insulted: **xamnimut** to feel insulted, **xamnmacw** to insult each other

2022 **xamlayc** one's eyesight is returning

2023 **xamlc** to be stuck, not moving (away from): **alhxamlcnu alh+Nuxalk** you will never leave Bella Coola, **xamxamlctu-** to make somebody stay with oneself, **xamlcaqw's** to stay in bed; to die in one's sleep

2024 **xamu** (tr.), **xamwa** (itr.) to dip something out of a container

2025 **xapa, *xapn** (tr.) to pack, carry something: **xapayalhta** packstrap, **nusxapaasta** knapsack, **xapnamktsut** to mount a horse, **alhxapaliikw** horse, **as7alhxapaliikw** to travel on horseback

2026 ***xaq'akw** protruding horizontally: **alhxaq'akw** tree having many short lower branches, **anuxaq'akwalh** series of lower branches that have been trimmed so as to form a flight of stairs

2027 **xaq'ants** crane, great blue heron

2028 **Xatii** a man's name

2029 **xawis** galvanized, tin, metal: **xawisaalh** metal spoon, **xawisals** tin can, **xawisaltwa** the sky is tin-colored, grey, **Xawisus** a man's name

2030 **xaw7li** large mussel

2031 **Xawxawaalis** a geographical name

2032 **xaxaq'** goose: **xaxaaq'i** dim.

2033 **xayaq'a, *xayaq'n** barnacle: **xayaq'nanlh** mythical house made of barnacles

2034   **xayulh** west wind

2035   **xi** (tr.), **xya** (itr.) to peek through a hole at somebody: **alhxitits** I am peeking at them, **alhxyanaw** they are busy peeking, **alhxyaynicis** he caught a glimpse of him

2036   ***xi** to be visible, shine, (be) light, bright: **nuxi** light, bright, **nuxyals** it is bright in the house, **nuxyakta, snuxyak** torch, lantern, flashlight, **sinuxi** lamp; window, **sinuxyalsilh** window, **nusxyals** cataract of the eye, **xilcus** to emerge from a hole or forest, **xilcustimut** to stick up one's head from behind something, **Snuxyaltwa** a chief's name

      xim early daylight, dawn: **xiximi** dim., **sxim** daybreak, **ximuts** to bloom, blossom, **sximuts** blossom, flower, **sxiximuuts** flowers, **sxiximuutslh** picked flowers, bouquet, **Anuxim** a chief's name, **Anuximalus** a man's name, **S7anuximaqw's** a man's name, **Nunuximtimut** a woman's name, **Alhximlayc** a personal name, **Ximximana** a woman's name, **Anuximana** a woman's name, **Nuximalhlayc** a woman's name, **Sinuximalh** a woman's name, **Nuximaksta** a woman's name, **Alhximik** a woman's name, **Ximtswa** a woman's name, **Ximximikuutslayc** a woman's name

2037   **xiku** = **qiku**

2038   **Xila** a woman's name

2039   **xilaax** (tr.) to tilt a boat: **alhxilaaxtu-** = **xilaax, xixlaax** boat is unsteady, "tippy"

2040   **xilh** to be frequent, be or do something often: **xilhalh** to go often, **xilhak** to do something often, **ala+xilh wa+malacw** for many a year

2041   **-xin** formative suffix (22.3)

2042   **xitl'** lean, skinny: **xitl'anaats** very skinny, **xinxitl'alh** having thin legs, **xitl'aaxuts** tea or coffee has no sugar in it

2043   **xits'** raw: **isxiixts'** to eat something raw

2044   **xits'** metal axe: **xits'lh** iron, **xixts'uulh** coins

2045   **Xixays** Carrier native(s) from the vicinity of Ootsa Lake

2046   **xixi** marten: **xiixî** dim.

2047 **xl** to be sent, directed: **x𝑰xl** messenger, **xltu-** to send somebody, **sx𝑰xltcw** postillon d'amour, **xlaktum ska+...** he was told to ...

2048 **xlamanta** animal's den

2049 **xlh** to lack, be deprived: **alhxlh** widow in mourning, **xlhalhh** hungry

2050 **xlq'** (tr.) to cause something to go around or across something: **xlq'iixw** (tr.) to turn something around, **xlq'aaxm** to go across a road or body of water

2051 **xm** (tr.), **xma** (itr.) to bite something

2052 **xm** dead, decayed: **xmaaxuts** dead vegetation, rotten trees, **xmlc** tree is decaying (lying on the ground), **xmlciixwlayc** one's knees are "dead", feeling numb

2053 **xmxmaatslh** minnow

2054 **xnk** (see **uuxnk**)

2055 **Xnulh7a** name of a witch doctor

2056 **xp'** (tr.) to permeate, penetrate something: **(alh)xp'** permeated with water, saturated, soaked, **alhxp'aqw's** to penetrate with one's eyes, see through, discern, **anuxp'ik stsitumas** he is sound asleep

2057 **xs** fat: **sxs** fat, grease, **xsaaxutsm** to apply grease or vaseline to one's beard, **xsalh** "precipitation is fat" = it is raining heavily, **xsalhmtinilh** it is raining heavily in our area, **xsaaxuts** drink is very sweet

2058 **xsasa** salmon roe on a skein: **nuxsasa** it has roe inside, it is a female fish, **xsaasay** stonecrop

2059 **xt** brittle: **xtlc** to become brittle, wither

2060 **xtl'** to be half, incomplete, defective, faulty: **xtl'** (tr.) to find fault with, chide, reprimand somebody, **xtl'uuts** (tr.) to criticize somebody for what he has said, **anuxtl'ikm** (tr.) to be dissatisfied with somebody

nuxtl' to make a mistake: **nuxtl'uts** to make a speech error, **nuxtl'amktsut** to have made a mistake, be in trouble, **icnuxtl'liwa** to continually make mistakes

nuxtl'ikayc to be halfway through: **nuxtl'ikayc ti+tl'uk'** it is half moon, **nuxtl'ikayc ti+7amlh** half a summer has elapsed

2061 **xts'a, qts'a** stick, rod: **xts'ats'ay** sapling, young tree, **asqts'ayak** to hold a stick in one's hand

2062 **xts'a, qts'a** little furry thing: catkin, pussy willow; chipmunk

2063 **xts'us = qts'us**

2064 **xul** (tr.) to push or press something down: **xulalulh** (tr.) to launch a boat, **xulayc** to have been launched; to return to the spouse one has deserted, **xuxulusm** to buck the wind, **nuxuliixwakm** (tr.) to cause a person's health to deteriorate, **nuxuliixutsm** (tr.) to say negative things about somebody, **xulikit+ts' tu+sulhaw+txw** now they pushed it off the roof of their house, **xultsut** to push off, commence a boat trip, **nuxulaaxtsut = xultsut**, **nuxuluulh** (tr.) to fold a corpse down into a semi-cubic coffin

2065 **xulxulis** spring tide (? "it pushes (it) back"): **xulaaxmis** the tide is going up

2066 ***xum** to flow, stream: **xumaqw's** one's tears are running, **sxumaqw's** tears, **nuxumtu-** to make water run, **anuxum** stream, river, **anuxuuxumi** creek, **anuxumikiixw** to have a running nose, **anuxuxumiiklayc** to have gonorrhoea

2067 **xup** (tr.), **xupa** (itr.) to insert something; to cook something in an oven: **alhxuplh** oven-baked, roasted (food), **is7alhxuplh** to eat something roasted, **alhxuptnm** to have a roast in the oven, **xupats c+a+ kusi** I am roasting potatoes, **nusxuupsta** cooky sheet, **xuplqsak** (tr.) to put a ring on somebody's finger, **xupm** to get stuck in, sink into mud

2068 **xuq'** (tr.), **xuq'a** (itr.) to rasp, file something: **xuq'ta** file, **xuq'aalhta** rasp, **xuq'uts** (tr.) to file, sharpen a blade

2069 **Xuq'ulhis** a man's name

2070 **xuta** dipnet: **xutam** to fish with a dipnet

2071 **xuts** (tr.), **xutsa** (itr.) to soak something in water, soften, make pliable: **xutsm** to soak dried fish in water, **xutsalhm** to put one's feet into the water, wade, **xutslc** to become soft, pliable, **xutslc-anlh** clothes get soft, "broken in", **xunxutslqs** "dipped tip" = crown pen, writing pen, **xuuxwtsi** supple, bending readily, **xuuxwtsliwa** lithe, flexible (person), **xuxutsi** young mountain goat

2072 **xwalt** to snore: **nusxwaltmc** snoring habitually

2073 **xwaxwi** eggs of housefly

2074 **xway** to melt

xwalc (/xway⌃lc/) = **xway**: **xwalctu-** to melt something, **xwalxwalc** solder

2075 **xwiita** (tr./itr.) to eat eulachon flesh

2076 ***xwiits** = ***xwits**

2077 **xwiixn** a type of box

2078 **xwiq'm** to grate, creak, squeak: **xwiq'miilh** door creaks, squeaks, **anuxwixwqw'mikiiqwalits** to grind one's teeth

2079 ***xwis** fun, pleasure, play: **sxwis** game, **xwism** to play, joke, **xwism** (tr.) to make fun of somebody, **xwismuutsm** (tr.) to give somebody a nickname, **xwisxwismuuts** to be saying funny things, joking, **sxwis-xwismuuts ŝkwatstas** it is a nickname, **sixwis(m)ak** toy

2080 ***xwits**, ***xwiits** (tr.) to shake something: **alhxwitstsut** to shake oneself, **alhxwitsakm** to shake one's hands, **sxwits** dance, **xwiitsana** restless, playful, **Anuxwitsakm̲layc** a personal name

2081 ***xwlh** (tr.) to cross a barrier, press into, pass (through), surpass, exceed something: **xwlhtsut** to press on, keep going, **ays+ts' c+txw sxwlhaycs** at that moment he had already moved past, **alhxwlh-(iiqw)is+ts' alh+ti+suncwt snusk'lutss** today it is much colder, **alhxwlhiiqwis ti+tl'msta+tc ulh+ti+ŝc** "the man is going deeper and deeper into badness" = the man is becoming increasingly evil, **anayk ska+xwlhikuutsalhms ulh+tu+taqw'lh+tski+t'axw** he wanted to travel further down that river, it appears

2082 **xwlhtn** (tr.), **xwlhtna** (itr.) to brace something

2083   **xwɫxwluulhi** stocky, short (person): **sxwluulhi = xwɫxwluulhi**

2084   **xwꞥxwnm** hummingbird: **xwꞥxwn<u>m</u>i** dim., **xwꞥxwnmulh** hummingbird's egg

2085   **xws** (tr.) to oil, grease, lubricate something: **alhxws** oiled, lubricated, **xwsta** ointment, oil, **xwsuulhutsta** butter

2086   **xwsanim** a game (now obsolete)

2087   ***xwtn** (tr.) to hold something open: **xwtnutsta** sail pole, **(nu)xwtnusta** frame made of sticks used for drying salmon, **nuxwtnutsta** stick used to open eulachon net

Y

2088   **-y = -i(i)**

2089   **ya** good: **kanusyam** to have a good flavor, be sweet, **yalc** to recuperate, get well, **yalcnic** (tr.) to cure somebody, **yalcnimut** to cure oneself, **yalctnm** to be a healer, **yalayc** to be lucky, successful, **yalculh ti+tl'uk'** it is full moon, **nuyalcikta** object from which one derives pleasure, **nuyalciktutim c+ti+qiqti+tc** they enjoy the child, **nuya ti+qla** water is clear, **yalikt** to have a good personality, **yanimut** to boast, **7yanimut** to observe chastity, abstinence, **yanic** (tr.) to like something or somebody, **yayxuts** to be talkative, **nuyayanlh** generous, **yayaqw's** to have good eyesight; brightly colored, **yayaliwa** to be in good physical shape, **yayatsuti** to go easy, take one's time, **nuyayalsuts** to have a strong voice, **nuyayulhalxi** to be balanced, have equilibrium, **yayulhlamim ska+...** he is allowed to ..., **usya** to have a smooth top (surface), **usyayik, usyayayk** to have a smooth upper surface, **usyayayc** to have a good spouse, **usyayak tsi+cnass** he has a good wife, **Yayuulhus** a location at Kimsquit characterized by the presence of small pretty pebbles

2090 **+ya** you know, eh?, right? (28.3.15, 28.3.24)

2091 **yacw** (tr.) to approach, call somebody's attention: to wake somebody up; to ask somebody a favor or offer employment: **nuyacwtsinu** I ask you a favor, **anuyacw** hired, employed

2092 **yacwm7maylh** old female sealion

2093 **Ya7is** a bay situated southwest of **Nuk'lat**

2094 **yaki** mountain goat: **yacyaakî** dim., **yakîixw** mountain goat's head, **yakyanlh** blanket made of mountain goat fur, **yakyaalh** spoon made of goat's horn

2095 **Yalaclhay** Goose Island

2096 ***yalh7ay** possibility, opportunity, availability: **yalh7ayakmitsut** to succeed, manage to get something done, **axw ti+ka+yalh7ayakmits ska+ nitsmnicits** I do not have the means to revive him, **clhyalh7ayliwa** to have the time to do something, **snuyalh7ay** guts, intestines **yalh7ay** (tr.) to pledge, give somebody in marriage: **yalh7aytinits ulh+ta+kwtmtsts+tx** I was given to my husband in marriage, ours is an arranged marriage

2097 **yalhkayc** to be overly ..., too much: **yalhkayc t'ayc st'ss** this is too salty, **yalhkutsayc** to overeat, **nuyalhkiikaylayc** to accidentally add too much water to food

2098 **yalit, yallit** to be (a) brave

2099 **yallak** to be sleepy

2100 **yalli** to be a good swimmer

2101 **yallit** = **yalit**

2102 ***yalq, *yalx** round, circular, spherical: **nuyalqaaq** bowl, **nuyalqiilh** hoop, **yalqiilhm** ring-throwing (game), **yalquulh** ball, sphere, **anu- yalx** to be round, **nuyalxmtu-** to arrange objects in a circle, **yalxus** (tr.) to loop a rope, **anuyalxus ti+tpiksta** it is a round drying frame, **yalxutsayc** to have gone around the world, **yalxalhm** (tr.) to circle, walk around somebody, **yalquulhla** (tr.) = **yalxalhm**

2103 ***yamlh** music, singing: **nuyamlh** to sing, **nuyamlhik** to want to sing;

(recorded) music, record, **nuyamlhiknm** to play a record or musical instrument, **nuyamlhalsim c+a+tsitstsipii** birds are singing in his house, **nuyamlhusits+lu** I am still singing a lullaby to him, **nunuyamlh** (to be a) singer, **nusyamlh** (to be a) habitual or professional singer, **nunusyamlh** a group of professional singers, choir, **k'iŝyamlh** to lack singing talent, **yayuuts ti+snuyamlh** he is good at singing

2104 **(7)yanahu** turnip: **7yanahwi** dim., **nu7yanahuuta** turnip bed

2105 **yank** to pole a boat: **yanyanklaycm** to be poling clumsily, **Yanklayc** a man's name

2106 **yants** driftwood: **yayntsi** dim., **yantsanlh wa+sulh** it is a house made of driftwood, **snuyantsaqw's** watersnail, **Nuyants** location east of **Putsla**

2107 ***yaqas** round: **yaqasuulh** ball (a Kimsquit word), **yaqasuulhm** to play with a ball, **yaqasiilh** hoop

2108 **Yaqulhlas** a man's name

2109 **Yaqwla** a personal name

2110 **yatn** rattle

2111 **Yatsalt** name of a female chief

2112 **yaw!** hi!, hello! (29.4)

2113 **Yaxasila** a personal name

2114 **yaxat** (tr.) to ridicule somebody: **Yaxat** a man's name

2115 **Yaxlhn** a man's name

2116 ***yaxw** to be allowed, have permission: **yaxwnictsinu ska+tl'apnu** I allow you to go, **axw alhyaxwnicim ska+7usqas** he is not allowed to go out, **axw yaxwnimutmim c+tx** he was not allowed by him (to ...), **yaxwnimutnicis ska+...** he agreed to ...

2117 **yayaasi(i)** to be pretty, handsome

2118 **yayaatwi(i)** happy: **yayaatwamktsuti** to be happy about oneself, to enjoy oneself, **ik'axw yayaatwis ska+7alhpss** he does not like to eat

2119 **yayax** small type of horn played in **kuŝyut** dance: **yayaxi** toy, **tam-**

yayaxiitu- to make a toy for somebody, **yayaxm** (tr.) to make fun of, make a fool out of somebody

2120 **Yayaxtsi** a man's name

2121 **-yi** = **-i(i)**

2122 ***ynuc** bound allomorph of **inacw** (23.7)

2123 ***yul** (tr.) to turn, rotate, roll something: **yulm** to walk in a circle, around something; to return from the dead, be reincarnated, **alhyulmlh** having returned from the dead, reincarnated, **nuyulmaax** to return to point of departure, **alhyulaaktmacwm** (tr.) to roll something between one's hands

yul (tr.) to stir, rub, stroke something: **yulakm** to stir soapberries, **yulaakm** to rub one's hands, **yulapsm** (tr.) to rub or stroke somebody's neck, **yululhik** (tr.) to rub or stroke somebody's back, **yulyulm** to start a fire with a firedrill or by rubbing sticks, **yulmta** firedrill, **Yulyulmlh** a mountain west of Kimsquit

2124 **Yulatimut** a man's name

2125 **Yulkwmay** a woman's name

2126 **yum** shy, ashamed: **yumyum** = **yum**, **yumnictss** he made me feel ashamed

2127 **yumalcw** to be sour: **yumalcwlhp** sourgrass, sheep sorrel

2128 ***yup** (tr.) to move (over), make room for somebody: **yupalhtsx!** get out of my way!, **yupaaxtsx!** get out of my chair!, **yuupalh** to start dancing, **Yuyupaaxani** a location south of Sit'xt

2129 **yup'alcw** to arrive at a point of land: **syup'alcw** point of land

2130 **yutlc** to get used to something: **yutlcnic** (tr.) to let somebody get used to something

2131 **yuyucw** bracelet

* * * *

Canadian Museum of Civilization	Musée canadien des civilisations
Canadian Ethnology Service	Service canadien d'Ethnologie
Gratis	Gratuit

The following Canadian Ethnology Service papers are available from:

On peut obtenir les dossiers suivants du Service canadien d'Ethnologie de:

Publications	Publications
Canadian Ethnology Service	Service canadien d'Ethnologie
Canadian Museum of Civilization	Musée canadien des civilisations
100 Laurier Street	100, rue Laurier
P.O. Box 3100, Station B	C.P. 3100, Succursale B
Hull, Québec	Hull (Québec)
J8X 4H2	J8X 4H2
Canada	Canada

1   PRELIMINARY STUDY OF TRADITIONAL KUTCHIN CLOTHING by Judy Thompson (1972). 92 pages.

2   SARCEE VERB PARADIGMS by Eung-Do Cook (1972). 51 pages.

3   GAMBLING MUSIC OF THE COAST SALISH INDIANS by Wendy Boss Stuart (1972). 114 pages.

6   INKONZE. Magico Religious Beliefs of Contact-Traditional Chipewyan at Fort Resolution, N.W.T. by David Merrill Smith (1973). 21 pages.

7   THE MIDDLE GROUND: Social Change in an Arctic Community, 1967-71 by Joel S. Savishinsky and Susan B. Frimmer (1973). 54 pages, 1 map, 2 figures, 2 tables.

10   PAPERS IN LINGUISTICS FROM 1972 CONFERENCE ON IROQUOIAN RESEARCH, ed. by M.K. Foster (1974). 118 pages.

11   MUSEOCINEMATOGRAPHY: Ethnographic Film Programs of the National Museum of Man, 1913-73 by D.W. Zimmerly (1974). 103 pages, 22 figures.

13   RIDING ON THE FRONTIERS CREST: Mahican Indian Culture and Culture Change by T.J. Brasser (1974). 91 pages, 5 plates, 1 map.

16   AN EVALUATIVE ETHNO-HISTORICAL BIBLIOGRAPHY OF THE MALECITE INDIANS by M. Harrison (1974). 260 pages.

17   PROCEEDINGS OF THE FIRST CONGRESS OF THE CANADIAN ETHNOLOGY SOCIETY ed. by J.H. Barkow (1974). 226 pages.

18   KOYUKUK RIVER CULTURE by A. McFadyen Clark (1974). 282 pages, 5 maps.

23   PAPERS OF THE SIXTH ALGONQUIAN CONFERENCE, 1974 ed. by W. Cowan (1975).
       399 pages.

26   A PLACE OF REFUGE FOR ALL TIME: Migration of the American Potawatomi into
       Upper Canada 1830-50 by J.A. Clifton (1975). 152 pages, 3 maps, 7 plates.

42   A PRACTICAL DICTIONARY OF THE COAST TSIMSHIAN LANGUAGE by John Asher Dunn
       (1978). 155 pages.

66   THE INUIT LANGUAGE IN SOUTHERN LABRADOR FROM 1694 TO 1785/LA LANGUE INUIT AU
       SUD DU LABRADOR DE 1694 À 1785 by/par Louis-Jacques Dorais (1980). 56 pages,
       1 map/1 carte.

70   ANALYSE LINGUISTIQUE ET ETHNOCENTRISME: Essai sur la structure du mot en
       Inuktitut par Ronald Lowe (1981).

79   MUSICAL TRADITIONS OF THE LABRADOR COAST INUIT by Maija M. Lutz (1982).
       89 pages, 2 maps, 1 table.

80   NORTH-WEST RIVER (SHESHATSHIT) MONTAGNAIS: A Grammatical Sketch by Sandra
       Clarke (1982). 185 pages.

81   MOOSE-DEER ISLAND HOUSE PEOPLE: A History of the Native People of Fort
       Resolution by David M. Smith (1982). 202 pages, 1 table, 3 figures, 10 maps.

82   MUSIC OF THE NETSILIK ESKIMO: A Study of Stability and Change, Volumes I and
       II by Beverly Cavanagh (1982). 570 pages, 16 figures, 10 plates, 1 vinyl
       record.

84   OOWEKEENO ORAL TRADITIONS: As Told by the Late Chief Simon Walkus Sr.
       Transcribed and translated by Evelyn Walkus Windsor. Edited by Susanne
       Hilton and John Rath (1982). 223 pages, 2 maps.

86   THE MUSICAL LIFE OF THE BLOOD INDIANS by Robert Witmer (1982). 185 pages.

87   THE STOLEN WOMAN: Female Journeys in Tagish and Tutchone Narratives by Julie
       Cruikshank (1982). 131 pages.

88   AN ETHNOHISTORIC STUDY OF EASTERN JAMES BAY CREE SOCIAL ORGANIZATION, 1700-
       1850 by Toby Morantz (1983). 199 pages, 6 tables, 4 maps.

89E   CONSCIOUSNESS AND INQUIRY: Ethnology and Canadian Realities. Edited by
       Frank Manning (1983). 365 pages.

89F   CONSCIENCE ET ENQUÊTE: L'ethnologie des réalitiés canadiennes. Marc-Adélard
       Tremblay, rédacteur (1983). 407 pages.

90   AN OJIBWA LEXICON. Edited by G.L. Piggott and A. Grafstein (1983).
       377 pages.

91   MICMAC LEXICON by Albert D. DeBlois and Alphonse Metallic (1983). 392 pages.

92   THE BELLA COOLA LANGUAGE by H.F. Nater (1983). 170 pages.

93   COAST SALISH GAMBLING GAMES by Lynn Maranda (1984). 143 pages.

96   BEAR LAKE ATHAPASKAN KINSHIP AND TASK GROUP FORMATION by Scott Rushforth
        (1984). 204 pages, 11 figures, 16 tables.

97   EDWARD SAPIR'S CORRESPONDENCE: An Alphabetical and Chronological Inventory,
        1910-25. Edited by Louise Dallaire (1984). 278 pages.

98   INTERPRETIVE CONTEXTS FOR TRADITIONAL AND CURRENT COAST TSIMSHIAN FEASTS by
        Margaret Seguin (1985). 114 pages, 2 maps, 1 table, 2 figures.

100   THE RED EARTH CREES, 1860-1960 by David Meyer (1985). 231 pages, 5 tables,
        24 figures, 21 plates.

102   BEOTHUK BARK CANOES: An Analysis and Comparative Study by Ingeborg Constanze
        Luise Marshall (1985). 159 pages, 34 figures, 11 tables, 1 map.

PE3   FAMILLE ET PARENTÉ EN ACADIE par M.A. Tremblay (1971). 174 pages, 5 annexes,
        47 tables.

PE5   THE QUEST FOR FOOD AND FURS: The Mistassini Cree, 1953-54 by E.S. Rogers
        (1973). 83 pages, 17 plates, 7 figures, 6 tables, 9 maps, 7 graphs.

PE8   THE "MOTS LOUPS" OF FATHER MATHEVET by G.M. Day (1975).

PE9   LABRADOR ESKIMO SETTLEMENTS OF THE EARLY CONTACT PERIOD by J.G. Taylor
        (1974). 105 pages, 1 figure, 26 tables, 4 maps.

B138   BELLE-ANSE by M. Rioux (1957). 125 pages.

B176H   THE LYNX POINT PEOPLE: The Dynamics of a Northern Athapaskan Band by J. Helm
        (1961). 193 pages, 8 figures, 6 tables. Hard cover.

B176S   THE LYNX POINT PEOPLE: The Dynamics of a Northern Athapaskan Band by J. Helm
        (1961). 193 pages, 8 figures, 6 tables. Soft cover.

B179H   BAND ORGANIZATION OF THE PEEL RIVER KUTCHIN by R. Slobodin (1962). 97 pages,
        4 plates, 3 figures, 2 maps. Hard cover.

B179S   BAND ORGANIZATION OF THE PEEL RIVER KUTCHIN by R. Slobodin (1962). 97 pages,
        4 plates, 3 figures, 2 maps. Soft cover.

CER1   MYTHS AND TRADITIONS FROM NORTHERN ALASKA, THE MACKENZIE DELTA AND CORONATION
        GULF by D. Jenness (1924). 90 pages.

CER2   COMPARATIVE VOCABULARY OF THE WESTERN ESKIMO DIALECTS by D. Jenness (1928).
        134 pages.